Wellington
Against Soult

Oh, Christ! It is a goodly sight to see
What Heaven hath done for this delicious land:
What fruits of fragrance blush on every tree!
What goodly prospects o'er the hills expand!
But man would mar them with an impious hand:
And when the Almighty lifts his fiercest scourge
'Gainst those who most transgress his high command,
With treble vengeance will his hot shafts urge
Gaul's locust host, and earth from fellest foemen purge.

George Byron, *Childe Harold's Pilgrimage**

---

* George Byron, *The Complete Poetical Works of Lord Byron*, 3 vols (London, George Routledge and Sons, 1886), Vol. 1, p. 261. This quotation is verse XV from Byron's epic *Childe Harold's Pilgrimage*.

Wellington Against Soult

The Second Invasion of Portugal, 1809

David Buttery

Pen & Sword
MILITARY

First published in Great Britain in 2016 by
Pen & Sword Military
an imprint of
Pen & Sword Books Ltd
47 Church Street
Barnsley
South Yorkshire
S70 2AS

ISBN 978 1 47382 143 9

Typeset in Ehrhardt by
Mac Style Ltd, Bridlington, East Yorkshire
Printed and bound in the UK by CPI Group (UK) Ltd,
Croydon, CRO 4YY

Pen & Sword Books Ltd incorporates the imprints of Pen & Sword
Archaeology, Atlas, Aviation, Battleground, Discovery, Family
History, History, Maritime, Military, Naval, Politics, Railways, Select,
Transport, True Crime, and Fiction, Frontline Books, Leo Cooper,
Praetorian Press, Seaforth Publishing and Wharncliffe.

For a complete list of Pen & Sword titles please contact
PEN & SWORD BOOKS LIMITED
47 Church Street, Barnsley, South Yorkshire, S70 2AS, England
E-mail: enquiries@pen-and-sword.co.uk
Website: www.pen-and-sword.co.uk

Contents

List of Plates

In 1809 the French army under Napoleon I appeared invincible but this was about to change. Engraving by Denis Auguste Marie Raffet (1804–60).

Napoleon's need to overcome Great Britain's naval supremacy lay behind the French invasion of Portugal. Engraving from the *Leisure Hour*, 1868.

Marshal Jean de Dieu Soult, one of Napoleon's most experienced generals, was ordered to invade Portugal for a second time in 1809.

General Sir John Craddock faced the unenviable task of defending Portugal while the British and Portuguese were uncertain about how to respond to the French threat. Painting by Sir T. Lawrence.

General Sir Arthur Wellesley (later Duke of Wellington) decided to march north and stop Soult's invasion in its tracks rather than adopt a passive defence.

French soldiers risked a grisly fate if they fell into the hands of Portuguese or Spanish guerrillas. Painting by Francisco José de Goya y Lucientes.

Outraged by guerrilla attacks, the French often responded in kind and summary executions and atrocities were common during the Peninsular War. Painting by Francisco José de Goya y Lucientes.

The British government debated whether to continue the war after General Moore's death at Corunna and the evacuation of his army from Spain. Engraving by Rouget.

Napoleon underestimated the strength of resistance he would encounter in the Peninsula as the Portuguese and Spaniards had been whipped up into a fury by the clergy. Engraving by Rouget.

A sentry guards a printing press shut down by the French authorities. Press restrictions were commonplace during the Napoleonic Wars and all sides published extensive propaganda. Engraving by Rouget.

A view of the Douro with the Bishop's Seminary visible in the background under the bridge and the Serra Hill on the right. (*S. Hadaway*)

A view across the river with the modern bridge looking towards the Serra Hill where Wellesley placed his artillery to cover the attempted crossing. (*S. Hadaway*)

Constant skirmishing took place between French light infantry and Portuguese peasants and militia as Soult retreated through the hills and mountains.

Despite terrible losses, the British infantry stubbornly resisted French attacks at Albuera in 1811, causing Soult to comment, 'We had won the day but they did not know it and would not run away!'

Following Napoleon's final defeat, Soult ingratiated himself with succeeding governments and became a pillar of French society. From a painting by Pierre-Louis de Laval, engraved by T. Johnson.

Maps

Portugal, 1809.

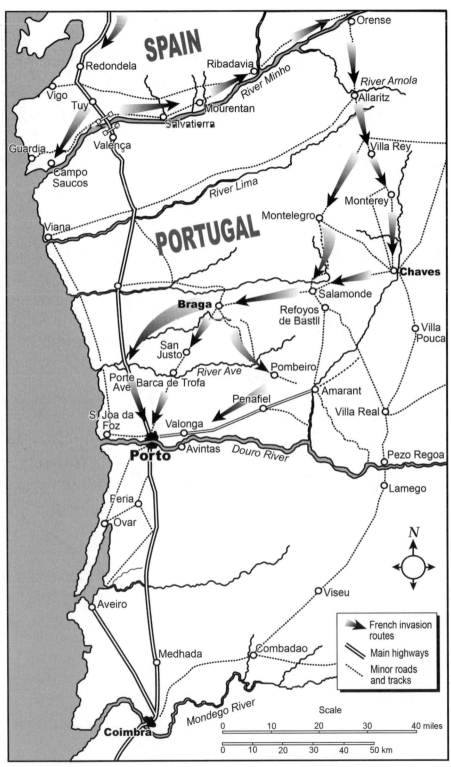

Second Invasion of Portugal, February–March 1809.

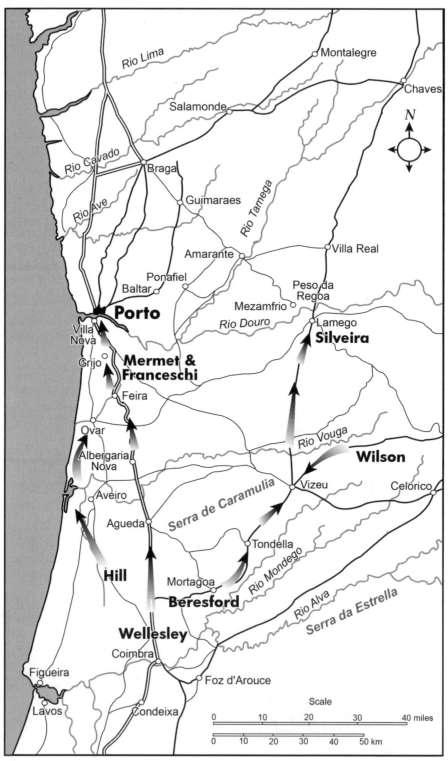

The Allied March North.

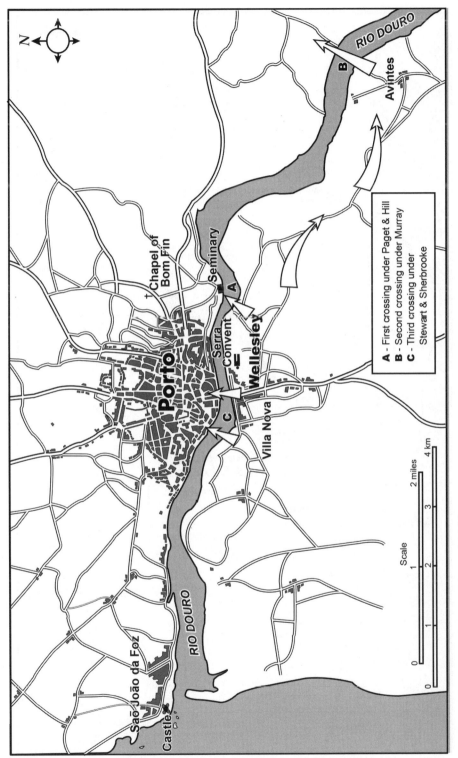

The Passage of the Douro, 12 May 1809.

Map labels:

N

RIO DOURO

Avintes

B

Chapel of Bom Fin †

Seminary

A

Serra Convent

Porto

Wellesley

C

Villa Nova

São João da Foz

Castle

RIO DOURO

A - First crossing under Paget & Hill
B - Second crossing under Murray
C - Third crossing under Stewart & Sherbrooke

Scale

0   1   2   3   4 km

0   1   2 miles

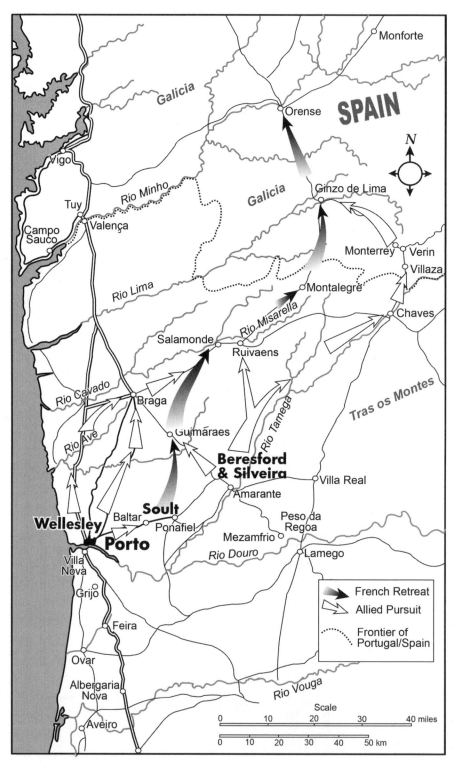

Soult's Retreat.

Chronology

1769	29 March	Birth of Jean de Dieu Soult (at St-Amans-Labastide, Tarn)
	1 May	Birth of Arthur Wesley (later Wellesley)
	15 August	Birth of Napoleon Buonaparte (surname spelling later changed)
1781		Death of Lord Mornington
		Wesley enters Eton
1785	16 April	Soult enlists in *Régiment Royal Infanterie*
1787	7 March	Wesley joins the army as an ensign
	13 June	Soult promoted corporal
	25 December	Wesley promoted lieutenant
1790	30 June	Wesley becomes MP for Country Trim, Ireland
1791	31 March	Soult promoted *corporal fourrier* (Quartermaster)
	30 June	Wesley promoted captain
	1 July	Soult promoted sergeant
1792	17 January	Soult elected drill instructor
	20 April	France declares war on Austria and Sardinia
	21 September	Establishment of the National Convention Government
	22 September	French monarchy abolished
1793	21 January	Louis XVI executed
	31 May	Reign of Terror begins
	7 September	Siege of Toulon begins
	30 September	Wesley promoted lieutenant colonel
	16 October	Execution of Marie-Antoinette
	19 November	Soult promoted to captain on General Taponier's staff
	18 December	Toulon falls
1794	4 March	Bonaparte takes command of the artillery in the Army of Italy
	25 June	Jourdan defeats the Austrians at Fleurus (Soult present)
	June	Soult commands a brigade in *l'Armée de Sambre et Meuse*
	27 July	*Coups d'état* of 9 Thermidor – fall of Robespierre
	21 September	Battle of Dego
1795	5 April	Peace of Bâle between France and Prussia
	4–5 October	*Coups d'état* of 13 Vendémaire (whiff of grapeshot)
	1 November	The Directory replaces the Convention government
1796	2 March	Bonaparte appointed commander of the Army of Italy
	26 April	Soult marries Louise Berg at Solingen
	3 May	Wesley promoted full colonel

1797	14 January	Battle of Rivoli
	2 February	Surrender of Mantua
	4 September	*Coups d'état* of 18 Fructidor
	17 October	Treaty of Campo-Formio between France and Austria
1798	21–5 March	Soult serves at Stockach
	21 April	Soult promoted *gènèral de division*
	19 May	Bonaparte sails for Egypt
		Soult fights at Ostend in Championnet's division
	29 December	Second Coalition against France
1799	25 March	Austrians defeat Jourdan at Stockach
	4 May	Seringapatam falls
		Wellesley appointed Governor of Mysore
	June–September	Soult serves under Massena
	4 June	First Battle of Zürich
	17–19 June	Battle of the Trebbia
	18 June	*Coups d'état* of 30 Prairial
	15 August	Battle of Novi
	25 September– 10 October	Second Battle of Zürich
	9 October	Bonaparte returns to France
	9 November	*Coups d'état* of 18 Brumaire
1800	15 May	Bonaparte crosses Great St Bernard Pass into Italy
	6 April–13 May	Soult fights near Genoa – wounded and taken prisoner
	4 June	Massena capitulates at Genoa
	14 June	Battle of Marengo
1801	9 February	Peace of Lunéville between France and Austria
	13 February	Soult given a command under Murat in Italy
	14 March	Prime Minister William Pitt resigns
		Viscount Henry Addington becomes Prime Minister
	23 March	Tsar Paul I dies – succeeded by Tsar Alexander I
1802	25 March	Peace of Amiens between France and Great Britain
	29 April	Wellesley promoted major general
	June	Soult's Italian command (under Murat) ends
1804	16 May	Great Britain declares war on France
	6 August	Second Mahratta War
	12 August	Ahmednuggur falls
	28 August	Soult appointed to command St-Omer camp near Boulogne
	23 September	Battle of Assaye
	29 November	Battle of Argaum
	15 December	Gawilghur capitulates
1804	7 April	Execution of the Duc d'Enghien
	10 May	William Pitt becomes Prime Minister
	18 May	Bonaparte crowned Napoleon I Emperor of France
	19 May	Eighteen generals created Marshals of Empire

		Soult created *Maréchal de l'Empire* (eighth in seniority) and Colonel General of the Imperial Guard
	1 September	Wellesley awarded Order of the Bath
	2 December	Napoleon's Coronation at Notre-Dame
1805	10 March	Wellesley leaves India
	March	Soult given command of IV Corps in Austria, Prussia and then Poland – holds post until 1807
	9 August	Third Coalition against France
	19 October	Mack surrenders at Ulm
	21 October	Battle of Trafalgar
	2 December	Battle of Austerlitz (Soult commands IV Corps)
	26 December	Treaty of Pressburg between Austria and France
1806	1 April	Joseph Bonaparte created King of Naples
		Wellesley becomes MP for Rye, Sussex
	10 April	Wellesley marries Kitty Pakenham
	14 October	Battles of Jena and Auerstädt
	21 November	Napoleon issues Berlin Decrees
1807	7 January	Britain declares a blockade of French ports and colonies
	8 February	Battle of Eylau
	3 April	Wellesley appointed Chief Secretary of Ireland
	14 June	Battle of Friedland
	7–9 July	Treaty of Tilsit between France, Russia and Prussia
	29 July	Napoleon orders a concentration of troops in Bayonne
	11 August	Portugal ordered to sever diplomatic relations with Britain
	2 September	Copenhagen bombarded by the British
	4 September	Dutch ports closed to Britain
	5 September	Junot takes command of the Corps of Observation of the Gironde
	7 September	British capture Copenhagen and seize Danish fleet
	25 September	Portugal offers to join the Continental System
	1 October	French and Spanish ambassadors withdrawn from Lisbon
	17 October	Corps of the Gironde enters Spain
	20 October	Portuguese close ports to Britain
	27 October	Treaty of Fontainebleu between France and Spain
	13 November	The Second Corps of Observation of the Gironde under General Dupont enters Spain
	18 November	Portuguese ports blockaded by Royal Navy
	23–4 November	Junot's army reaches Abrantes
	27–9 November	Prince Regent João VI and his court sail for Brazil
	30 November	Junot's vanguard enters Lisbon
	1 December	Spanish division under General Solano enters Portugal via Elvas to occupy southern Portugal
	13 December	Spanish Division under General Taranco enters Portugal
	15 December	Rioting in Lisbon

	18 December	Spanish Division under General Carrafa enters Portugal
	22 December	Junot disbands the Portuguese army
	23 December	Indemnity of 100 million francs imposed on Portugal
1808	1 February	Junot created Governor General of Portugal
	25 April	Wellesley promoted lieutenant general
	2 May	Major revolt in Madrid
	6 June	Revolt breaks out at Porto and Vila Real against the French
		Joseph Bonaparte proclaimed King of Spain
	8 June	Revolt against the French at Braga
	9 June	Disorder in Porto – Spanish troops disarmed
		Revolt against the French at Braganza
	15 June	General insurrection throughout Portugal
	16 June	First Siege of Zaragoza begins
	19 June	The Bishop of Porto appointed head of the Supreme Junta
	21 June	Loison repelled at Teixeira by General Silveira
	25–6 June	Vila Vizosa and Beja are sacked by the French
	27 June	Fort of Santa Catarina at Figueira da Foz seized by the Portuguese
	29 June	Soult created *Duc de Dalmatie*
	5–6 July	General Margaron captures Leiria then retires towards Lisbon
	12 July	British troops under Wellesley sail from Cork
	16 July	Portuguese militia surround Almeida
	20 July	Dupont surrenders at Bailén
	29–30 July	Portuguese and Spanish defeated before Évora
	1–8 August	British land at Mondego Bay
	11–12 August	Wellesley meets with General Freire at Leiria
	14 August	First siege of Zaragoza ends
	17 August	Battle of Roliça
	21 August	Battle of Vimeiro
		Sir Harry Burrard takes command
	22 August	Sir Hew Dalrymple takes command
		Armistice at Vimeiro
	30 August	Convention of Sintra
	September–October	French evacuate Portugal
	21 September	Wellesley sails for England
	11 October	Junot disembarks at La Rochelle
	27 October	General Moore marches into Spain
	3 November	Soult given command of II Corps
	5 November	Napoleon takes command of the Army of Spain
	4 December	Napoleon occupies Madrid
	20 December	Second siege of Zaragoza begins
1809	1 January	Soult commands pursuit of Moore's army as Napoleon returns to France
	11 January	Moore's rearguard reaches Corunna
	13 January	Spanish army defeated at Uclés

16 January	Battle of Corunna
23 January	Soult garrisons Corunna and marches against Ferrol
26 January	Ferrol surrenders to Soult
2 February	Elements of Soult's cavalry reach the Portuguese frontier
15–16 February	Soult unsuccessfully tries to cross the River Minho into Portugal
20 February	Zaragoza falls
21 February	Soult's army reaches Orense
4 March	Soult invades Portugal
28–9 March	Spanish defeated at Medellín
	Vigo retaken by Portuguese guerrillas and Royal Navy
29 March	First Battle of Porto (Oporto) Soult storms and occupies the city
April	Wellesley resigns as Chief Secretary of Ireland and sails for Portugal
6 April	Archduke Charles invades Bavaria –war between France and Austria
12 April	Alcantara falls taken by the Allies
20–3 April	Battle of Eckmühl
22 April	Wellesley disembarks at Lisbon
23 April	Wellesley assumes command of the army in Portugal
10 May	Wellesley tries to encircle Soult's advance guard at Ovar (using an amphibious flanking manoeuvre)
	Beresford drives Loison from Pezo de Ragoa
11 May	Action at Grijo as the British approach Porto
	Loison is repulsed by Silveira's forces
	Elements of Wellesley's army reach the Douro River
12 May	Battle of Porto/Passage of the Douro – Wellesley defeats Soult
	Soult attempts to retreat along line of Douro
	Loison falls back from Amarante
	French begin retreat over Serra de Santa Catalina towards Galicia
13 May	Napoleon enters Vienna
	Soult abandons artillery and baggage
14 May	Soult combines with Loison at Guimaraes
	Wellesley advances north hoping to cut off Soult's retreat
	Victor takes Alcantara
14/15 May	Major Dulong storms the Ponte Nova (bridge)
	Beresford/Silveira advance in pursuit of Soult's army
15 May	Silveira attempts to block Soult's retreat by marching on Salamonde
	Wellesley reaches Braga
	Beresford reaches Chaves
16 May	Dulong storms Saltador bridge
	British vanguard fall upon French rearguard at Salamonde

	17 May	Napoleon annexes the Papal States
	19 May	Soult's army reaches Orense (Spain)
	20–3 May	Battle of Aspern-Essling
	3 July	British army under Wellesley enters Spain
	5–6 July	Battle of Wagram
	6 July	Pope Pius VII arrested by the French
	27–8 July	Battle of Talavera
	4 September	Wellesley created Viscount Wellington
	16 September	Soult appointed major general to King Joseph
	September–October	Wellesley orders the construction of the Lines of Torres Vedras
	July–September	British expedition to Walcheren
	4 October	Spencer Perceval becomes prime minister
	14 October	Treaty of Schönbrunn between France and Austria
	20 October	Construction of the Lines of Torres Vedras begins
	30 October	Duke of Portland (British prime minister) dies from a stroke
1810	2 April	Napoleon marries Archduchess Marie-Louise of Austria
	14 June	Soult commands *l'Armée d'Andalousie*
	24 July	Combat on the Côa
		Third Invasion of Portugal under Marshal Massena
	27 September	Battle of Busaco
	10–14 October	French halt before the Lines of Torres Vedras
	14 November	Massena withdraws to Santarém
1811	5 March	Massena begins to retreat
	11 March	Badajoz falls to the French
	3 April	Battle of Sabugal
		French leave Portugal
	3–5 May	Battle of Fuentes de Oñoro
	10 May	Massena relieved of command
	16 May	Soult narrowly defeated at the Battle of Albuera
1812	19 January	Wellington takes Ciudad Rodrigo
	6 April	Wellington takes Badajoz
	11 May	Prime Minister Spencer Perceval assassinated
	24 June	Napoleon invades Russia
	22 July	Battle of Salamanca
	18 August	Wellington created Marquess of Wellington
	14 September	Napoleon enters Moscow
	22 September	Wellington created Generalissimo of Spanish Armies
	27–9 November	French retreat over the Beresina
	14 December	French rearguard reaches the River Niemen
1813	3 January–1 July	Soult commands Old Guard (of the Imperial Guard)
	16 March	Prussia declares war on France
	3 May	Battle of Lützen
	21–2 May	Battle of Bautzen
	21 June	Battle of Vittoria – Wellington promoted field marshal

	6 July	Soult commands armies in the Pyrenees (until mid-April 1814)
	20–30 July	Battle of the Pyrenees
	12 August	Austria declares war on France
	31 August	San Sebastian falls to Wellington
	16–19 October	Battle of Leipzig
1814	1 March	Treaty of Chaumont
	31 March	Allies enter Paris
	10 April	Battle of Toulouse
	11 April	Napoleon abdicates
		Treaty of Fontainebleu
	26 April	Louis XVIII proclaimed King of France
	3 May	Wellington created Duke of Wellington
	4 May	Napoleon reaches Elba
	20 May	First Treaty of Paris
	5 July	Wellington appointed Ambassador to the French Court
	1 November	Congress of Vienna begins
	4 December	Soult appointed Minister of War
1815	26 February	Napoleon escapes from Elba
	1 March	Napoleon lands at Golfe-Juan
	20 March	Napoleon enters Paris
	9 May	Soult appointed major general in *l'Armée de Nord*
	16 June	Battles of Ligny and Quatre Bras
	18 June	Battle of Waterloo
	22 June	Napoleon's final abdication
	26 June	Soult's officially leaves *l'Armée de Nord*
	7 July	Allies enter Paris
	5 October	Napoleon reaches St Helena
	20 November	Second Treaty of Paris
	7 December	Execution of Marshal Ney
1816	12 January	Soult flees France
1819		Soult permitted to return to France
1821	5 May	Napoleon I dies in exile
1830	17 November	Soult appointed Minister of War (until mid-July 1834)
1832	11 October	Soult appointed President of the Council of Ministers (until July 1834)
1838	28 June	Wellington and Soult are present at Queen Victoria's Coronation
1839	12 May	Soult reappointed President of the Council of Ministers (until March 1840)
1840	29 October	Soult reappointed Minister of War (until 1845) and President of the Council of Ministers (until 1847)
1847	26 September	Soult appointed *Maréchal-Géneral de France*
1851	2 December	Napoleon III crowned after seizing power in a *coup d'état*
	12 December	Death of Marshal Soult at St-Amans-Labastide
1852	14 September	Death of the Duke of Wellington

Preface

The early campaigns of Sir Arthur Wellesley (soon to be created Duke of Wellington) usually receive far less attention than his later exploits during the Peninsular War. This titanic struggle strongly influenced the outcome of the Napoleonic Wars with the French invading Portugal no less than three times, hoping to conquer the Portuguese and drive their British ally into the sea. The Third French Invasion of Portugal, by forces under Marshal Massena in 1810, usually garners the most scrutiny from writers and historians, while the first invasion under General Junot in 1807 gains less coverage. Yet in comparison with both of these, the Second French Invasion of Portugal in 1809 is even more obscure.

Why this should be so is puzzling as this invasion includes numerous incidents that should be of interest to historians and enthusiasts of this period. Perhaps the lack of a large battle accompanied by the enormous casualties typical of the Napoleonic Wars goes some way to explaining this with some assuming that little can be learned from the campaign as a consequence. Examination of the invasion and the conflicts fought during the campaign prove this to be anything but the case. For example, incidents that occurred during the First Battle of Porto made this an immensely important event in Portuguese history. Furthermore, Marshal Soult's invasion was beset with difficulties including a treacherous conspiracy that appears more akin to fiction rather than reality, and which fatally undermined his command.

The end of the campaign also witnessed a remarkable river operation that surprised one side so much that great strategic advantages were gained for relatively little loss of life when compared with other Napoleonic battles. Bafflingly, costly victories that gained far less in strategic terms have received far more attention from historians. The retreat that followed earned the opposing commander great plaudits and the entire campaign had enormous political repercussions in Portugal at a time when the population wavered between resisting or reluctantly embracing the French cause. In addition to providing valuable insights into the personalities of Wellesley and Soult (who both became hugely influential during this period), the outcome of the second invasion had a great effect on the way in which the Peninsular War would be fought. Consequently, those studying the Napoleonic Wars should find this campaign both historically relevant and of great interest.

This title is part of the 'Wellingon Against' series and it should be borne in mind that in May 1809 Sir Arthur Wellesley had not been honoured with the ducal title by which he is so well known. Nevertheless, he is referred to as Wellington in the title for its recognitive value and to maintain the spirit of the series. I am not alone in this as there are many other publications, such as Jac Weller's *Wellington in India*, Charles Grant's *Wellington's First Campaign in Portugal* and Ian C. Robertson's *Wellington at War in the Peninsular 1808–1814* and others books, that describe events prior to Wellesley gaining his peerage.

In this volume, I have used modern Portuguese spelling in the main body of the text. Therefore, for example, rather than referring to the city of Oporto (commonplace in British accounts of the time) the Portuguese Porto has been used. However, regarding quotations from contemporary works of the time, the original spellings have been retained as the original writers intended.

I have made great use of the libraries and archives of my former university (the University of Leicester) during my research and this has provided access to many sources that would otherwise have been unavailable to me. I would particularly like to thank librarian David Charlton of the David Wilson Library, whose help has extended far beyond what I have a right to expect. Indeed, he has sought out books and Internet sources that I would probably never have found but for his assistance. I am profoundly grateful for his help during the compilation of this book.

Likewise, my old friend Stuart Hadaway has given me access to his personal library and photographs and once again provided me with helpful advice and support. As the two founder members of Historians Inc., we have often collaborated to produce books and other works and travelled far and wide together in our quest to discover more about the past, visiting sites in Britain, Portugal, France, Spain, Belgium and Israel among others.

Having worked as a proofreader in the past, I would like to acknowledge the help I have received with this in relation to this book and other projects from Pauline Buttery, A.E. Godley and Stuart Hadaway, and Pamela Covey (of Pen & Sword), who have all checked through my work for me. They have saved me from committing errors on several occasions and their help is greatly appreciated. Books are rarely free from mistakes and any that remain are entirely my responsibility.

Finally, many thanks to all those wonderful people I met in Portugal who gave me an insight into the Portuguese view of the Peninsular War. Foremost among these are Jorge Estrela, Rodolfo Beghona, Helena Rafael, João MacDonald, José Sardica, Rui Ribolhos Filipe and his partner Dina Spencer da Graça as well as many others. Their hospitality and kindness made my research visits to Portugal a great pleasure. I hope they enjoy the book and feel that I have shown their nation and people due respect through this work.

Chapter One

Under Threat

Between 1808 and 1809 the outcome of the Napoleonic Wars lay in the balance and there was great uncertainty throughout Europe as national leaders pondered over whether to support France, which had dominated the Continent for nearly a decade, or to oppose her. Napoleon I, Emperor of France had reached the zenith of his power by 1807 but cracks were appearing in his First French Empire and his army no longer seemed invincible.

The Revolutionary Wars during the late eighteenth century had shocked observers when the French revolutionaries not only successfully defended their new republic but also turned on the monarchies set against them and brought the war across the frontiers of France to challenge the old order. Although the rise of Napoleon and his imperial form of government tempered revolutionary fanaticism to an extent, warfare continued throughout the imperial period.

The French army humbled the powers of Austria, Prussia and Russia in a succession of conflicts that ultimately saw France emerge victorious. Renouncing his former allies, Tsar Alexander I of Russia signed the Treaty of Tilsit in July 1807, which saw Napoleon and the tsar dividing much of Europe between them. France had become incredibly strong with numerous allied and satellite states supporting her. Yet, this had been accomplished at great cost with Napoleon coming close to losing the Battle of Eylau in 1807 and only achieving a decisive victory at Friedland a few weeks afterwards with both sides sustaining horrific casualties.

Great Britain was the only major power still at war with France by the end of 1807, stubbornly refusing to make peace until the balance of power was restored. British military efforts to damage French interests had only enjoyed limited success up to this time, but the Royal Navy dominated the oceans and, until the French navy could overcome their sea power, Britain was secure against invasion. Safe on their island, the British could employ their impressive financial muscle to support France's enemies, fermenting rebellion and giving hope to defeated nations who dreamt of challenging France once more.

Napoleon's solution to this dilemma was to introduce his 'Continental System' – a commercial embargo designed to bankrupt Britain by preventing the British from trading with Europe. The French employed diplomatic pressure to close Continental ports to British ships with varying degrees of success since, although the British were unpopular in some quarters, business with them was commercially lucrative. For example, the Royal Navy relied upon Russian timber for shipbuilding and the Russian nobility refused to cancel contracts that yielded great revenue, regardless of what they thought of their mercantile partners.

Portugal was also reluctant to conform to Napoleon's wishes. Following centuries of disputes and conflicts with Spain (their only neighbour on land), Portuguese trade was heavily reliant on seaborne commerce, which the Royal Navy could easily disrupt. Furthermore, Portugal was England's oldest ally and British and Portuguese merchants had trade agreements dating back centuries, particularly within the wine industry. Portugal's best policy was clearly neutrality and, although politically hostile to former French revolutionary governments, the Portuguese had remained so except for one brief conflict in 1801. With their small army they realised they had little hope of successfully fighting France on land but severing trade links with Britain could see their coastline blockaded and potentially destroy their economy.

The emperor viewed Portuguese neutrality with a cynical eye due to their strong links with England and knew that the Royal Navy frequently used Portuguese ports for supply and refitting. This could result in the British landing troops if the Portuguese chose to allow it. Furthermore, after the catastrophic defeat of the combined French and Spanish fleets at Trafalgar in 1805, Napoleon wished to rebuild the French navy so that it could challenge British naval power. If the Portuguese navy fell into his hands, he would gain valuable ships of the line to add to his fleet. After all, the British could only be truly overcome by invading across the Channel, and until the French navy could challenge the Royal Navy's supremacy at sea this would never be possible.

While the French were busy constructing new ships, it was better to acquire existing vessels and (even more crucially) experienced crews. Therefore, the emperor hoped to employ the Portuguese fleet, which comprised eleven ships of the line, ten frigates and numerous smaller vessels.[1] The British had already attacked Copenhagen on 2–7 September 1807 (even though Denmark was a neutral state) and seized the Danish fleet there to prevent it falling into French hands. While Britain had strong ties with Portugal, the government might be prepared to seize their ally's fleet rather than risk invasion.

Consequently, Napoleon applied diplomatic pressure to the Portuguese, demanding that they sever all links with France's enemy and seize British-owned assets and property in their country. British diplomats attempted to convince the Portuguese to remain neutral and implied that Portugal would face a naval blockade and risk the seizure of their navy should they side with France. Caught between two superpowers, Prince Regent Dom João and his government made every effort to placate Napoleon while privately assuring the British that any war against them would be in name only. Although the Portuguese agreed to most of Napoleon's demands, he decided to invade and occupy their nation nonetheless. On 13 November 1807, General Junot led a French army into Spain, tasked with capturing Lisbon, securing the navy and deposing the Bragança royal family. While Junot entered central Portugal, two Spanish armies would invade simultaneously, marching into the northern and southern provinces.

Although the Portuguese chose not to resist militarily, Junot encountered enormous difficulties as a result of the appalling weather, dreadful roads, poor supplies and the harsh terrain he was forced to march through. Large numbers of men were lost through illness, starvation and exposure to the elements, rendering the bulk of his army ineffective. Determined to fulfil his promise to the emperor, Junot reached the capital with a small advanced guard on 30 November. Lisbon capitulated and its fall was accounted a major triumph in Paris, one source commenting, 'As everyone knows, Junot took possession of Lisbon, of the army that was there, and of the entire kingdom, without having at hand a single trooper, a single gun, or a cartridge that would burn ...'.[2]

However, the Prince Regent, his court and many officials set sail from the capital as Junot's army approached, taking the fleet with them. Dom João had made an agreement with Britain and took ship for the Portuguese colony of Brazil, re-locating his court there. While disappointed by the loss of the fleet and the significant amount of wealth the Regent had taken with him, Napoleon was pleased at this propaganda coup as the nation was now under his influence in return for relatively little bloodshed and loss of equipment, which would have been high if the Portuguese had chosen to fight.

Yet, the ragged appearance of Junot's soldiers shocked Portuguese observers. Their clothing, weapons and accoutrements were in a pitiful state after gruelling forced marches and deprivation. The army was widely dispersed along the invasion route and the sight of ragged groups of soldiers staggering into barracks was uninspiring. Even a high-ranking officer like Thiébault (Junot's chief-of-staff) presented a poor appearance, 'The state we were in when we entered Lisbon is hardly credible. Our clothing had lost all shape and colour; I had not had a change of linen since Abrantes; my feet were coming through my boots ...'[3] Witnesses were unimpressed by these worn-out soldiers, whom they had previously considered the finest in Europe. Consequently, when the French raised their flag over Lisbon, a serious riot ensued. The Spanish armies also failed to conform to Junot's invasion plan with Porto, Portugal's second largest city, remaining unoccupied until 13 December when General Taranco's army arrived. Although General Solano's Spanish troops took control of Elvas on 2 December, the Spanish occupation of the south also proceeded slowly.

Junot did his best to rule from Lisbon but was handicapped from the outset. The Portuguese court had taken almost 50 per cent of the country's assets to Brazil and the value of the nation's currency had depreciated by about 30 per cent. Prices soared and, although the French froze the prices of basic commodities, the economy was slow to recover.[4] To make matters worse, Napoleon imposed an extraordinary tax of 100 million francs on Portugal to pay for the costs of Junot's expedition. The Portuguese deeply resented funding their own invasion and, with the Royal Navy blockading their coastline, it seemed unlikely that the country would be able to pay this indemnity.

Yet, Napoleon had little desire to win favour with the Portuguese people, believing their links with his greatest enemy were so strong that he would never gain their friendship or loyalty. To this end, he ordered Junot to disband their army and incorporate the best soldiers into the French army if they were willing to serve. Frenchmen replaced many Portuguese officials and acts of civil unrest were commonplace by February 1808.

Meanwhile, the emperor had decided that he could no longer rely upon the uneasy alliance that existed between France and the Spanish Bourbon royal family. The French ambassador, François Beauharnais, knew the Spaniards well and outlined his fears about their precarious regime:

> It is beyond understanding how this government can continue without governing, how it can support itself with an empty Treasury and without foreign credit. All Spain is longing for things to change. Everyone is waiting patiently for the day when the Emperor will turn his attention to this country so that things may be put right.[5]

As Napoleon's brother-in-law and ardent admirer, Beauharnais was somewhat biased and perhaps had too much faith in what he and France could achieve in Spain. Yet, the Spanish rulers had little enthusiasm for the French form of government and their future as long-term allies was doubtful. Napoleon viewed the dynastic struggle between King Carlos and his son as contemptible and deemed the old-fashioned Spanish society and form of government as incompetent, unjust and corrupt. He had some reason to suppose that many progressive Spaniards would welcome a change of government.

Therefore, he sent large numbers of troops into Spain on the pretext of supporting Junot's invasion and subsequent occupation of Portugal. With Prince Ferdinand conspiring against his father, Napoleon persuaded the royal family to come to France where he offered to act as a mediator and help resolve their disputes. Instead, he forced both father and son to renounce their claims to the throne (effectively deposing them) and proclaimed to the Spaniards:

> Your princes have made over all their rights to the Spanish crown to me; I have no desire to reign over your provinces; but I do seek an everlasting claim on your love and the recognition of generations to come in Spain. Your monarchy is ancient; my mission is to give it new

life; I shall improve your institutions and I shall give you the benefit of reform … Spaniards: I have convoked a general assembly of the delegates of all provinces and all cities. I myself want to know what your wishes are and what are your needs.[6]

The French army already occupied numerous Spanish fortresses and garrisons, alarming some Spaniards. With a sizeable French military presence in Madrid, Napoleon declared his brother Joseph as King of Spain. King Joseph received a cautious welcome as he travelled through his new kingdom and the crowds that greeted him in the capital were friendly but not overly enthusiastic. He was dismayed by the muted response to his coronation and his new subjects made it clear that they were loath to accept a foreign ruler. It took him little time to realise that serious military power would be necessary to support his monarchy, as he outlined in a letter to his brother: 'We must have fifty thousand more men and fifty million francs within three months. Respectable people here have no more use for me than the rabble has. You are making a mistake, Sire; your glory will not avail you in Spain. I shall fail and the limits of your power will be exposed …'[7] Discontent grew and culminated in a violent uprising on 2 May in Madrid, which became known as the *Dos de Mayo* (immortalised in paintings by the artist Francisco Goya). The crowd fell upon French civilians, soldiers and sympathisers and there were many brutal murders in the streets. Serious fighting erupted in the capital and was only put down after the French fired musket volleys into the mob and scores of Madrileños were cut down by the elite Mameluke cavalry (originally recruited from Egypt) as they charged into the crowds. Incensed by the killing of many of his soldiers, Marshal Murat exacerbated the situation by ordering summary executions of hundreds of Spaniards in a grisly aftermath to this bloody incident.

News of the unrest quickly spread throughout Spain, provoking widespread revolts and many declared themselves against the French and hailed the new Supreme Junta (established in Seville) as their government in the king's absence. The French encountered serious opposition at Zaragoza when the city resisted from 16 June–14 August and they were eventually obliged to lift the first siege. Zaragoza's example inspired resistance throughout the nation but it was the defeat and surrender of an entire French army under General

Dupont at Bailén on 20 July (in southern Spain) that really lent hope to the rebellion and the regional juntas that had declared themselves against the occupation.

Eventually, Napoleon admitted that he had underestimated the difficulties he would encounter in Spain, acknowledging: 'I thought the system easier to change than it has proved in that country, with its corrupt minister, its feeble king and its shameless, dissolute queen.'[8] Yet, although many had been discontented under Bourbon rule, most were deeply conservative and had an instinctive dislike of foreign intervention in Spanish affairs. Consequently, the French had a serious problem in the Peninsula.

Uprisings in Spain encouraged the Portuguese to revolt and after the Spanish troops occupying Porto left to join their compatriots the small French garrison there was overwhelmed when the local population rose up against them. Don Antonio de São José de Castro, the Bishop of Porto, agreed to head a Supreme Junta established in Porto and began raising forces to oppose the French. Revolts also took place in the south where small French outposts were attacked and many *anfrancesados* (Portuguese who had collaborated during the occupation) were murdered.

While Junot remained secure in Lisbon and the central provinces were relatively quiet compared with the rest of the country, he knew that he must suppress these uprisings quickly as he could not expect swift reinforcements from Spain or France. He had around 25,000 troops in Portugal but many were garrisoned in key fortresses like Elvas and Almeida, which he was reluctant to abandon. Therefore, he chose to dispatch flying columns to suppress centres of rebellion. However, attempts to reach Coimbra and Porto were thwarted and, although French forces were not seriously defeated, they encountered such strong resistance that Junot considered the north lost for the present. In the south revolt was brutally suppressed. A combined force of Spanish regular soldiers and Portuguese militia was defeated before Évora on 29 July and the town was subsequently stormed and sacked with a ferocity recalled with horror in Portugal to this day. Indeed, for two months the French carried out numerous reprisals to discourage rebellion, burning villages and towns and executing all those suspected of joining or aiding the insurgents. Consequently, Portuguese guerrillas took a fearful revenge on French soldiers who fell into their hands.

Had the French had time, they probably would have crushed resistance in Portugal but the arrival of a British army under General Sir Arthur Wellesley in early August at Mondego Bay halted their operations. With the limited number of troops at his disposal, Junot could not match a regular army and suppress revolt simultaneously. Therefore, he concentrated his forces and marched out from Lisbon to give battle, only to be defeated at the Battle of Vimeiro on 22 August 1808. He fell back on Lisbon but the city was largely unfortified and offered little protection, especially as the British landed numerous reinforcements and soon outnumbered French forces in Portugal. Moreover, Junot knew that his regime faced widespread resistance from the people and that more troops and supplies were unlikely to reach him until 1809 at the earliest. Consequently, he chose to negotiate a settlement with the British.

The resulting Armistice, later formalised at the Convention of Sintra 30 August 1808, gave remarkable concessions to the French. While the British liberated Portugal without further fighting, they allowed the French to evacuate their army along with its arms and plunder. In his eagerness to reach a settlement, General Dalrymple, the British Commander-in-Chief, even agreed to sail Junot's army back to France using the Royal Navy. The formidable border fortresses of Almeida and Elvas surrendered without a fight as a result of the convention and the British now had a foothold on the Continent. However, the extremely lenient terms outraged the Portuguese Supreme Junta and the British government was dismayed. Ultimately, generals Dalrymple, Burrard and Wellesley were recalled to face an official inquiry. While his superiors' reputations were tarnished, only Wellesley's recent victory and good conduct during the hearings saved his career from irreparable harm.[9]

In the wake of the catastrophic defeat at Bailén, King Joseph abandoned Madrid, considering a defence of the Spanish capital untenable with the loyalty of its citizens in doubt. The French established themselves in a defensive line along the Ebro River, yielding almost all French-held territory except for northeast Spain. Outraged by such defeatism, and knowing his brother's flight was a propaganda gift to his enemies, Napoleon crossed the Pyrenees to assume personal command of the campaign. He brought an army of at least 200,000 men, which included the Imperial Guard.

Meanwhile, Spanish armies took up positions in the Ebro River region. General Blake assembled some 31,000 men in the north around Reynosa, while General Castaños had 34,000 men in positions around Logrono. General Galuzzo had 13,000 men near Burgos and Don José Palafox y Melzi (who had recently risen to prominence after leading the defence of Zaragoza) led a further 25,000 men towards the front. General Moore spent most of the autumn reorganising British forces in Lisbon and left the capital on 27 October to aid the Spanish defence with an army of 30,000 men.

While the Spanish Supreme Junta had a grand strategy of cutting off French communications before attacking along a wide front, effective co-ordination was hampered by disputes between the generals and they failed to agree upon a senior commander. Shortly after his arrival, Napoleon launched a major offensive on 6–7 November 1808, aiming to draw the Spandiards into attacks into the mountains on his flanks before smashing their centre. He then intended to cut off their lines of retreat and advance on Madrid.

Blake was defeated at Espinosa and then Gamonal, and Napoleon was soon able to move on Burgos, where he ordered Marshal Soult to Reynosa and Marshal Ney to attack on the opposite flank. Soult seized the well-stocked port of Santander on 16 November and Marshal Lannes won a victory at Tudela on 23 November. With French forces moving to cut off their withdrawal, the Spanish armies were soon in full flight and only General San Juan's small army of 12,500 men made a serious effort to prevent the French from recapturing Madrid by defending the Somosierra Pass from 29–30 November. They were overwhelmed by Napoleon in command of 45,000 veteran soldiers and San Juan was lynched by his own men as he tried to halt the ensuing rout.

Napoleon reoccupied Madrid on 4 December 1808 and, with his customary energy, immediately began making new laws, banning the Holy Office of the Inquisition and placing other restrictions on the power of the Church. He introduced reforms with the best intentions but they undermined his brother's authority and Napoleon refused to allow Joseph to rule unless he was seen to have popular support. To this end, registers were opened and the 27th French Army Bulletin subsequently recorded:

The city of Madrid has particularly distinguished itself; 28,500 heads of families have taken the oath of Allegiance upon the Holy Sacrament. The citizens have promised his Imperial Majesty, that if he will place his brother on the throne, they will serve him with all their efforts, and defend him with all their means.[10]

While contemporary historian General Sir William Napier believed these Spaniards were not placed under duress, it should be borne in mind that Napoleon had entered the city after defeating the Spanish armies in the field and the threat was implicit. Napoleon's bulletins were also propaganda and, while not necessarily inaccurate, the figure of 28,500 should be judged in this context. After this and other announcements, King Joseph was restored to his throne.

In other parts of Spain, savage fighting continued and Zaragoza was besieged a second time on 20 December. Ferocious street fighting occurred once the French broke into the city:

The Aragonese maintained their positions on the opposite side, throwing up batteries at the openings of the streets, within a few paces of similar batteries of the French. The intervening space was soon heaped up with dead, either thrown from the windows of the houses in which they had been slain, or killed in the conflicts below.[11]

Zaragoza did not fall until 20 February 1809 but the city's resistance became legendary and produced popular heroes such as Augustina Zaragoza, one of the many women who fought there.[12] Although regular Spanish soldiers helped defend the city under Don José Palafox, huge numbers of ordinary townspeople participated in the defence and fought determinedly for their city. This inspired many to resist and was widely used by propagandists to show how the majority of the people opposed French interference in the Peninsula.

By 1809, the vast majority of the common people in the Peninsula had turned against the French occupation. Catholic opposition to French revolutionary doctrine (the power of the Church had been suppressed during the Revolution) was sufficient to turn many against them, despite

Napoleon's efforts to moderate republican policies during the imperial period. Furthermore, while some aspects of his regime appealed to progressive areas of society, Napoleon's deposition of the Spanish king was widely seen as treachery on the part of a former ally, alienating many who might have supported France.

Most importantly, the war was inflicting incredible damage on the Peninsula in both urban and rural areas. Large numbers of dispossessed and vengeful people enlisted in the Spanish armies or joined the guerrillas, who could easily hide out in mountainous areas or conceal themselves among the common people in the cities. They struck with increasing confidence at isolated groups of French soldiers or small outposts and the resulting reprisals were often indiscriminate and alienated the people even more.

The Supreme Junta in Seville attempted to establish itself as the new government. Although this official body was composed of noblemen and respectable Spaniards, they were rabidly anti-French, as a decree published in February 1809 reveals:

> His majesty, considering that the French, in the unjust and barbarous war which they wage against Spain, pay no regard to any principle of the law of nations, that they shamelessly violate the most solemn of treaties ... they imprison, persecute and banish peaceable citizens and respectable magistrates, imposing, at the same time, the most disgraceful punishments on other unfortunate persons on the slightest suspicions and most frivolous pretexts.[13]

The decree continued in the same vein citing atrocities such as the death of a nun who cast herself into a well to avoid rape by a French soldier, the mutilation of a young mother and the casual murder of her infant immediately afterwards. The Junta then took the astounding decision to exclude the French from the rules of war, a proclamation issued to the Spanish armies stating:

> That no quarter shall be given to any French soldier, officer or general, who may be made prisoner in any town or district, in which acts contrary to the laws of war have been committed by the enemy, but that

such persons shall be immediately put to the sword, as an example to their companions and a satisfaction to outraged humanity.[14]

The Marquis of Astorga endorsed this measure which reveals just how terrible the war in the Peninsula had become, with a supposedly enlightened nobleman condoning reprisals that flouted the rules of war. Indeed, although savage acts were committed throughout the Napoleonic Wars, this conflict became notorious for horrific acts of violence (including torture, rape and murder) committed against soldiers and civilians.

The military theorist Jomini commented on how difficult it was for a regular army to suppress partisans unless the occupying force ruled justly and refrained from imposing excessive punishments and won the people over to its side. Without achieving these aims, guerrillas would find shelter, support and (after striking) could withdraw rapidly and disappear among the civilian population to their opponents' frustration. This often provoked reprisals against the innocent, perpetuating the cycle of violence and atrocity. Jomini believed guerrilla warfare so brutal that, 'The immense obstacles encountered by an invading force in these wars have led some speculative persons to hope that there should never be any other kind, since then wars would become more rare, and, conquest being also more difficult, would be less of a temptation to ambitious leaders.'[15]

Yet it must not be assumed that an anti-French attitude was universal in Portugal and Spain. Some of the minor gentry, radicals and the emerging middle class initially welcomed the prospect of French-style reform. The Spaniards had endured a corrupt government that had been permeated with nepotism and favouritism and dominated by the Church for centuries so some quietly approved of the removal of the incompetent Carlos IV and his son Ferdinand. Furthermore, the royal family's reputation had been damaged by the actions of Manuel Godoy (President of the States Council) who was widely perceived as corrupt and promoted beyond his abilities as he was the queen's favourite.

Previously, when the Spanish permitted the French to march through their country to invade Portugal, General Thiébault commented on the 'enthusiasm with which our troops were received in Spain, especially in Biscay. It proved, no doubt, that the sound of our fame had reached even the villages of Spain, but still more the degree of the Spaniards' discontent with their government. If our march seemed like a holiday for them, it was a triumph for us.'[16] Yet, he went on to observe on how quickly this situation changed once Napoleon ousted the Spanish monarchy and government. As a French officer Thiébault was somewhat biased, though there is no reason to disbelieve his claim that the French were warmly received as allies fighting against Spain's traditional foe. Furthermore, many Spaniards and Portuguese had been attracted by the reforms that French revolutionary doctrine promised and were eager to see change, even if it involved direct French military intervention. While *anfrancesados's* accounts are rare, the Portuguese historian Ramos acknowledged:

Amongst the liberal, republican and radical segments of the Spanish and Portuguese populations there was much support for a potential French invasion, despite Napoleon's having by 1807 abandoned many liberal and republican ideals. Before the invasion, the term *afrancesado* ('turned French') was used to denote those who supported the Enlightenment, secular ideals, and the French Revolution. Napoleon relied on support from these *afrancesados* both in the conduct of the war and administration of the country. But while Napoleon – through his brother Joseph – fulfilled his promises to remove all feudal and clerical privileges, most Spanish liberals soon came to oppose the occupation because of the violence and brutality it brought.[17]

Yet, in both of these nations the harsh reality of the French occupation from 1807–8, accompanied by the brutal repression of rebellion and enormous damage to land, property and the economy, made the French highly unpopular. Repressive French actions in Portugal turned many sympathisers against them and those who still felt that republican aims justified these means were inclined to stay silent, fearing a violent reaction from their compatriots.

In Madrid Napoleon had discovered the position of Moore's army and swiftly marched against him, hoping to trap and encircle his forces. He considered the Spanish armies beaten and that Moore was 'the only general [in Spain] now worthy to contend with me'.[18] Knowing his army was massively outnumbered, Moore began to retreat on 23 December 1808. In the wake of recent defeats, the Spanish could offer little assistance and there was scant enthusiasm to combine forces for a stand against an army led by Napoleon himself. Almost 350,000 French soldiers were now in Spain and the emperor could bring as many as 230,000 against Moore and his Spanish allies.[19]

Closely pursued through hilly and mountainous country in terrible weather, the British turned to fight numerous rearguard actions, notably at Sahagún, Benavente, Lugo and Cacavellos. The Spanish were also hounded but Napoleon believed catching Moore was the priority since his army was yet to suffer a defeat. Although the Spanish fought some costly actions to cover their withdrawal, they ultimately evaded the French. Realising that the campaign was lost, Moore decided to evacuate Spain and divided his army in order to fall back on both Corunna and Vigo from where it would embark for Britain.

Considering the campaign virtually won, Napoleon handed over command of the pursuit to Marshal Soult on 2 January 1809. Disturbing news had reached him from Paris and he was keen to return. Before leaving, he sent the Imperial Guard back to Valladolid, Debelle's division to garrison Madrid, Bonnet's division to garrison Santander and Lapisse's division south to suppress insurrection. Soult was ordered to drive Moore into the sea and was given 25,000 infantry, 6,000 cavalry and a further 16,000 men under Marshal Ney acting in support. Deeming Moore's army undernourished, poorly supplied and exhausted by their retreat, Napoleon considered these numbers more than sufficient for the task.[20]

After the emperor's departure, the French continued to press Moore's retreat and, although the British reached Corunna first, Soult arrived before the troops could board ships waiting in the harbour. The Battle of Corunna took place on 16 January 1809 and was a hard-fought action (see Chapter 2). Moore was killed towards the end of the battle but inflicted sufficient losses on Soult's forces which allowed his army to embark without serious interference.

While the British had achieved a victory, it was tempered by the fact that they had been forced out of Spain and Moore's army had suffered considerably. In addition to losses sustained during the retreat and battle, many of the soldiers who returned from the campaign were sick after suffering severe privations. People were shocked by their ragged appearance and the state of their arms when they disembarked in southern England, which did nothing to inspire the country's confidence in future military expeditions. Although an army remained in Portugal, many thought the British had been rudely ejected from Spain and had avoided a serious defeat by a miracle.

The first few months of 1809 marked a low point for Prime Minister William Bendinck, Duke of Portland's Tory ministry. After the debacle of the Convention of Sintra, some questioned the competency of the army's command and the outbreak of a fully-fledged scandal regarding the Duke of York's behaviour (as Commander-in-Chief of the British Army) caused immense embarrassment for the government. This concerned his former mistress, Mrs Mary Ann Clarke, who allegedly took bribes to use her influence with the duke to bestow military appointments, commissions and promotions. Attempting to exhort money from him in return for private letters she retained, Clarke had persuaded Colonel Wardle to raise the matter in the House of Commons on 27 January 1809. While eventually exonerated, the duke's reputation was tarnished and enormous damage done to the Establishment and the army. Obliged to resign on 18 March, the duke's scandal could not have occurred at a more difficult time with the Cabinet debating whether to reinforce or evacuate British forces in Portugal.[21]

The reaction in the British press to the end of Moore's campaign varied considerably. *The Times* commented: 'Alas! Our victory is as useless as our retreat ... and neither in flying nor fighting, do we appear to have had any other object in view than that of saving ourselves and deserting the cause we sent troops to sustain.'[22] Unsurprisingly, the French newspapers also made great capital out of the British army's abrupt departure, as this passage from *Le Moniteur* illustrates:

The English will learn what it is to make inconsiderate movement in the presence of the French army. The manner in which they have been driven from the kingdoms of Leon and Galicia and the destruction of part of their army will, no doubt, teach them to be more circumspect of their operations on the Continent.[23]

Although 1808 began well for the Allies, with promising victories like Bailén and Vimeiro, it ended with the Spanish armies defeated and fleeing in disarray. Furthermore, Moore's narrow victory over Soult had merely allowed the British to evacuate with no tangible gains other than avoiding a serious defeat.

On 25 January 1809, Viscount Robert Castlereagh (Minister for War and the Colonies) bravely accepted responsibility for the overall failure of the campaign to support the Spanish, an offer greeted with scorn by some Whig MPs. Yet, he moved for a vote of thanks to honour the victory, remarking on the:

> distinguished conduct and exemplary valour displayed in the battle of Corunna, whereby the complete repulse and signal defeat of the enemy, on every point of attack, was effected, and the safe and unmolested embarkation of the army secured in the presence of a French army of superior force.[24]

Castlereagh continued that Moore had also conducted the army's withdrawal under extremely difficult circumstances and by choosing his line of retreat carefully he 'had completely succeeded in drawing to the northern extremities of the peninsula the efforts of the French forces from the track of the Spanish armies …'.[25] By diverting the march of a substantial portion of Napoleon's army, he denied the French a chance to crush the retreating Spanish armies and strike deeper into southern Spain. Before seizing the opportunity to trap Moore, Napoleon had contemplated marching directly on Lisbon and, if Portugal fell a second time, then chances of further British intervention in the Peninsula were slim. Moore's actions had bought the Allies time and Castlereagh proposed a motion to exonerate Moore. Although this provoked some vocal protests, Lord Henry Petty (later Lord Lansdowne) rose and seconded the motion despite being a prominent member of the Opposition.[26] Even so, Moore's reputation suffered, his heroic death in battle notwithstanding, and the outcome of the campaign remained controversial.

British grand strategy for continuing the war remained in doubt. Although the Cabinet still wished to maintain a military presence in Portugal, it would be costly to send reinforcements overseas. They also hoped to intervene elsewhere on the Continent and troops would be needed for that purpose. Parliamentary objections were raised over the depletion of the fencibles, yeomanry and militias tasked with defending Britain itself, with men being enticed to enlist in the regular army to raise its strength. MPs on both sides of the House of Commons were concerned with the cost of defending Portugal and wished to know how money was being spent:

> Lord *Erskine* rose to make the motion … for accurate returns for the number of officers and men belonging to the infantry, the cavalry, and the artillery, who had embarked at different ports of this country and Ireland, for Spain and Portugal. He also wished to have an account delivered of the expenditure, under the different heads, of money, arms, clothing, etc which had been sent at different times to the Spanish patriots.[27]

Parliament had a right to know how much the country was spending in this regard but the Earl of Buckinghamshire asked for this request to be temporarily withdrawn as 'He had received information … which he feared was but too correct, that the French had re-entered and re-occupied Portugal. It was for his majesty's ministers to say whether this was the case or not, for they no doubt must have received advices of such an event.'[28]

He feared the consequences of the French seizing the ports and fortresses of Portugal, which was a concern also voiced by the Earl of Liverpool who rose as the next speaker. He explained that such complex figures would take time to compile and present to the Commons. This ended the debate over the financial cost of continuing the Peninsular War but, interestingly, it took place on Friday, 3 February 1809 and Marshal Soult (while certainly marching towards the frontier at that point) only attempted to cross the Minho and enter Portugal on 15–16 February. In any case, the country was certainly not under French occupation as suggested, implying that this was an attempt to stifle debate over the vast expense of pursuing war with France.

On 7 March, Sir Arthur Wellesley submitted a memorandum to the Cabinet where he stated, citing his recent experience, that the situation in Portugal was far from hopeless:

> I have always been of the opinion that Portugal might be defended whatever might be the result of the contest in Spain ... My notion was that the Portuguese military establishment of forty thousand militia and thirty thousand regular troops ought to be revived, and that in addition ... His Majesty ought to employ an army in Portugal amounting to about twenty thousand troops ... even if Spain should have been conquered, the French would not have been able to overrun Portugal with a smaller force than one hundred thousand men ...[29]

Although Sir Arthur later amended his estimate of the number of British soldiers required to 30,000 (with 4,000 of them being cavalry), his point that the mountainous nature of the country made it easy to defend appealed to the Cabinet. If Portugal were secured against invasion, the British would have a base to intervene on the Continent and support her allies. Wellesley's well-founded analysis was persuasive and, with Castlereagh's patronage, he was able to gain the promise of another senior command in Portugal.

The Cabinet were impressed with Wellesley's reasoning and optimism. Nevertheless, it still entertained the possibility of military expeditions to Sicily, Italy, Catalonia or Holland (designed to support Austrian operations). Although it eventually agreed to send reinforcements to Portugal, 'in truth, the Cabinet seems never to have favoured the despatch of troops to this quarter ... the choice of Ministers was determined in great measure by circumstances'.[30]

Following his return to France from Spain, Napoleon found his Empire under grave threat from several quarters. Foreign states were contemplating war with France, Royalist revolts had flared up in the Vendée and even members of his own government had conspired against his rule. Baron Stein was fermenting rebellion in Prussia, but far more seriously Metternich (Austrian Minister of Foreign Affairs and Chancellor) had brought Emperor Francis I to the brink of declaring war.

Like all dictators, Napoleon feared being overthrown by those in his own camp and when he returned to Paris was aghast to discover his own ministers had conspired against him in his absence. Charles Maruice de Talleyrand Périgord (Prince of Benevente) had been distancing himself from Napoleon as early as 1807 when he resigned his post as Foreign Minister. He strongly disapproved of Napoleon's deposition of the Spanish monarchy and believed a war in the Peninsula would be costly and almost impossible to win.

It was rumoured that Talleyrand had opened secret communications with the British and, during the Erfurt Conference, secretly informed the tsar of Napoleon's policies. During the emperor's absence, he joined with Joseph Fouché (Minister of Police) and others to alter the line of imperial succession if the emperor failed to return from Spain.[31] Talleyrand now considered Napoleon a megalomaniac who would bring about his own downfall, allegedly telling the tsar (through Metternich) that:

It is up to you to save Europe, and you will not succeed by giving Napoleon his head. The French people are civilised; their sovereign is not. The sovereign of Russia is civilised; his people are not. Therefore, it is up to the sovereign of Russia to be the ally of the French people. The Rhine, the Alps, the Pyrenees are the conquests of France. The rest is the conquest of the Emperor; they do not belong to France.[32]

Talleyrand was among the most able politicians of the period and had been of great service to Napoleon prior to 1807. However, the emperor now distrusted him and once commented, 'The triumph of Talleyrand is the triumph of immorality.'[33] While he declined to punish Fouché, supposedly one of the few men Napoleon actually feared, he decided to make an example of Talleyrand.

Summoning Talleyrand to an audience on 28 January, Napoleon left him standing in an adjoining chamber (Talleyrand was disabled and required a cane for support) for three hours. When he finally deigned to see him, the furious emperor berated him in front of witnesses in the crudest terminology, culminating in the famous insult, 'You are nothing but a shit in silk stockings', and dismissed him from the post of Grand Chamberlain of the Empire.[34] Although Talleyrand was humiliated, it is worth noting that Napoleon did not seriously punish any of those who had plotted against him, even though their disloyalty amounted to treason. A more ruthless monarch would have had the conspirators imprisoned or executed.

The most serious of Napoleon's problems was impending war with Austria, which was the main reason he had returned from Spain. Austria was now sure of receiving backing from the Turkish Porte and their government believed they could put as many as 400,000 troops into the field. What Metternich lacked was financial support and he was busily engaged in securing a loan from Britain of £2.5 million to help meet the costs of Austrian mobilisation and a further £5 million per annum once war was declared.[35] By the standards of the day, this was a staggering amount of money, which Parliament would be reluctant to risk with the outcome of a conflict against Napoleon so uncertain.

Nevertheless, the Tory ministry did send Mr Adair as an ambassador to negotiate with the Austrians and Turks in Constantinople. Eventually, the Austrians received a firm promise of financial assistance once action against France had begun. By April, the British Cabinet also decided to support this Fifth Coalition against France militarily and planned a large-scale intervention on the Continent. This was the Walcheren Expedition, which began with landings on 29 July 1809 and saw the British commit 40,000 men in an attempt to seize French territory and capture Antwerp.

Napoleon did his utmost to disrupt the plans of the Allies, writing to the Russian tsar asking him to apply diplomatic pressure on the Austrians to avert war. However, in spite of previous claims of friendship, Alexander had been forced to ally with France in 1807 and was exasperated by Napoleon's constant demands. By 1809, the Russian nobility were already complaining to him about the financial pressures Napoleon's trade embargo had placed them under and, having gained Finland and the Danubian provinces at Tilsit, Alexander already had most of what he wanted out of his union with France. The tsar did threaten to withdraw the Russian ambassador from Vienna but his attempts to prevent another military coalition against France were unenthusiastic.

France was now in the unenviable position of fighting wars on two fronts. Napoleon's decision to become embroiled in the Peninsular War had a crucial effect on the outcome of the Napoleonic Wars. The tsar, his most important ally, had become increasingly indifferent to his requests, the German states were restive and Britain showed no sign of bowing to the commercial pressure France was applying. With hindsight, Napoleon's Continental System was flawed, since its success relied upon monitoring a vast stretch of coastline to deter smuggling in addition to enforcing mercantile compliance in Continental ports. Furthermore, Britain could rely on her colonies for trade to an extent and maintain her financial security for some time.

Even the vaunted French army would have difficulty fighting against Austria and in the Peninsula simultaneously. Napoleon would be unwise to wage wars on two fronts if they could be avoided so his boundless ambition was both a strength and a weakness, as Jomini conceded:

It is true that he loved war and its chances; but he was also a victim to the necessity of succeeding in his efforts or of yielding to England. It might be said that he was sent into this world to teach generals and statesmen what they should avoid. His victories teach what may be accomplished by activity, boldness and skill; his disasters, what might have been avoided by prudence.[36]

The Peninsular War had already placed the First Empire under great strain and the news of war with Austria was greeted with dismay in Paris. It began on 12 April 1809 when the Archduke John's army invaded Italy without a formal declaration of war, defeating Napoleon's viceroy (Eugène Beauharnais) at Sacile on 16 April. The Tyrolean provinces rose in revolt against the Bavarians (French allies) and the Archduke Charles led an army across the Inn River on 12 April to invade Bavaria. By 14 April, Napoleon had left Paris to take command in what would become one of his greatest campaigns.

The emperor was now too deeply committed in the Peninsula to pull out, having placed his brother on the throne of Spain and being forced to maintain thousands of troops there. Withdrawal would be a humiliating disaster for French arms and would weaken the emperor's political position on the Continent. His only option was to finish what he had started and this meant invading Portugal a second time. With the emperor occupied in central Europe, the responsibility of carrying out this invasion lay in the hands of his marshals.

Chapter Two

The Duke of Damnation

A corporal in the Royal army at the time of the French Revolution, Jean de Dieu Soult rose swiftly during the wars fought to protect the French Republic. Soult gained the emperor's trust and was among the first of those appointed Marshal of France, fighting under Napoleon's command in Austria, Prussia and Poland. Although he had proved himself capable in independent commands, he fought better under the eye of his emperor, and was renowned for his strategic ability as a chief-of-staff. By 1809, Soult's career included an impressive array of campaigns but Napoleon's command to lead the Second Invasion of Portugal was a daunting challenge for him.

By the time of Jean's birth in 1769, the Soults had lived in the Languedoc region of France for generations. Originally named Soulz, the family was Protestant but changed their surname due to the Revocation of the Edict of Nantes in 1685, when many Protestants were persecuted on the grounds of their religious beliefs. Protestant marriages were annulled and children declared illegitimate among other restrictions placed upon their religion. Many Protestants fled France but the Soults chose to convert to Catholicism and assimilate.

Most of Jean's forebears had been tradesmen or minor local government officials and his father, also Jean, was the local notary in St-Amans-Labastide, a remote hamlet near the Black Mountains. His father married Marie-Brigitte de Grenier de la Pierre, whose family hailed from minor gentry who had prospered in the glass-making trade. Her family disapproved of the match but the marriage went ahead in 1765 nonetheless. When young Jean was born, he was followed by a further five siblings – four brothers and one sister.[1]

Marie-Brigitte was a pious woman and gave her eldest son the unusual Christian name of Jean de Dieu in memory of the Portuguese founder of a small Catholic religious order who had previously fought as a soldier for Emperor Charles V in Andalusia during the sixteenth century. Although often referred to as Nicolas, this was not his baptismal name and was largely used as a derisory nickname, which probably originated during the period when Soult fought along the Rhine. It was more widely used after the Second Invasion of Portugal in scathing reference to his desire to become king, with his detractors calling him 'Roi Nicolas'. Interestingly, the use of the name Nicolas as an insult was commonplace in rural areas of France around this time, being associated with someone who was foolish or had been caught out in a ludicrous scheme.[2] In later life, jealous and hostile associates referred to him so often by that name that many historians incorrectly assumed that Nicolas was his actual Christian name.

Living in such an isolated region, the family had to be self-sufficient and young Jean had regularly to gather and carry firewood, water and other supplies. He also had to till the family vegetable plot and these chores made him strong and physically active. The family lived in a small stone cottage, which was one of only five residences in the hamlet, but were obliged to share this abode with the local curé and only occupied the upper floor. The Soults had little money and this was a hard existence. In his later years, Soult would recall his childhood mainly to revel in the fact that he had come so far since those unfortunate days rather than out of any sense of nostalgia.

Soult always spoke French with a strong Languedoc accent, partly influenced by the Black Mountains patois of his region. Although this would not be a problem in his future military career, he tried to lessen his accent as it handicapped his efforts in politics later on, but he was only partially successful in doing so and spoke with a strong regional accent throughout his life. Young Jean received no official schooling and was only given intermittent instruction by Abbé Soult, his uncle, who only visited St-Amans occasionally.[3] His lack of a formal education was something he always regretted in later life.

Jean's father died when he was 10 and his mother, who took over the notary business, hoped that he would adopt his father's trade. To this end, she apprenticed him to a notary in a nearby village but Jean fell in with local ruffians and had to be apprenticed to a second master when dismissed by the first. Yet, he had little desire to pursue this career and instead dreamed of becoming a soldier. In February 1785 he absconded but soon returned to St-Amans. Striding back into the family home, Jean was confronted by bailiffs who were seizing possessions in lieu of his mother's arrears. Shortly thereafter, Jean enlisted as a 16-year-old volunteer in the *Regiment Royal Infanterie* at the Château La Rembergue. He immediately sent the 10 crowns he received on enlistment to his mother to help settle the family debts.

Jean was posted to St-Jean d'Angély for the next two years but became discontented with army life for a number of reasons. A man of his class, lacking formal education, was unlikely to rise far in the army and officers bought their commissions, which commanded high prices. A private income was therefore desirable and his family were poor and he had no patron to rely upon. Most officers hailed from the aristocracy or gentry and obtaining sufficient credit to overcome this bar was a problem. He also had trouble with army discipline and was almost court-martialled for brawling on one occasion. Soult briefly contemplated leaving the army, hoping to return to St-Amans to start a bakery, but he failed to secure his release from service.[4]

Soult had become a non-commissioned officer by the time of the French Revolution. Years later, when the monarchy returned, Royalist critics claimed he was a revolutionary firebrand during this period, preaching dissent in revolutionary societies and the army. This is almost certainly untrue as Soult, far keener on making a success of his military career, was never a radical. His memoirs contain few partisan observations, even though he lived through a period of enormous political turmoil. Rumours of fanaticism probably arose due to his speaking out against the foreign powers threatening France and owed more to patriotism than revolutionary fervour.[5]

The Revolutionary Wars provided a great opportunity for Soult due to his useful military experience, which included being a drill sergeant and the French equivalent of a quartermaster (*corporal fourrier*). He had also demonstrated a flair for army administration duties, which would boost his career. Now France was threatened by invasion, Soult saw action in the Army of the Rhine, serving with the 1st Battalion of the Haut-Rhine, defending the Vosges region of northeast France. During this period, officers were often elected by the rank and file and, being an experienced sergeant, he swiftly rose through the ranks.

Although Soult probably took part in skirmishing around the fortress of Wissembourg, he first saw serious action at Uberfelsheim on 29 March 1792. After winning a victory at Mainz, General Custine's forces were falling back when the pursuing Prussians fell upon the French rearguard. Soult's battalion took almost 50 per cent casualties but held the line and Custine gave a Soult a commendation for the role he played in this engagement.

He next saw action at Bodenthal Camp against the Austrians on 13–14 September and, although only a lieutenant, commanded two battalions which took part in the assault on enemy positions there. During this period, experienced officers were in such short supply that junior officers found themselves with far larger commands than their rank would usually permit them to hold. He continued to fight in numerous small engagements along the French frontier, culminating in the Battle of Saverne on 18 October 1793, where Soult suffered personal loss when his cousin was killed and one of his brothers wounded.[6]

Soult rose rapidly through the ranks and he gained an appointment in General Hoche's army. Subsequently, he became chief-of-staff in Lefebvre's division in the Army of the Meuse. As further promotions followed, he joined the Army of the Sambre and Meuse for the Invasion of Belgium 1794 under General Jourdan. He fought at the Battle of Fleurus on 26 June and was in the thick of the action, having five horses shot from under him as he carried dispatches. The National Convention Government, which ruled France from 1792–5, had anticipated a defeat and only General Jourdan's narrow victory over the Austrians here prevented a purge. Some years later Soult was horrified to learn that the Representative of the People (a political officer accompanying the army) had a list of officers marked for execution in the case of defeat and it included his name.[7]

Soult developed a friendship with General Lefebvre and they would both rise to the rank of marshal in 1804. As Lefebvre's division approached Brussels, it found its march blocked by a combined Dutch/Austrian force at Mont St Jean on 6 July 1794. The division attacked and was delayed by resistance for some hours, but the Allies beat a swift retreat when French reinforcements arrived. Ironically, Soult would meet another adversary here in very different circumstances twenty-one years later when he acted as the emperor's chief-of-staff.

Until October 1794, Soult was occupied in securing Belgium and Luxembourg and later wrote that participating in the sieges of fortresses and helping administer regions falling under French control was the hardest work of his career.[8] Nevertheless, his hard work paid dividends and he was a general by the end of that year, having been a sergeant only three years before.

At this time, the Vendée region was a hotbed of Royalist sympathisers and in a state of revolt against the National Convention. General Hoche was ordered to suppress the rebellion and asked Soult to transfer onto his staff for this campaign. Scorning to fight against his fellow Frenchmen in what amounted to an anti-guerrilla operation, Soult turned down this invitation, even though it came from an old comrade.[9]

Soult was serving on Lefebvre's staff when he met Louise Berg. She was 24 years old, a Protestant and came from Solingen (near Düsseldorf). Soult was billeted in her house and first met her as they passed on the staircase. Duffieux de la Grange-Merlin, a French Royalist émigré recruiting in the German states for the British army, was also courting Louise. However, Soult's status had far more appeal to her mother and she approved and assisted him in his courtship of her daughter.

They were married in April 1796. Soult was not very religious and, with his family's history of Protestantism, the divide between his Catholic faith and her Protestant beliefs seemed irrelevant to them both. They hailed from similar backgrounds and got along very well, their fifty-five-year marriage surviving occasional infidelities on both sides.

Their marriage remained strong throughout Soult's career and Louise accompanied him on some campaigns, although he refused to allow her to travel with him in the Peninsula due to the savage nature of that war. She proved a fine hostess during his later career when they maintained a large house in Paris, and made great efforts to get along with his friends and colleagues in both his military and political life. Although not a great beauty, she found favour with Napoleon who acknowledged that Soult had found a fine partner by remarking, 'Soult is very ambitious but it is his wife who manages him.'[10] The emperor even made Louise a Dame of Honour to his mother, who he loved dearly, signifying his great regard for her.

Fighting continued along the frontiers of France and one of Soult's most renowned exploits during this period was executing the withdrawal of a brigade from Herborn on 16 June 1796. Faced with an overwhelming number of enemy cavalry, which were supported by other arms, he had the infantry form squares and retire in echelon. This required careful timing but Soult achieved this feat and only took minimal casualties, much to the surprise of the rest of the army who had considered this brigade lost. The brigade was eventually relieved by cavalry reinforcements under General Ney.

It was around this time that serious rivalry developed between Soult and Ney. Soult transferred to Championnet's division in 1797 and became more familiar with Ney under this command. Soult probably viewed Ney as a reckless, over gallant, glory-hunting fool while his rival saw him as a staff lackey who purposely avoided the risks of front-line combat. Both of these assessments were unfair and it is likely that these proud, ambitious men simply had conflicting personalities.

By 1798, Soult was stationed in northern France and became involved in preparations for an invasion of England, carrying out administrative work for this operation. In an attempt to frustrate French efforts, the British carried out a raid on the French-controlled port of Ostende, hoping to destroy the port's canal link with Bruges and prevent a concentration of transport vessels there. The raid began on 19 May but Ostende's guns discouraged a serious assault on the town and the British prepared to embark after destroying a canal sluice and several transport ships. A daring counter-attack by the Ostende garrison saw most of this force captured on the beaches before they could embark, but whether Soult was present is uncertain. Although he claimed to have been at the surrender in his memoirs, some factual errors on his part imply that he may not have been.[11]

Returning to the Army of Mainz (soon to be renamed the Army of the Danube), Soult was involved in a campaign where the enemy usually possessed more men and resources. The Battle of Stockach in 1799 was a typical battle with the French heavily outnumbered, and when Lefebvre was wounded Soult assumed command of the division. Despite losing 1,800 casualties, he managed to hold his ground and the fiercest fighting occurred on 25 March when Soult's division suffered 50 per cent losses in a major Austrian attack.[12] Despite heavy losses on both sides, the battle was indecisive but, as the French felt obliged to adopt a defensive strategy along the Rhine, Stockarch is usually considered an Austrian victory. Yet, his superiors noted Soult's able performance in command.

Following an incredibly successful campaign in Italy, Bonaparte became the foremost general in France and gained great political influence. In 1798, having dismissed an invasion of England as impractical, he embarked upon a campaign in the Middle East. His main objectives were to seize Egypt and challenge British commercial dominance of the region. Soult was not part of this famous military expedition but the campaign he was engaged in, while overshadowed by Egypt, was far more important for France and the survival of the Directory Government that ruled France from 1795–9.

Soult was sent to the Army of Helvetia under General André Massena. The course of the war had turned and the forces of the Second Coalition opposing France were swiftly recapturing their lost territory. The Russians and Austrians mounted strong offensives and the French suffered serious defeats in Italy. They were also defeated and forced into retreat along the northern frontier, and with the Allies poised to invade France, only Massena's army in Switzerland (the central sector of the French defence) stood in the way. Yet, Massena was an excellent general who knew the mountainous Swiss terrain would favour a defensive strategy, despite the overwhelming number of the enemy forces ranged against him.

Soult's first duty was to pacify Swiss guerrilla activity in the Reuss Valley area, an assignment that was likely to be dangerous and distasteful but came with an independent command. During this period, guerrillas were considered brigands and most armies adopted stern measures to deal with them, executing captured patriots and carrying out reprisals to discourage uprisings. To his credit, Soult chose another path since he believed most Swiss favoured the French cause.

Despite the murder of French soldiers, Soult treated captured guerrillas well and convened a conference at the Monastery of Einsiedeln with Swiss leaders on the condition that they would discourage further attacks while negotiations were in progress. During these talks, he downplayed the recent violence, arguing that their common enemy (the Austrians) was the natural foe of the Swiss. His approach was successful and the Landemann of Schwyz encouraged locals to enlist in the French army. Soult formed a high opinion of the Swiss recalling that, 'I shall never forget the welcome I had from these good people and I get renewed pleasure from thinking about them as I write …'.[13] Surprised and impressed by Soult's diplomatic success, Massena was pleased to see the Swiss enlisting in considerable numbers.

Soult was present at the first Battle of Zürich, 4–7 June 1799, when the Archduke Charles tried to break through Massena's defences (founded on the Zürichberg) and in the woodlands around the city itself. Fighting was intense and the French repulsed many Austrian assaults but Massena chose to pull back across the River Limmat on 5 June, leaving a number of cannon behind in the process. Yet, the French benefitted from their fortified positions, suffering approximately 1,700 casualties while the Austrians lost almost twice that number.

A lull now ensued as the Austrians were reluctant to attack over the river and deployed around Zürich to await reinforcements. An Allied victory at Novi on 15 August allowed the Russian General Suvorov to quit Italy for Switzerland as most of northern Italy fell under Allied control. A Russian army under Korsakov had already reinforced the Austrians at Zürich but it pleased Massena when he learned that the Archduke Charles (a formidable opponent) had been ordered to the Rhine. The Allies were doing well there too with the city of Mannheim falling on 18 September. French defeats to the north and south of Switzerland caused great alarm in Paris and for weeks Massena bravely refused demands from the Directory that he should mount an immediate counter-attack (generals had been executed for lesser acts of insubordination during this period). He insisted on timing his attack with great care and refused to be rushed.

The Second Battle of Zürich took place on 25–6 September. Taking advantage of Suvorvov's delay as he marched through the St Gotthard Pass, Massena divided his 50,000 troops to assail the Austrian and Russian armies, which were stationed on both sides of Lake Zürich. The central sector of the Austrian position was protected by the lake, a stretch of the lower Linth River and the Walensee. Surprise was a vital element his battle plan and Soult played a critical role in organising the amphibious crossings. He scouted the area dressed as a private soldier as, during the lull in the fighting, sentries usually declined to fire upon each other. By these means, he was able to approach closely and reconnoitred the positions of marshland and numerous flooded channels in the area.

Soult trained and selected 160 men who were good swimmers, and this tiny vanguard swam the Linth at 2.30 am on 25 September. Clad only in their breeches and shirtsleeves, they carried swords or knives in their teeth while others tied pistols and cartridges (wrapped in bundles) to their heads to avoid getting their powder wet. Once they gained the enemy bank, they silenced Austrian sentries in an action that seems more akin to a modern commando raid than Napoleonic warfare. Some of their number had dragged ropes behind them and these were used to pull rafts, platforms and fascines across to construct a bridge. Before the alarm could be raised, a whole battalion had crossed the Linth. Simultaneously, attempts were made to cross downstream at Schloss Grynau and by boats across Lake Zürich.[14]

The success of this difficult and unconventional operation had a major effect on the battle and Soult gained great credit for the role he had played in it. The enemy mounted numerous counter-attacks but all were repulsed and Austrian General Hotze killed during one engagement. Soult's forces managed to seize enemy stores and a flotilla of boats on Lake Zürich early on in the action and this unexpected attack greatly assisted Massena's ultimate victory in the battle.

After defeating the Austro-Russian armies at Zürich, Massena ordered Soult to block Suvorov's march from the St Gotthard Pass. He achieved this, skilfully using three divisions in an attempt to ensnare the Russians in the mountains, ultimately forcing Suvorov to withdraw. This demonstrated considerable skill in command as, while many generals could handle a brigade, not every commander was capable of commanding at corps level and Suvorov was an experienced opponent. Soult demonstrated considerable ability as a strategist in mountain warfare with the intricate manoeuvring and risk of ambush involved. After Suvorov's repulse, he rejoined Massena to complete the pursuit of the Austro–Russian forces fleeing Zürich. It was a decisive victory as the Allied offensive was stopped in its tracks.

Massena, himself a master of mountain warfare and the defensive, was particularly impressed with Soult and singled him out for praise after the campaign. The successful crossing of the Linth drew his attention in particular and he wrote of his 'falling upon the enemy with such skill and energy and beating them everywhere'.[15] When Bonaparte returned from Egypt, leaving his army behind, he justified his actions by the need to save the Republic as France itself was threatened. To his embarrassment, politicians in Paris pointed out that Massena had effectively achieved this in his absence.

The Brumaire *coup d'état*, 9–10 November 1799, saw the Directory Government in Paris swept away and replaced by the Consulate. Initially, three consuls were selected to rule but, as First Consul, Napoleon Bonaparte soon took precedence. Justly proud of his achievements in Italy in 1796, Napoleon was outraged that nearly all of his conquests had been lost in his absence and decided to regain them for France. Massena was given command of the Army of Italy and ordered to halt Allied progress, while Bonaparte assembled an Army of Reserve near Dijon for an invasion.

Soult's able performance in Switzerland led directly to his appointment to command an entire wing of Massena's Army of Italy. Prior to their departure for the front, he was appalled by the extent of the corruption he witnessed in the Army of Italy's commissariat. While usually financially astute, Massena had been swindled out of resources set aside for his army according to Soult, who wrote, 'Is our army to be the plaything of this foul horde who enrich themselves at the soldiers' expense?'[16]

Perhaps it was Soult's observation of corruption that persuaded him that if others could profit from war, why should he refrain from doing so? Certainly, his chief was already notorious in the French army for looting and observing Massena's actions may have affected him somewhat.[17] Soult appears to have taken an interest in furthering his own cause at around this time and is said to have confiscated goods and money in Italy, which seldom ended up in the government's coffers.

Soult was aged 31 when he joined Massena in Italy and at the height of his military capabilities. Unfortunately, there was little Massena's army could do to stem the Austrian advance in northern Italy. Although the departure of Russian forces left the Austrians with only 45,000 men in this theatre, the French defeat at the Battle of Genola in autumn 1799 allowed the Austrians to consolidate their gains and bring up reinforcements. Massena's army was forced back and took refuge in the Port of Genoa. The Austrian General Melas laid siege to the city on 20 April 1800, having 90,000 troops at his disposal to hem in Massena's army of some 18,000 men.

Gaining possession of Genoa was strategically vital for the Austrians in order to attempt an invasion of southern France. In addition to being an important supply base, they could not afford to have a hostile force occupying this port in their rear as they advanced. Accordingly, Bonaparte ordered Massena to hold the city at all costs, promising to cross the Alps and relieve the city. In addition to being surrounded on land, the port was under blockade by the Royal Navy and conditions inside the city deteriorated as supplies could not reach the garrison.

Yet, Massena mounted a stubborn defence, sending scores of sallies into the Austrian siege lines to disrupt their operations. Soult led numerous raids and the enemy were astounded at how well the garrison held out under such appalling privations with starvation rampant in the city. On 11 May, Soult was wounded during a sortie, receiving a musket ball through the knee. Conveying him upon an improvised stretcher (a blanket tied between two muskets), his men were forced to abandon him as the effort of carrying him caused him too much pain. He was left behind in the company of his brother and an aide-de-camp and all three were taken prisoner.[18] Elated by their capture of a French general, the Austrians took Soult back to their lines and mounted renewed assaults against Genoa's ramparts, only to be repulsed.

Capture spared Soult from having to endure the extreme privations in the city. Massena was even reduced to forbidding funeral services (due to their negative effect on morale) and only allowing those capable of carrying a musket to receive rations. Nearly 30,000 soldiers and civilians perished during the siege, largely from disease and starvation. Although news that Bonaparte had crossed the Alps and was marching towards them raised the garrison's spirits, Massena capitulated on 4 June and the Allies granted him generous concessions as a tribute to his gallant defence.

Soon afterwards, Bonaparte won a narrow victory at the Battle of Marengo on 14 June 1800, but Massena's stubborn resistance had bought him valuable time. Louise Soult was allowed into the Austrian camp to tend her husband and, hearing the guns at Marengo, they guessed that he would not remain a prisoner for long. During peace talks, General Berthier attempted to placate an Austrian delegate saying, 'It must be a consolation to have been beaten only by a fine army under the greatest general in the world.' The Austrian officer replied briskly, 'The battle of Marengo was not lost here, but before Genoa.'[19]

After a period of convalescence, Soult received an administrative command under Murat in Italy, holding this post during the brief cessation of hostilities in the Napoleonic Wars following the Peace of Amiens on 25 March 1802. With war declared once more on 16 May 1803, he was put in command of St-Omer Camp near Boulogne on 28 August. Here preparations were made for a proposed invasion of England, with Soult overseeing much of the training and organisation of what would eventually become Napoleon's *Grande Armée*. The operation was cancelled after Nelson's naval triumph at Trafalgar in 1805, but it is uncertain whether Napoleon ever really intended to cross the Channel owing to the Royal Navy's unchallenged supremacy at sea. In later years, when questioned about French military intentions, Soult was evasive, limiting himself to the comment, 'Ah, Monsieur, that is the great question.'[20] With his level of responsibility at Boulogne, it is almost certain that he knew Napoleon's mind regarding the proposed invasion but chose never to reveal the truth.

Bonaparte crowned himself Emperor Napoleon I of France on 18 May 1804 and created the Marshalate the following day. Soult was one of eighteen Marshals of Empire created and the eighth in terms of seniority. He also gained the rank of Colonel General of the Imperial Guard, but the title of Marshal of Empire was more a civic honour than a military rank and partly designed to give the army political voice for ruling France.[21] His elevation to the Marshalate also placed Soult among an elite group of generals who enjoyed great influence in the army and held the emperor's confidence.

Some of the recipients of this honour owed their position to political reliability more than their military talent but there were some excellent commanders among them. Foremost among these were Massena, Suchet and Davout, who rivalled the emperor himself in terms of command skills. Others were good fighting soldiers, such as Ney, Murat and Soult's old chief Lefebvre. They came from a variety of backgrounds and it is interesting to note that the sons of tradesmen, soldiers, innkeepers and lawyers were among them. Theoretically, the Revolution had swept away tradition and privilege with this practice continuing into the imperial period: 'It was a saying among the rank and file of the armies of revolutionary France that every soldier carried in his knapsack the bâton of a marshal. This was to prove truer than is usual with such dicta; far more than half of Napoleon's marshals did actually arise from the ranks.'[22] Napoleon regularly quoted this saying (usually attributed to him alone) and it is true that the system he established was a meritocracy allowing far more movement between social classes than the monarchy ever permitted. Indeed, without noble birth or wealth it would have been nearly impossible for those from working class origins to attain such heights previously. This was also true of the emperor himself, whose father only obtained the status of minor nobility as a reward for supporting the French, and whose family origins and homeland were obscure.

While Soult was pleased to see some old comrades elevated to the Marshalate, he had developed a fierce rivalry with Ney and found his relationship with Berthier strained at the best of times. This was probably due to professional jealousy between them as both Berthier and Soult were renowned for their ability in the role of chief-of-staff, although Berthier was probably superior. However, nearly all of the marshals still on active service were proud, competitive and ambitious men who viewed themselves as answerable to the emperor alone. When they were not under Napoleon's personal command, they were unlikely to co-operate effectively – as some campaigns later proved.

The fact that Napoleon deliberately fostered rivalry between his marshals was unhelpful. He did so because these men had witnessed and, in some cases, contributed to the fall of a king, making them difficult to command and impossible to intimidate by the force of his personality alone. Furthermore, although most of them admired the emperor, Napoleon had seized power rather than inheriting it like a hereditary monarch. This led to the obvious conclusion that other capable men could do the same if an opportunity presented itself, so it was in Napoleon's interest to ensure his subordinates did not gain enough fame and prestige to challenge him. By the adept use of favouritism, he was able to keep them at each other's throats and distract them from pondering on opportunities to oust him when these arose.

Many negative remarks have been written about this group, as Delderfield recorded, 'they were to wear a variety of labels. They were to be called callous, greedy, treacherous, rapacious, brutal and a hundred other things. There is only one word that no writer has ever dared to use in respect of any one of them. That word is "coward".'[23] In spite of their faults, all twenty-six men eventually appointed to the Marshalate were selected on merit, having proved themselves as brave and capable soldiers. Some gained great influence during a period when France practically challenged an entire continent. Soult was now a member of this inner circle and would become one of the giants of the Napoleonic era – a stunning rise for a man from such a humble background.

With the Invasion of England cancelled, Napoleon now redirected the *Grande Armée* against the Austrian and Russian armies marching against France. Demonstrating exemplary staff work, Marshal Berthier planned a long and complicated march for almost 160,000 men in 7 infantry corps, 1 cavalry corps and the Consular Guard (soon to be renamed the Imperial Guard). The roads the army had to use often amounted to little more than forest tracks and Berthier (at Napoleon's direction) ensured that these nine huge units could convey artillery and baggage through difficult terrain and received adequate supplies. In only forty-five days, men who had been camped around Boulogne, Brest and Hamburg converged on the enemy with incredible speed. They surprised and cut off an entire Austrian army under General Mack, who surrendered at the small Bavarian town of Ulm on 20 October 1805, allowing Napoleon an almost bloodless victory. Soult commanded the IV Corps of the *Grande Armée* and now participated in the Austerlitz campaign, which ended in Napoleon's most celebrated victory. However, difficulties were already beginning to emerge in the command structure as the marshals vied for their emperor's approval. Soult, Murat and Lannes were in conference at Murat's headquarters on 28 November when Lannes proposed a temporary withdrawal, to which they agreed. When Napoleon arrived, he expressed surprise that the usually aggressive Lannes thought retreat necessary and when he asked Soult's opinion he received an evasive reply. This drew an angry response from Lannes, as recorded by Thiébault:

I have not been here a quarter of an hour, and I know nothing about our position but what these gentlemen have told me. My opinion was founded and formed on their statements … Marshal Soult's answer is that of a dirty sneak, and such as I was far from expecting. I regard it as an insult, and I will have satisfaction for it.[24]

From a fighting soldier like Lannes, a challenge to a duel was serious, despite the emperor's attempts to prohibit the practice. While Soult tried to placate Lannes, Napoleon simply paced up and down, seemingly deep in thought. 'Suddenly he stopped short, and after saying, "I too think a retreat necessary" [abruptly left]'.[25] Thiébault implies that Napoleon only said this to prevent a duel as the resulting manoeuvre was more an evolution than an actual withdrawal. This would not be the last time that Napoleon's marshals came close to exchanging blows.

The decisive battle of the campaign took place in Moravia at Austerlitz on 2 December 1805 (the first anniversary of Napoleon's Coronation). It was known as the Battle of the Three Emperors because, although the Russian General Kutusov was technically the commander-in-chief, Tsar Alexander I and the Austrian Emperor Francis II were also present. Unsurprisingly, this raised questions over who was truly in command, such divisions giving the French an advantage.

Napoleon had abandoned the strategically important Pratzen Heights in the centre of the battlefield, hoping to entice the Austrians and Russians into mounting an attack. His strategy worked and while Lannes held the French left, the enemy assailed the French right flank as Napoleon had hoped. Parts of this area were bordered by lakes and some units were forced to deploy upon marshy ground, placing them at a disadvantage. Soult's IV Corps, Bernadotte's I Corps and the Guard Cavalry under Bessières held the French centre. Napoleon intended to counter-attack with these forces but the manoeuvre required careful timing and Lannes (supported by Murat's cavalry) withstood a series of ferocious attacks before he was able to do so.

Once the bulk of enemy troops had marched down to assault the French right, Napoleon ordered Soult to recapture the Pratzen Heights. The counter-attack was a stunning success, with Soult's IV Corps seizing the heights and cutting off many enemy troops. All attempts to regain the position by the Allies were firmly repulsed and the French trained artillery on the frozen lakes as the enemy tried to retreat across them, killing many and forcing large numbers to surrender. With the heights in French hands, the position of the Allied army became untenable and it began to retreat having suffered severe losses. The Austrian emperor personally sued for peace that night and the decisive defeat of the Allies at Austerlitz effectively destroyed the Third Coalition against France.

Soult was exultant over the effective role he played during the battle, especially during the crucial counter-attack, which Napoleon acknowledged had been the decisive manoeuvre. In contrast, Lannes was so angry over the lack of recognition he received from the emperor for his stubborn defence that he rode back to Paris without even asking his commander's permission to leave.

This was the *Grande Armée*'s first great victory and more were to follow. Over the following years, Napoleon rewarded his marshals with many titles and Soult believed that he should have been made Duke of Austerlitz in recognition of his achievements there. However, some officers like Thiébault (who commanded a brigade in IV Corps) alleged that he stayed out of the firing line and actually left the field due to inflammation of the eyes on one occasion and questioned his contribution to the victory.[26] He believed Soult gave few orders and even then from a distance, with General Vandamme (one of Soult's divisional commanders) deserving the real credit for the assault on the Pratzen Heights. He argued that the emperor was right to deny Soult a battle-related title:

> Marshal Soult, who no more fought the enemy that day than he fought Lannes, reckons Austerlitz among his titles to fame. The fame belongs by right not to him but to his army. The Emperor made no mistake, and when he gave him a title he did not call him – I will not say Duke of Austerlitz – Lannes would not have stood for that – but after any town or village recalling the name of a victory.[27]

Yet, Thiébault was biased as his memoirs contain some vitriolic passages castigating Soult, whom he accused of opposing his promotion.[28] The military historian Paddy Griffith also casts some doubt on Thiébault's theories, as the emperor himself believed Soult was responsible for the attack, calling him 'the *premier manoeuvrier* in Europe'.[29] Many historians believe that the real reason Napoleon refused to award a title associated with Austerlitz to anyone was due to his desire to keep all the glory of this victory for himself alone.

Over the next decade, the emperor would make some marshals dukes, princes and even kings and Soult received the title Duke of Dalmatia on 29 June 1808. Napoleon's reason for honouring him with this association is obscure as he had never even been to the Illyrian coast where this province was located. Soult wanted a title commemorating a feat of arms in preference, having seen many of his fellow marshals receive battle-related titles. For example, Marshal Lefebvre was created Duke of Danzig, Ney the Duke of Elchingen, Massena the Duke of Rivoli and Lannes the Duke of Montebello. Indeed, this caused discontent among other Marshals of the Empire but, in Soult's case, the fact that rivals like Ney and Lannes received such titles while he was denied one must have particularly rankled. He believed that he had been cheated out of the title Duke of Austerlitz right up to the end of his life.[30]

In the aftermath of the Austerlitz campaign, Soult took the opportunity of improving his education. Intriguingly, Griffith records that he made use of his aides-de-camp for this purpose. Knowing that many subordinates had benefitted from a better education than he had, Soult would debate with them about a variety of subjects – historical, literary and military topics among others.[31] France's ascendancy after Napoleon's great victory did not remain unchallenged for long with Prussia joining an alliance with Great Britain and Russia against France on 15 September 1806. Refusing to wait until these states assembled a united force, Napoleon mounted a pre-emptive strike, inflicting two serious defeats on the Prussians at the battles of Jena and Auerstädt on 14 October 1806. Prussia's army was considered among the best in the world and Napoleon's lightning campaign and overwhelming victory shocked observers and resulted in Berlin being occupied by the French less than two weeks later.

Soult's IV Corps was present at Jena but only engaged in the fighting to a limited extent. Sainte-Charmans, one of Soult's staff officers, commented on his alleged reluctance to expose himself to danger, stating that he chose to concentrate on strategic planning, relaying his orders to his staff to an unusual extent. He believed that:

in war he loved vigorous enterprises, but only on condition that he did not expose his own person too far. He was far from sharing the brilliant courage of Marshal Ney and Marshal Lannes; one could not even reproach him of the opposite excess, of sheltering himself too carefully. This defect came to him with the great fortune he had amassed.[32]

Allegations of this nature were often levelled against senior officers and perhaps the contrast between Soult and marshals like Ney, who adopted a more active approach, magnified this fault to an unfair extent. Furthermore, when commanding officers did expose themselves to hazards, they often drew criticism for running the risk of leaving their troops leaderless if they fell in battle. Soult had displayed his personal courage as a junior officer on many occasions in the past and, having attained senior rank, it was not his duty to put himself at risk.

However, this was not the first time that he had been accused of avarice and, by implication, looting in occupied territories. It was rumoured that he was second only to Massena among the Marshalate for his eagerness to acquire money and works of art and accusations of this kind followed him throughout his career.[33] Indeed, it was alleged that he appropriated art treasures from all over Europe but most especially during his four years of service in the Peninsula. For example, Bartolomé Esteban Murillo's *The Assumption of the Virgin* famously came into his possession and eventually became a valued item in the Louvre's collection.[34]

Although Prussia had suffered a major defeat, King Frederick William III stubbornly refused to agree terms with Napoleon, placing himself under Russian protection. Therefore, the *Grande Armée* marched into Poland to fight the Russians and Soult was present at the Battle of Eylau, 7–8 February 1807, where IV Corps was heavily engaged. The battle was fought in bitter weather conditions and Marshal Augereau's division lost its way in a blizzard, accidentally marching into the concentrated fire of several Russian artillery batteries and infantry formations. It was later said that Augereau lost 15,000 men in only fifteen minutes. The French suffered 15,000–25,000 casualties compared with the Russians who lost around 15,000 men.

After the battle, Soult accompanied Napoleon as he visited the makeshift hospitals overloaded with wounded men. "'Marshal," said the Emperor to him next day, "the Russians have done us great harm," to which Soult, nothing daunted, replied, "And we them. Our cannon balls were not made of cotton.'"[35] Soult was placed on the right during the battle and had done much to stop that flank from crumbling under a succession of furious Russian attacks. He was among the first to detect signs of a Russian withdrawal and inform the emperor and, during a battle when the high command was placed under great strain and serious mistakes were made, 'Soult was one of the few senior officers who emerges from Eylau with credit.'[36]

Soult gained the emperor's favour during the campaign in Poland and this was probably due to his grasp of the strategic situation. Napoleon sought his counsel on several occasions to the extent that Marshal Berthier made his dislike of Soult very plain.[37] An exemplary chief-of-staff, Berthier was nicknamed the 'Emperor's Wife' by the troops because of the amount of time he spent in close conference with Napoleon and his disapproval was probably a result of professional jealousy.

The Russians were finally defeated at the Battle of Friedland on 14 June 1807 and the tsar sued for peace. The two emperors met on a raft moored symbolically in the middle of the River Nieman near the town of Tilsit on 25 June. Terms were agreed between 7 and 9 July and the resulting Treaty of Tilsit effectively divided much of Europe between them and united the two nations against Britain.

France was now the dominant power in Europe and Napoleon conveyed his pleasure by bestowing decorations, honours and titles on his soldiers. The Marshalate were foremost in this as many of them had made invaluable contributions to the emperor's victories and Napoleon was careful to acknowledge this. Soult already had private sources of income but was now awarded a stipend of 300,000 francs per annum in addition to the title Duke of Dalmatia. To place this in context, an infantryman received roughly 250 francs per year (before stoppages) and this stipend was in addition to Soult's army pay.

The next time Soult saw active service was in Spain after joining the *Grande Armée* for Napoleon's strike over the Ebro (see Chapter 1) which shattered the Spanish armies. Soult performed well, commanding II Corps from 9 November onwards and sweeping forward to take Burgos before heading southwest during the attempt to cut off General Blake's army. Up to that point, the campaign had been a French triumph and, when Napoleon marched from Madrid against Sir John Moore's army, he wrote to Soult from Tordesillas, saying, 'Our cavalry scouts are already at Benavente. If the English pass to-day in their positions they are lost.' Although Moore avoided the trap, the emperor remained confident, writing to his brother that:

> great events will take place. If the English have not already retreated they are lost. Even if they have already moved they shall be chased to the water's edge and not half of them shall re-embark. Put into your newspapers that 36,000 English are surrounded, that I am at Benavente in their rear while Soult is in their front.[38]

Although the appalling weather effected mobility, Soult very nearly cut off General Romana's army as it withdrew across the Plains of Leon. Even so, he fell upon the Spanish rearguard at Mansilla on 29 December capturing over half of this 3,000-strong force along with their artillery, although this action allowed Romana's main army to escape.

Napier expressed his admiration of how Napoleon reacted once aware of an opportunity for outmanoeuvring a British army, but also praised Soult:

> [Napoleon] put fifty thousand men in movement on a totally new line of operations, and in the midst of winter execute a march of two hundred miles ... Nor is Soult's indefatigable valour to be overlooked, as contributing to the success. It is remarkable how he and the emperor, advancing from different bases, should have combined their movements, that after marching, the one about a hundred and the other above two hundred miles through a hostile country, they effected their junction at a given point and at a given hour without failure ...[39]

Soult had lost none of his ability when it came to strategic planning during his absence from active service and made a major contribution to Napoleon's Spanish campaign. One lesson he learned from the emperor was that, while clever manoeuvring on the battlefield often brought success, it was precise planning and thorough logistics that frequently enabled such victories. He later wrote 'inspiration is nothing but rapid calculation'.[40]

Napoleon handed over command of the pursuit to Soult on 2 January 1809 but, while he pushed on as hard as weather conditions would allow, the French troops were tired after marching for hundreds of miles through challenging country. The British troops were equally exhausted and demoralised by having to retreat but fought a series of effective rearguard actions nonetheless. Soult pressed the British retreat as closely as he could, the cavalry of his vanguard killing or capturing numerous stragglers. Yet, the rules of war were usually observed and those taken prisoner were well treated.[41]

It was around this time that Soult gained the sobriquet 'Duke of Damnation', a corruption of his official title Duke of Dalmatia. This nickname is thought to have originated in the lower ranks of the British army and probably referred to the fact that Soult's forces harassed them mercilessly during the retreat and 'that damned Duke' was rarely more than one step behind them. It also implied a grudging respect that those in the ranks had for their enemy and, during the time he spent campaigning in the Spanish Peninsula, he was often referred to as 'The Damned Soult' and other variations upon this nickname in the Spanish, Portuguese and British newspapers.

Moore decided to delay the French pursuit by fighting a strong rearguard action at Lugo. The River Minho was running high and was virtually impossible to ford near the town, which influenced his choice of ground. The river valley also provided a good defensive position, sloping down to the river at a gentle angle with the whole area marked by numerous dry stone walls, hedges and narrow lanes. Rough hills on the British right flank also protected Moore's position.

Observing that the enemy was present in some force, Soult's vanguard halted and waited for support. When he arrived on 7 January, Soult probed the position, suspecting that a brief engagement with the rearguard would ensue and the British would swiftly withdraw. He ordered a preliminary bombardment with one horse artillery battery, while preparing to advance with four squadrons of cavalry. The French were surprised when the fire of this battery drew counter-fire from at least fifteen guns, which rapidly silenced it.

Realising that a serious engagement was likely, Soult brought up infantry and additional artillery, mounting a feint against the British right while directing his main attack against their left. After a preliminary cannonade, the infantry advanced in column, initially gaining ground but meeting serious resistance from Leith's Brigade. Leith was pushed back but the personal intervention of Sir John Moore prevented a serious reverse when he rode to the point of crisis and steadied the line. General James Leith then brought up a battalion of the 59th Regiment and the French withdrew.

Surprised by the stubbornness of the British defence, Soult consolidated his position and waited for the rest of II Corps to reach him. He also sent a dispatch to Ney requesting that he detach a division of VI Corps and send it by the Val des Orres to Orense and assail the British right. However, with food supplies low and being eager to reach the coast, Moore withdrew in the night before he could be outflanked. Lugo was the last major attempt by the British to delay the French pursuit and Moore's army reached Corunna on 11 January, a day before Soult's advance guard.

A fleet of over a hundred transports, escorted by twelve ships of the line put into Corunna's harbour on 14 January. Moore was eager to embark before the French could intervene, destroying the main gunpowder storehouse in the town and beginning the embarkation of cavalry and artillery immediately. He was aware that Ney's VI Corps was hurrying to join Soult and knew his army was not strong enough to survive a simultaneous attack, which would see him pushed into the small peninsula the town stood upon and forced to surrender. Despairing of loading the horses in time, he ordered the bulk of them shot dead on the beaches but as skirmishing began on 15 January, he realised that he would have to fight a battle to allow all of his soldiers to evacuate.

Owing to lack of numbers, the British had abandoned the Penasquedo Heights and Soult took full advantage of their prominence, deploying his guns there effectively. On the morning of 16 January 1809, Moore had only 15,000 infantry, 9 cannon and a tiny force of 90 cavalry against Soult's 16,000-strong force supported by 40 guns. Hoping that Ney would arrive to support his attack, Soult delayed until the afternoon but ordered the attack to begin at 1.30 pm.

Soult's intention was to attack and occupy Moore's left and centre while mounting a cavalry based assault on their right to cut the British off from Corunna. The British resisted strongly, refusing to let their flank be turned by the cavalry on the right and the fighting began to centre on the village of Elvina, which lay slightly to the right of Moore's centre in a shallow depression. Soult ordered a heavy preliminary bombardment and: 'The assault was made upon the English by the first brigade of the division of Mermet, which overthrew them, and drove them from the villa of Elvina. The 2nd regiment of light infantry covered itself with glory. General Jardon, at the head of the Voltigeurs, made a terrible carnage.'[42] Jardon had deployed 600 skirmishers, which effectively prepared the way for Mermet's infantry but the British refused to abandon the village and fighting raged there and on the ridge behind it.

General Baird was wounded and Moore rode with his staff to rally the troops behind Elvina at 3.00 pm, when he ordered the 42nd to counter-attack as the French 31st Regiment advanced beyond their support. By 3.30 pm Mermet's attack was faltering but the village was still fiercely contested, the British 42nd and 50th regiments having fought almost to a standstill. Moore now felt free to concentrate on repulsing the assault on his right flank and brought up reinforcements from General Warde's Guards Brigade from his reserve.

The French 47th Regiment attempted to outflank the British positions on the ridge, only to meet fierce resistance as Moore ordered General Bentinck's brigade to form a new line to counter them. The fighting came to close quarters and the 47th almost lost their eagle standard: 'The Colonel of the 47th regiment distinguished himself. An Ensign of the 31st infantry killed with his own hand an English Officer, who had endeavoured to wrest from him his eagle.'[43]

General Baron Armand Lahoussaye's cavalry had made steady progress on the British right but found itself opposed by elements of the 95th, which had taken up position on broken ground. Lahoussaye ordered his dragoons to dismount and skirmish with the riflemen but they found themselves easily outmatched by these elite skirmishers and, as Moore brought up five more battalions to reinforce his flank, they broke off the assault. By 4.30 pm, most of the French were retreating to the Penasquedo Heights and the fight on this flank was virtually over.

General Moore was attempting to rally elements of the 42nd and 50th around Elvina, when he was struck by a cannon ball that shattered his shoulder. General Hope assumed command at about 4.50 pm and Moore was carried from the field. The French mounted one last attack at 5.15 pm but were driven off with relative ease compared with former assaults and Soult ordered a general withdrawal to the heights. Moore lived long enough to hear that the French had been repulsed but died soon afterwards and was buried that night.

The British lost between 800 and 900 men at Corunna but the French suffered nearly twice as many casualties. Soult decided to await Ney's arrival before mounting another attack but was caught unawares as the British quietly proceeded with their evacuation overnight. Once he realised what was happening, Soult ordered artillery batteries brought forward onto the Heights of Santa Margarita overlooking the anchorage to fire upon the fleet. 'The Duke of Dalmatia had caused a carronade [cannonade] to be discharged among the vessels from the fort of Santiago. Several transports ran aground, and all the men who were on board were taken.'[44]

Soult swiftly took possession of Corunna and later claimed to have captured military stores (including 3,000 muskets) including large amounts of ammunition, and estimated that at least 2,800 of the British who had embarked were wounded. Yet, the French Army's 29th Bulletin claimed that a significant portion of Moore's treasury was seized but that was almost certainly erroneous. Despite their successful embarkation, the British expedition had met with an ignominious end, the French recording:

> The air about Corunna is infected by the carcases of 1200 horses that the English killed in the streets. Gen. Alzedo, Governor of Corunna, who appears to have taken part with the insurgents only from force, took the oath of fidelity to King Joseph Napoleon with enthusiasm. The people manifest the joy they feel at being delivered from the English.[45]

While the French were understandably triumphant at expelling the British from Spain, Moore's successful retreat and defence allowed 27,000 troops to evade capture (when combined with the rest of the army that embarked from Vigo). Soult was also so impressed by Moore's defence that he purchased a stone monument to be erected over his grave as a mark of respect. Nevertheless, with the British gone and Spanish forces scattered, Soult and

Ney could now set about occupying northern Spain and the way to Portugal lay open.

Up to January 1809, Soult had enjoyed a spectacularly successful and varied career. Yet, while some excellent biographies on Soult exist, historian Jean Tulard believes that a definitive account of the man will not be written until the Soult family releases his personal papers in their entirety, which is an important consideration for those studying his career.[46] Although Soult wrote manuscripts for four volumes of memoirs, only two have been printed so far, leaving yawning gaps about his thoughts on the Peninsular War and the Bourbon Restoration, among other topics. If his descendants allow these books to be published, historians will a have more complete picture of these events from his perspective.

Judging by what Soult did publish, combined with the views of others, it is clear that he was an ambitious and capable soldier who rose to exalted rank through personal effort in a manner that would have been impossible but for the French Revolution. His early campaigning speaks of a soldier who carried out his duties energetically and did not hesitate to place himself in danger if necessary. He proved highly competent during the frontier campaigns with the Army of the Rhine but it was his performance at the Second Battle of Zürich where he truly excelled. Furthermore, the fighting in the aftermath of Zürich against Suvorov gained him recognition as a strategist and planner of extraordinary ability. The fact that this won him accolades from Massena, who did not bestow praise lightly, reveals much about his abilities.

Being posted to the Army of the Rhine in 1796, denied Soult the chance to serve under Bonaparte during his first Italian campaign. Consequently, he was excluded from that special inner circle of officers whom the future emperor favoured due to their early association with him. Veterans of the Army of the Rhine often complained that Bonaparte never granted them the same consideration displayed to former comrades from the Army of Italy. Although hardly Soult's fault, this fact may explain why Napoleon occasionally supported other officers over him, although his bias lessened over time. Bonaparte also sailed without Soult on his Egyptian venture in 1799, but his campaigns in the East, while spectacular, never held the same appeal for the emperor, probably because of the manner in which they ended.

While some questioned his personal courage, he was present in the thick of the fighting during the campaigns along the Rhine, risked his safety reconnoitring the crossing of the Linth and was wounded at Genoa, casting doubt over this criticism. Yet, Griffith believes that he never quite fulfilled the initial promise he showed at Genoa. Up to that time, he had fought almost continuously for nine years but a series of administrative appointments in Italy and elsewhere followed, rather than combat commands. Furthermore, the pain and illness he undoubtedly suffered as a result of his knee wound could well have changed his personality, and Griffith writes that he consequently felt less inclined to take personal risks and succumbed to the temptations offered by senior rank.[47]

Yet, his failure to rise to the challenges and provocations of other marshals speaks more of noble self-restraint than cowardice to modern eyes. Napoleon strove to eradicate duelling in the army, with only limited success, and the last thing he wanted was his marshals fighting each other, setting an example of ill-discipline to subordinates. France had many enemies and the potential loss of senior commanders over petty disagreements could only weaken Napoleon's empire.

Historian Laurence Currie believed that, while a strict disciplinarian, Soult was prone to reaping the spoils of war and therefore became self-indulgent in his later career, winning an unsavoury reputation as a looter.[48] Yet, the French army of this era became notorious for liberating works of art and other treasures and continued to follow the revolutionary principle of making war pay for itself. While it is true that the emperor attempted to curb excesses during the imperial period, the example that he and other members of the marshalate set in this regard left much to be desired and Soult was far from being the only officer to indulge in the misappropriation of goods.

There is also much to be admired in Soult's career. He was an able diplomat and this was clearly demonstrated through his actions in discouraging revolt in Switzerland by persuasion rather than the reprisals to which many of his contemporaries would have resorted. Indeed, he always dealt well with foreigners, taking a German wife and proving adept at negotiation both with the military and at political soirées in Paris as a member of Napoleon's elite.

Soult had proved himself as a commander many times but this was usually at divisional rather than army corps level. While Massena permitted him considerable latitude in Switzerland, he was used to acting in a subordinate role to the emperor. After the Battle of Corunna and the subjugation of northern Spain, the campaign that lay ahead for him would be an independent command. Although Napoleon planned for him to act in concert with other French armies, the invasion of Portugal involved marching into hostile territory, initially unsupported, and ranged against the best commanders the British could put into the field. Whether he would be up to this challenge remained to be seen.

Chapter Three

Invasion from the North

In Napoleon's view, having made judgements based largely on the reports he received in Paris, the task of invading Portugal must have appeared straightforward. There were far fewer regular troops to oppose the French in comparison with his own campaign in the Peninsula, allied to the facts that the British only maintained a small force in Portugal, the Spanish armies were scattered and the Portuguese levies were inexperienced and unlikely to be effective (in the emperor's opinion). Yet, the news he received was often weeks old and the situation looked very different making calculations from maps compared with being there on the ground.

However, Napoleon took care to gather serious intelligence about Portugal before ordering Soult to attempt another invasion. For example, he interviewed General Thiébault (Junot's chief-of-staff in Portugal from 1807–8), questioning him closely about the country and openly taking notes as he did so. Unfortunately, the emperor could not resist comparing Soult's success in expelling a British army from Spain with the disastrous end of Junot's campaign at the Battle of Vimeiro. As he had been a key member of Junot's high command, this brought Thiébault's own actions into question, making him defensive and resentful.

The emperor was primarily concerned with the practicality of the routes Soult could take when he marched from Galicia to Lisbon with a large fully equipped army, observing that, 'It is a case of crossing rivers instead of crossing mountains.'[1] While conceding that an invading army would be obliged to cross the Minho, Douro, Vouga and Mondego (in addition to minor rivers), Thiébault downplayed the risks such an operation would face, remarking that the marshal:

'will only have to act along practicable roads; he will march through a land of plenty; he will be able to operate everywhere, and in order to cross the three chief rivers he will have at his disposal the resources of Tuy, Oporto, and Coimbra.' He relished this reply, which justified his plan, and everything made me think that the interview had satisfied him.[2]

Stung by Napoleon's criticism of his failures in 1808, Thiébault was also no friend to Soult and these factors probably motivated him to give the emperor misleading information.

With the main British army ousted from Spain, the emperor saw the city of Zaragoza as the focal point of Spanish resistance and correctly predicted that it would not withstand siege for more than two months. As the Spanish had suffered numerous defeats, he believed resistance from the Spanish juntas would rapidly crumble. If his forces pressed closely on the heels of the retreating Spanish armies, Portugal and Andalusia lay open to invasion. As General Junot had disbanded the regular Portuguese army in 1807 and 1808, he deemed the Portuguese incapable of offering serious resistance and predicted the small British forces in the nation would swiftly embark and desert their allies if threatened. Considering the scale of recent French successes, it is not hard to see why he formed this over optimistic assessment.

Napoleon planned for Ney to pacify Galicia and protect Soult's rear while he marched into northern Portugal. He estimated that Porto, which was Portugal's second largest city, would fall by 1 February 1809 and that Lisbon would capitulate to Soult's army a mere ten days later. He believed that only 8,000–10,000 British troops remained in Portugal and totally dismissed the numbers of Portuguese ordenanza (militia) as poorly trained levies, who would be easily outmatched by regular troops. Having encountered guerrillas before, he underestimated their capabilities, considering them as little more than a nuisance for a professional army and stating that they could without difficulty be dispersed by punitive actions made by flying columns of regular troops.

Napoleon ordered Marshal Victor to advance into Estremadura with his I Corps as Soult crossed the Portuguese frontier. He was to occupy Mérida and then seize the fortress city of Badajoz, protecting the Spanish–Portuguese frontier, before establishing links with Soult along the River Tejo once Lisbon had fallen. If all went to plan, Soult would reinforce Victor with a division, and I Corps would then march on Seville and subdue resistance in Andalusia. The only serious obstacle he anticipated was the possibility of a British force landing in Lisbon or Cadiz which might bolster Iberian resistance, but as historian Sir Charles Oman commented:

> Even granting that all had gone as the Emperor desired, the estimate was too short by half. It was midwinter; Galicia and northern Portugal form one of the most mountainous regions in Europe: their roads are vile; their food supplies are scanty; their climate at that season of the year detestable. Clearly the task given to Soult could not be executed in the prescribed time.[3]

Napoleon had underestimated the physical and geographical difficulties that Soult and Victor must overcome as well as the scale of resistance they would encounter. Nevertheless, while he may have miscalculated the time this would take, if both armies mounted their offensives with sufficient speed and aggression, there was a strong prospect of success.

While the French confidently prepared to invade, General Sir John Cradock's views about successfully defending Portugal were gloomy in the extreme. He had arrived in Lisbon on 14 December 1808 and provided able assistance and support for Moore's campaign. However, he shared Moore's view that if their Spanish allies were defeated, maintaining a British presence in Portugal would become untenable. Moore had believed that Portugal's frontiers were too long to protect from incursion without a sizable army and the British government was unlikely to commit such a large force to the defence of an allied state. Cradock concurred with these theories and despaired of raising a regular and well-equipped Portuguese army in time to oppose an invasion, lamenting, 'It will take time and labour,' he wrote, 'to make a Portuguese army.'[4]

Cradock was not alone in this despondent assessment. Don Forjaz, Military Secretary in the Portuguese Regency, argued that they could ill-afford to send more than 6,000 men to Alcantara to oppose the invasion, should it occur.[5] Indeed, the Regency government in Lisbon gave Cradock little in the way of support and isolated British soldiers were occasionally set upon by the Portuguese, many being convinced that their allies were about to desert them.

By January 1809, Cradock had the bulk of his troops stationed in Lisbon but maintained garrisons at Santarem, Scavem, Almeida, Elvas and forts along the Tejo. While retaining the border fortresses was strategically vital to monitor and protect the frontier, the garrisons of Almeida and Elvas were modest and Cradock entertained grave doubts about defending the border, contemplating a concentration of his entire force around the capital. The only presence the British army maintained at Porto was five companies of the 60th Foot and responsibility for the city's defence fell to the junta.[6]

The junta at Porto had nearly 30,000 men under arms. Yet, the vast majority of these were ordenanza and armed civilians formed around a core of about 5,000 regular soldiers. As political intrigues continued (the Regency government refused to recognise the junta), the bishop was keen to preserve his small regular army, which was only beginning to approach an effective state. He was prepared to send militia north to defend the frontier or mount delaying actions against the French but was reluctant to risk any of his regular troops and wished to keep them in reserve in case the city itself was threatened.

The best force of disciplined, regular troops available in northern Portugal was the Loyal Lusitanian Legion, just over 3,000-men strong and commanded by military adventurer Colonel Sir Robert Wilson.[7] While some of his officers were Dutch or German, the rank and file were overwhelmingly Portuguese and the legion was already developing a fine reputation as a fighting force.

Wilson had been able to raise this unusual regiment due to his influence with the British Foreign Minister George Canning, who enlisted the help of the Portuguese minister in London and persuaded Castlereagh (Secretary of War) to permit the unit's formation. Arriving in Porto on 18 August 1808, Wilson was well received by the bishop, who 'overwhelmed me with kindness and good intentions and never did a stranger possess his affections to so great a degree'.[8] His relations with the Portuguese were sometimes difficult as the junta wished to maintain firm control of the legion, but although Wilson was officially a brigadier in Portuguese service, he acted as if his command was independent.

Wilson marched the 1st Battalion of the Lusitanian Legion from Porto on 16 December (about 700–800 men). Cradock had made attempts to bring this command under his direct control but Wilson's semi-independent state under the Bishop's nominal orders suited his fiery temperament, as he recorded in private letters, 'To unite with the British army would be no advantage to my ambitious projects. The order and system of such a force would be fatal to my adventures. I must have freedom of action.'[9]

Cradock suggested that he garrison Vila Real to defend the border region but Wilson marched to Almeida, believing it far more important for protecting the frontier. The Bishop of Porto agreed but ordered him to reinforce the garrison and forbade him to venture into Spain. Circumstances had changed by the time Wilson arrived at the fortress as it now suited Cradock's plans to assist Moore, but he cautioned that he 'should reflect before you shut yourself up in a fortress'.[10]

Wilson had no intention of adopting a passive defence and, after spending two weeks in the area, concluded, 'I do not believe the enemy have any intention of advancing in this quarter.'[11] Furthermore, he believed that not only was it possible to repel French incursions but that the French army was contemplating a complete withdrawal from Spain. He saw an opportunity to conduct raids over the border and established a forward base well into Spain for this purpose. Since his light infantrymen were entirely Portuguese and therefore familiar with this kind of countryside, he deemed his command ideally suited to such warfare.

After Corunna, some British Cabinet ministers doubted that Portugal could resist another invasion and government policy regarding continuing the Peninsular War was uncertain. Many favoured Cadiz over Lisbon as a potential base for British operations and Colonel Sir George Smith was sent there on 10 December 1808 to mediate with the Spanish. Even Castlereagh was unsure, '"The employment of the British army in the south of Spain," he wrote in effect, "depends on the admission of a British corps into Cadiz. Without the security of that fortress we cannot after Moore's experience, again risk an army in the interior in Spain."'[12] The government dispatched 4,000 men under General Sherbrooke to Cadiz but John Frere (British ambassador in Spain), negotiating with the Marquis Villel and the Spanish authorities there, was denied permission for them to enter the city. The problem was that, after a long history of war with Great Britain, the Spanish distrusted the British and feared that the troops might take up permanent residence in Cadiz and create a situation similar to that in Gibraltar.

Frere wrote to Cradock assuring him that, following the resistance Soult had encountered in northern Spain, he would probably abandon the 'unaccountable project of entering Portugal and occupying Gallicia [*sic*] at the same time'.[13] His dilemma was that the government kept sending mixed messages. History has not been kind to Cradock and historians such as Oman and Chartrand dismiss him as indecisive but Napier gives a more charitable opinion:

> The few dispatches received from England led him to suppose the ministers designed to abandon Portugal; but as their intentions on that head were never clearly explained, he resolved to abide by the literal interpretation of his first orders, and hold the country as long as he could without risking the loss of his army.[14]

When Wellesley later assumed command, he was sympathetic to his predecessor, conceding that holding the capital without risking a major defeat was unlikely and commented, 'It is difficult if not impossible to bring the contest for Lisbon to extremities, and afterwards to embark the army.'[15]

Following the Battle of Corunna, Soult had good reason to feel satisfied, despite his failure to trap and defeat the British. Corunna was on a small peninsula and could have withstood a siege for months if the governor had not chosen to surrender immediately after the British left. Soult and Ney could now draw on resources from the II, VI and VIII army corps in order to pacify Galicia and mount an invasion of Portugal. However, while Soult had 40,000 men and Ney 16,000–18,000 on paper, the army was fatigued after a long pursuit and a hard-fought battle. In addition to caring for the wounded, Soult was obliged to garrison outposts such as Villafranca, Lugo and Betanzos along the route of the pursuit in addition to leaving substantial numbers of sick and exhausted men behind. Regardless of his orders from the emperor, Soult meant to consolidate his gains and reorganise his army before moving south, and it was unlikely that he would be able to field more than 30,000 men for the invasion.[16]

Insurgents were already a serious problem for the French in Galicia and stragglers and isolated groups of soldiers were regularly set upon and murdered. Guerrillas cut off French garrisons at Betanzos and Lugo immediately after Corunna fell, the countryside becoming impassable for small parties of soldiers and even large forces subjected to harassment. General Pierre Soult (Soult's brother) managed to assemble 2,000–2,500 men who had become detached from their regiments at Astorga, but it was some months before he was able to rejoin II Corps due to guerrilla activity.

While Soult had captured heavy artillery and stores at Corunna, his army badly needed refitting. Many soldiers had rusted arms, torn clothing and worn footwear after their hard march through difficult country in appalling winter conditions. While he had done his best to find resources in Galicia, most towns in the region were poor and their storehouses had been plundered during the recent campaign since both sides needed supplies. He knew that one of his biggest problems was the acquisition of horses and mules in a part of Spain where they were already scarce. Portugal had few roads capable of taking wheeled transport (let alone heavy guns) so sure-footed baggage animals would be invaluable, a fact not lost on the British, who took the drastic step of slaughtering horses and mules in their hundreds at Corunna to prevent them falling into French hands.

Therefore, Soult marched against Ferrol, which lies opposite Corunna across the Ares Bay. This was an important port housing one of Spain's largest naval arsenals and the French could expect to find large quantities of supplies there. Soult's army arrived at the port on 25 January and Admiral Melgarejo, Ferrol's governor, surrendered the town without a fight the following day. He had made an agreement with the French and immediately left for Madrid where he took up an office under King Joseph. At least 10,000 men garrisoned the town and, although the bulk were militia, Spanish General Marquis Pedro de La Romana had left a few hundred regular soldiers there along with 4,000–5,000 sailors, so Melgarejo could have resisted for some time. Unsurprisingly, the Supreme Junta was incensed and denounced the admiral as a traitor.[17]

The capture of Ferrol was a coup for the French since they not only gained supplies but also effectively deprived the Spanish of a centre of resistance in the region. Soult's army badly needed clothing, muskets and ammunition and they found these in plentiful supply in Ferrol's storehouses. The capture of Spanish shipping in the harbour (including eight ships of the line) would also support Napoleon's naval ambitions. The fact that Melgarejo failed to fire these ships before his capitulation strongly implies an intention to change sides from the outset.

While the army paused at Ferrol, Soult received a dispatch from Napoleon. He had written it at Valladolid on 17 January and now conceded that his initial predictions for the course of the invasion were miscalculated. Revising his estimates, Napoleon instructed Soult to take Porto by 5 February and Lisbon on the 16th. He would have to rely on his own resources up to that point but I Corps should have reached Mérida by 16 February and he had ordered Marshal Victor to assist him by sending a column to rendezvous with him near the capital. Furthermore, General Lapisse was operating out of Salamanca and should be able to tie down the garrisons of Ciudad Rodrigo and (possibly) Almeida. It might also be possible for Lapisse to send Soult reinforcements if all went well along the frontier.

The problem with the emperor's plan was that the armies concerned would need effective communications in order to co-operate. Soult was already experiencing difficulties in northern Spain with constant attacks on his troops as they travelled between French strongholds. Once Soult crossed the frontier into enemy-held territory, this situation was likely to get worse. In Oman's opinion, 'The Emperor had yet to realise that in order to make operations simultaneous, when troops starting from bases several hundred miles apart are to co-operate, it is necessary that their generals are to be in free communication with each other.'[18] When he heard of the emperor's orders to Soult, Marshal Jourdan (then military adviser to King Joseph) scathingly remarked that he 'must have supposed that the road was as freely passable as that from Paris to Lyons'.[19]

By 29 January, Soult was making serious preparations for an invasion of Portugal and reorganising his army accordingly. However, he could only procure a few hundred extra horses and mules for his army.[20] This was a serious problem as he would find himself short of ammunition on the journey to Porto because of the lack of pack animals to convey it, and was obliged to pause during his march for it to be brought up on at least two occasions.

Ney encountered difficulty in pacifying Galicia and Soult was obliged
to delay his invasion until he could transfer direct responsibility for recent
French conquests to his fellow marshal. He busied himself establishing a
hospital for II Corps's sick and garrisoning Corunna and Ferrol. Relations
between the two marshals were strained and Soult felt aggrieved that Ney
appeared to linger at Lugo for a considerable period before rendezvousing
at Corunna and taking command there. Indeed, mindful that the emperor
wanted results quickly, Soult had already dispatched his cavalry ahead of his
main army before meeting Ney.

The army Soult amassed for his invasion was formidable. In 1807, Junot's
invading force largely comprised second line regiments mixed with a large
proportion of conscripts but most of Soult's rank and file were veterans led
by accomplished commanders. Indeed, some had served in Portugal from
1807–8 and had directly applicable experience. Generals Lorge and Lahoussaye
commanded two heavy cavalry divisions with General Franceschi commanding
the light cavalry. The infantry was split into four divisions under generals
Mermet, Merle, Delaborde and Heudelet. Soult had 17 infantry regiments,
10 cavalry regiments and, combined with artillery and support troops, led an
army of between 20,000 and 30,000 men towards the frontier. The artillery
had fifty-four guns at the outset of the invasion, possibly supplemented by
heavy cannon captured from artillery parks in northern Spain.[21]

Franceschi's light cavalry moved south along near the coast hoping to
secure the towns of Vigo and Tuy. Meanwhile, Lahoussaye advanced further
inland towards the lower River Minho, which marked the Portuguese
northern frontier. It was several days before the infantry set out but the
cavalry encountered very little resistance at first, Lahoussaye taking
Salvatierra without a fight and Franceschi subjected to only brief harassment
by insurgents before arriving before the port of Vigo. Having only a few
recruits and poorly armed ordenanza to defend the port, the governor
immediately capitulated and Franceschi swiftly advanced on Tuy. Here the
local junta begged the governor to resist as he had 500 regular troops but
he also surrendered without attempting to defend the town. By 2 February,
Soult's cavalry were poised on the frontier having advanced virtually
unopposed. While behind schedule, Napoleon's prediction that few would
stand against him had been borne out so far.

General La Romana's battered Spanish army was in no position to oppose Soult's invasion and the general was reduced to making plaintive appeals for money, arms and ammunition to the Central Junta and the British in Lisbon. The appearance of General Marchand's division (part of Ney's VI Corps) persuaded him to retire across the Minho into Portugal and here he remained at Orense to rally stragglers and attempt to reorganise his army. His recent campaigning had brought a series of defeats but, after each setback, he withdrew to avoid the destruction of his army, allowing it to fight another day. As Franceschi astutely commented, 'Romana creates an army. When his voice is heard the whole population rises in arms. When one marches against him he escapes. When one returns he returns.'[22] This was already proving to be a common pattern with Spanish armies during the Peninsular War, which infuriated their French opponents.

By 13 February, the infantry and artillery had caught up and Soult massed his army in the border region. Once the French crossed the Minho, the Entre Minho e Douro and Tras os Montes regions of northern Portugal would lie open to invasion. Soult planned to use the best available roads for his heavy guns and wagons and the most suitable crossing point for this was at Valença. The fortress of Valença, strongly garrisoned by militia and some regular soldiers, straddled the river at this point and its guns could potentially wreak havoc on troops trying to force their way over the bridge. Once his army were across the river, this strongpoint could be isolated or attacked from both sides, but Soult wanted to avoid heavy losses at the outset of the campaign.

In a manner reminiscent of his operation on the Linth years before, Soult carefully reconnoitred the northern bank of the river with his staff. Unless the army made a detour by travelling further upriver, crossing at the mouth of the Minho seemed the best option and he selected a point near Campo Saucos. The fact that the river was in spate due to the snow melting in the mountains complicated the operation. As a commissary of II Corps recalled, 'From 2 February onwards it never ceased to rain: veritable torrents fell from the clouds, and the least stream became a river. Much swollen, the Miño burst its banks, and presented a barrier that was all the more difficult to cross in view of the army's lack of bridging equipment …'[23] Scanning the south bank meticulously through their spyglasses, Soult and his staff observed large numbers of insurgents. They had dug entrenchments and plainly intended to oppose the crossing, so Soult ordered Lahoussaye to have his cavalry engage the guerrillas with musket fire in the region of Salvatierra, where the river was narrow, once the operation began. He would also mass troops as if they intended to cross at Melgaço, hoping to fool the enemy into thinking this was where the main crossing would take place.

On the night of 15 February, Soult attempted to cross the Minho in force using fishing vessels and riverboats taken from Guardia. These were laboriously rolled overland on logs to the river by the infantry and the scale of this operation meant that French actions must have been observed. Lahoussaye's distraction attacks began upriver and the artillery opened a thunderous barrage against the insurgents' positions on the southern bank to cover the operation. Soult guessed that irregulars would be intimidated by cannon fire and frightened at the sight of such a large a number of troops crossing the river but they proved remarkably stubborn. Ensconced behind cover, the insurgents weathered the cannonade and opened a ragged but determined fire on the fishing boats, which stood out starkly against the river in the moonlight.

The infantry in the boats sustained losses but, while some vessels managed to land on the southern bank, they were assailed by hundreds of guerrillas and could not gain a foothold. Further attempts to cross were made but as one officer recalled, 'at daybreak, we saw a multitude of Portuguese peasants, lining the opposite bank. In spite of torrents of rain, their numbers grew with every minute that passed. They wore overcoats of straw, their form merged with that of rocks, several of them advancing to the edge, firing on all who approached the river.'[24] The river still ran high after the rains and this added to the difficulty of rowing boats across in formation. Soult's men were not sailors and the current foiled their attempts to beach enough vessels at a single point in order to concentrate a large force. Therefore, the French attacks were delivered piecemeal fashion and repulsed. While the insurgents' indiscipline lessened the effect of their musketry (most firing individually rather than delivering volley fire), their massed charges with pikes, swords and knives proved very effective in denying the French a foothold on the south bank. Observing this, Soult halted the operation and marched upriver to seek a better crossing point.

Had Soult been more determined and prepared to risk serious losses, he might have forced a crossing at Campo Saucos, thus gaining possession of the best road south. Now he felt obliged to send his heavy calibre guns back to an artillery park at Tuy and make do with sixteen cannon and six howitzers until the road was secure. Napier believed that a successful crossing here might have seen Soult's army reach Porto by 21 February and his repulse by a few hundred determined insurgents 'had a surprising influence on the issue of the campaign'.[25] There is much truth in this as the Allied strategy was in a state of confusion. Mackenzie's division was still at Cadiz (weakening Cradock's army by its absence), the Portuguese Regency contemplated coming to terms with France and British foreign policy remained unclear. Local levies and guerrillas had bought the Allies valuable time.

The Entre Minho e Douro region (known as the Costa Verde region today) was far more difficult to enter than Soult had anticipated. Circumnavigating Valença, his army moved upriver towards Orense. The roads north of the Minho were little more than tracks and artillery and wagons encountered great difficulty traversing them, slowing the pace of the march. Furthermore, the countryside was hilly and mostly uncultivated making it ideal for mounting ambushes. Guerrillas regularly sniped at the French from cover or attempted to cut off and kill stragglers, only to withdraw rapidly if the French counter-attacked.

Some militia were bold enough to block the army's progress. Lieutenant Joseph de Naylies of the 19th Dragoons recalled their fierce resistance at Maurentan:

> One could only approach this place via a long defile lined with hedges and overhung with rocks that ended at the river Sachas, a small stream that at this point fell into the Miño. To reach the town, one then had to cross a very long and very narrow bridge, and this was defended by 1,000 ... men, barricaded, and blocked by *chevaux de frise*.[26]

The bridge was too narrow for horses but dragoons were cavalrymen also trained to fight on foot, so some of the 19th dismounted and a charge was made over the bridge with about 200 men. The militia fired a volley over the barricade as they did so but fled into the village before this determined assault rather than come to close quarters as the dragoons dragged the barrier aside. The French fought their way into Maurentan as the militia fired at them from within the houses. An officer recalled that, 'In a few moments the first houses had been stormed, and very soon the whole village was on fire. The flames took everyone who was still alive ... More than 400 Spaniards died in them whereas we lost just two dragoons'[27]

Most of the villages the army marched through were deserted and eerily quiet but at Ribadavia the French were assailed by 'clouds' of partisans who came roaring down from the hills in brave but reckless assaults. The village was held by two battalions, repulsing the guerrillas and inflicting grievous losses. De Naylies saw the bodies of hundreds of Galicians scattered before the town:

> I saw a horrible tableau that summed up the effects of this odious war. Lying nude and disfigured in the midst of a pile of corpses, I saw the bodies of two women. One of them was middle-aged: beside her lay a musket, while she was wearing a cartridge box and sabre ... and had been killed by a bullet in the chest ... The other, who was entirely naked and could not have been more than seventeen years old, had evidently joined a group of peasants in trying to pull a mounted officer from his horse: she had been cut down by a blow from a sabre that had split her skull in two.[28]

Such scenes provided gruesome evidence of the strength of popular feeling against the invaders among the peasantry and, while these small actions simply delayed their advance, it was a dire portent of what lay ahead.

As he approached Orense, Soult received a dispatch from Marshal Ney informing him that the entire province of Galicia was in a state of revolt and requesting assistance. With incessant guerrilla attacks on his rearguard, Soult realised that communications between II and VI Corps would be severed as soon as he entered Portugal but he decided to carry out his orders and invade nonetheless. When Soult reached Orense, he remained there for nine days to concentrate II Corps and gather supplies. While harassment by insurgents was frustrating, Soult encountered no serious opposition and crossed the Minho into Portugal on 4 March 1809. La Romana's army lay around 20 miles away but made no effort to intervene. Soult took the opportunity of distributing pamphlets to the Portuguese, which informed locals that they had no need to fear his men as the French meant to bring peace and stability to their nation.

With incessant political arguments between the junta in Porto and the Regency in Lisbon, Napier believed that it took an actual invasion of Portugal to persuade the Bishop of Porto to concentrate upon repulsing the French. While he had instructed the province of Entre-Douro-e-Minho to resist, the bishop was not prepared to endanger the 50,000 men at his disposal and instead set to work on preparing a line of entrenchments in the hills north of the city.[29] These operations required the use of valuable manpower and his refusal to send troops virtually guaranteed that the northern provinces would fall.

Nevertheless, General Bernadino Freire led a largely militia based force north with the intention of holding Braga, while General Silveira (military governor of Tras-os-Montes) hoped to block Soult's progress at Chaves, which lies about 50 miles southeast of Orense. In order to do this, he sought La Romana's assistance but the difficult relationship between the Portuguese and Spanish made the likely success of a joint enterprise doubtful. As the two forces neared their rendezvous near Chaves, Soult altered his line of march to intercept the Spanish army and La Romana immediately fell back on Puebla de Senabria. Franceschi's cavalry set upon his rearguard as he did so, killing or capturing at least 700 men and dispersing the entire force.

Silveira sent small detachments to skirmish with the French and delay their advance but Soult's vanguard easily drove them off with heavy losses. Receiving intelligence of La Romana's retreat, Silveira prudently decided to fall back to the Heights of San Pedro, about 3 miles south of Chaves, on 7 March. Soult paused for three days at Monterrey to allow elements of his army to catch up but now mounted a determined attack, scattering the forward outposts of the Portuguese and advancing against Chaves. Having observed the size and strength of the force opposing him, Silveira decided to withdraw and yield the town but his men were outraged. Many refused to surrender Chaves without a fight and Silveira's life was threatened. Pacifying the hotheads with difficulty, Silveira withdrew to Vila Real with half of his force, while the rest re-entered Chaves to mount a defence.

Arriving before the town, Soult called upon the defenders to surrender but this was spurned and the French mounted an attack on Chaves. After a day's fighting, the town surrendered on 12 March. Soult could not afford to guard his prisoners and generously (considering that many of the irregulars fought out of uniform) allowed the ordenanza to disperse and return to their homes after disarming them. The regular soldiers who had been captured were offered the choice between captivity or joining the French army and a significant number changed sides. Some French officers such as General Loison, who had served in Portugal in 1807, advised Soult to execute those captured out of uniform and to carry out reprisals to ensure Portuguese compliance.[30] Soult refused, perhaps recalling how effective his measured approach had been in winning over the Swiss population in 1799. Therefore, he treated the locals leniently. Having established a small field hospital for the wounded, Soult set off from Chaves on 14 March, leaving a small garrison of 100 men to protect the 1,200 wounded he left behind.

Initially, Soult moved south, intending to deceive Silveira into thinking he was marching against him, but then turned west. His cavalry brought intelligence on 17 March that a sizeable Portuguese force was drawn up on the hills at Carvalho d'Este, 6 miles northeast of Braga, and Soult intended to defeat them before marching on Porto. St Chamans, one of Soult's aides-de-camp, recorded resistance encountered by the army from the peasantry (let alone organised guerrilla bands) was intense as they marched through hilly and mountainous terrain:

isolated peasants kept up a continual dropping fire on us from inaccessible crags above the road: at night they attacked our sentries, or crept down close to our bivouacs to shoot at the men who sat round the blaze. This sort of war was not very deadly, but infinitely fatiguing ... every man who strayed from the ranks, whether he was sick, drunk, tired, or merely a marauder, was cut off and massacred. The peasants not only murdered them but tortured them in the most horrid fashion ...[31]

Acts of savagery were on the increase with the peasantry stirred into a passionate hatred of the French by the clergy, who assured them a place in heaven if they opposed the 'atheist ideology' the enemy practised. Many

French soldiers recalled seeing priests and monks taking an active role in the fighting.

Meanwhile, events in Spain were equally dispiriting for the Allied cause. Captain D'Urban was a British liaison officer with General Cuesta's army and (unaware that Soult had already crossed the frontier at that time) recorded that the Allies lack of success against Victor's army, which was driving its way further into Spain, had grave implications for Portugal. Disgusted by numerous failures to block or even impede French progress, he wrote the following on 19 March when Truxillo fell to the French:

> Thus in a day, almost without fighting, has a position been abandoned which might have held out till Doomsday, and with it all the advantages which depended on it being maintained; the salvation of all the rich country between the Tagus and the Douro, the rising spirit of the people, which promised everything good, public opinion, public hope, all been sacrificed in four-and-twenty hours, and almost without an attempt to prevent it.[32]

At Braga Napier recorded that the local levies and armed locals were driven into a rage by the priesthood's anti-French rhetoric.[33] The priest not only assured them that the French were bent on murder and rape but also denounced their 'unholy' system of government. General Freire learned of the strength of the approaching French army but, hearing of Silveira's retreat, had serious reservations about matching his poorly armed militias (supported by an ill-disciplined mob) against Soult's veterans.

He proposed a steady withdrawal towards Porto while mounting delaying actions and ambuscades along the route, but was accused of cowardice and siding with the enemy by the locals. More fearful of his own men than the enemy, Freire abandoned his command and rode back towards Porto with his staff. Incensed, the locals set off in pursuit, eventually waylaying the general and bringing him back as a prisoner.

Lieutenant Colonel Baron Eben, a German officer in the Lusitanian Legion, was appalled to find his superior held captive by his own men, writing, 'I saw him on foot, conducted by a great armed multitude, who suffered no one to pass, and on my attempting it threatened to fire'.[34]

Despite the threats made against him, Eben appealed to the angry crowd and managed to lead Freire into the safety of a nearby house, although he and those with him were shot at. Promising the general would be held under close arrest and put on trial, Eben calmed their passions but the mob only dispersed when they heard the French were approaching. Eben was busily preparing a defence when he was informed that 'the people had put the general to death with pikes and guns. I was now proclaimed general'.[35]

Eben did his best to mount a defence of Braga but only had elements of the 2nd Battalion of the Lusitanian Legion to support the local levies, which lacked experienced artillerymen and were unlikely to withstand an assault by regular troops. Soult arrived before Braga on 18 March and, hoping to avoid a fight, sent twenty Portuguese prisoners into the town with a small escort. These men relayed his promise to receive an honourable surrender if the garrison capitulated but they were set upon and murdered and the escort seized and held as prisoners.

On 20 March, the French stormed Braga and swiftly overwhelmed the Portuguese positions. As many as 4,000 Portuguese were slain, not only during the assault but as the defenders fled back through the streets once their defences crumbled. French soldiers, having witnessed many atrocities after crossing the Minho, refused to give quarter and bayoneted many of those attempting to surrender. There were only 200 French casualties and 17 Portuguese cannon were captured in the action. One of the first sights to greet the French as they reached the centre of Braga was the body of General Freire, lying bloodied with numerous wounds and partly eaten by pigs in the town square. They also discovered the bodies of the prisoners Soult had released with proclamations announcing the good intent of the French.

Yet, Soult still wished to win the populace over and one of his first acts was to attend High Mass in Braga Cathedral along with his entire staff, an act that even his biographer Hayman conceded was motivated by 'political rather than devotional reasons …'.[36] Nevertheless, some locals were won over and the mayor of the nearby town of Barceles presented himself to Soult to assure him that his town would offer no resistance and co-operate with the French. Despite being a respected community leader of many years standing, the mayor was deemed a collaborator and murdered shortly afterwards.[37]

Soult's elation at the fall of Braga was short-lived when he heard Silveira had returned, invested Chaves and retaken it on the day of the battle. General Botilho had also moved down the lower Minho with a small force and blocked the road to Tuy. It seemed that northern Portugal was still far from pacified.

Soult was dismayed at the consequences of leaving Chaves ill-protected but learned from his error, installing an entire division to garrison Braga. The strategic position of the town near the centre of the province rendered it an ideal strongpoint for dominating the area and he wished to secure his rear before moving south. The army marched in three columns, the first led by Franceschi and Mermet advancing by Guimaraens and St Justo to force the passage of the upper Ave River and clear the country of insurgents towards Pombeiro. Soult led the second column in person upon Barca de Trofa, while General Lorge advanced with the third column to the Ponte d'Ave.

The French encountered little opposition until they reached the Ave River on 25 March, where light infantry were forced to fight a sharp action with irregulars who contested the bridge:

General Mermet ordered Jardon to seize control of the Negrelos bridge which was defended by 900 Portuguese. Jardon attacked the enemy with some sharp-shooters of the 17th Infantry, and took control of the bridge after a stubborn fight; but he was hit by a bullet above his right eye and fell dead at the feet of his nephew, sergeant of the grenadiers, whom he had taken as his aide.[38]

The insurgents and militia swiftly lost heart and fled in the face of a determined bayonet charge but, aside from the death of General Jardon, French losses were slight. By 27 March, Soult's vanguard was approaching Porto and the following day his army deployed before the city.

Chapter Four

The Fall of Porto

As Porto was the centre of commerce in the north, its fall would be a major step towards a successful conquest of Portugal for the French. Approaching from the north, the city outskirts began just beyond a range of hills and Porto's streets wound down the hillside towards the river where warehouses and docks were located. Porto lies near the mouth of the River Douro, which snakes lazily through the metropolis, dividing the city from suburbs lying along the southern riverbank. The Douro's width meant that constructing a stone bridge to connect the two halves of the city would be enormously expensive so a pontoon bridge of boats was the crossing point.

Renowned for its red wine from the seventeenth century onwards, numerous vineyards were situated on the slopes of the Douro Valley. English merchants had invested heavily in the area and many famous Anglo-Portuguese wine producers hailed from Porto, such as Sandeman, Taylor's, Warre, Graham and many others. From 1820 onwards, the type of fortified wine (unusually sweet grape juice mixed with brandy) produced in the area came to be known as 'Port/Porto', although the region was already justly famous for wine production, particularly in Britain and eventually throughout the world. At the end of March 1809, many ships lay moored along the docks, the vast majority of which were laden with wine casks.

The Portuguese loved to bestow titles upon their cities and Porto was celebrated as *'leal e invicta cidade'*, which translates as 'loyal and unconquered city'.[1] However, in common with many Portuguese towns and cities, Porto lacked a city wall and its defences were primarily designed to defend it from seaborne rather than land assaults, with the Portuguese relying upon their frontier fortresses to protect them. Porto's title was about to be put to the test by the French and this ill-fated city would be fought over three times during the nineteenth century.

The approach of Soult's army posed a serious dilemma for Don Antonio de São José de Castro, Bishop of Porto, 1754–1843. This venerable cleric was a remarkable man and the fact that his Junta had not fallen under the Regency's control was largely as a result of his popularity among all classes and the determination of the local people to govern their own affairs rather than submit to government rule. The fact that Porto was where serious resistance to the French began was significant in this regard. As the principal superior of the Order of Saint Bruno, the bishop had been asked to become President of the Supreme Junta when the city revolted again French rule in June 1808. Since the uprising was a perilous undertaking, this required considerable personal courage.

The bishop lacked military and administrative skills but was sincerely patriotic and determined to resist the invasion. His main strength lay in his political influence and the fact that he retained autonomy over Portugal's second city for some time, despite the fact that the junta's authority was unrecognised by the Portuguese Regency or British government, is testament to his effectiveness. Although he had made preparations for defence, Soult's swift progress southward alarmed the junta and the appearance of a large French army before the city made the bishop doubt whether defending the city with a force largely made up of militia and volunteers was practical.

Morale was high in Porto, which was reassuring, but this also led to some ugly incidents, such as the treatment of Brigadier General Luiz D'Oliveira and others accused of harbouring French sympathies. As *The Times* reported:

the populace of Oporto murdered JOAO DE CUNHA, of Badeninka, Major of the 2d regiment; and on the 22d, they went to the prison, where they dragged LUIS DE OLIVIERA out of his bed, and instantly dispatched him with their knives: fourteen others, who were confined there on suspicion of being attached to the French, were shot; the dead bodies were drawn in triumph through the streets, across the bridge, and thrown into the river. After having wreaked their vengeance on these unfortunate wretches, the mob threw open the prison doors, and released all the prisoners without exception.[2]

As the mob's blood was up, the bishop hesitated to intervene, fearing they might turn upon him and his officials. Ever since the expulsion of Junot's forces, accusations of collaboration with the French had been commonplace and often used as excuses for the violent seizure of goods and property.

The bishop knew that Cradock's army was steadily growing in strength and that Marshal Beresford was massing forces south of the Mondego River. Therefore, if Porto could withstand siege, there was a realistic possibility that a relief force would be sent. If the defences held, the French were unlikely to risk crossing the immense barrier of the Douro in force without taking the city beforehand as they would not want to be in the position of having an enemy held city to their rear. Since the city straddled a large river, it would also be difficult to surround and easy for the Portuguese to re-supply.

The Portuguese had created a formidable system of redoubts (small forts) and entrenchments to protect the approaches to the city from the north, directed by Portuguese and British military engineers. Great progress had been made during three weeks of intensive work and at least sixteen earth redoubts now stood along a defensive line with wooden palisades, abattis and ditches blocking the areas between them. Almost 200 cannon were mounted in these redoubts, the sloping north faces of which were designed to protect these guns from cannon fire (theoretically cannon balls hitting the slope or glacis would ricochet over the fort without striking the guns or defenders). Barricades blocked the streets leading into the city and some houses had had loopholes cut into them (so muskets could be fired from within) as a second line of defence. The line ran from the small castle of San João de Foz on the coast, overlooking the mouth of the Douro, to the chapel of Bom Fin on the east of the city on a front over 6 miles long.

The earthworks had been built upon hills that largely obscured Soult's view of the city as the land sloped down sharply behind them with the city streets winding down towards the river. The Douro was extremely wide as it meandered its way through the city and the only span crossing it was a bridge of boats about 300yd (274m) long, linking the main city with the suburb of Villa Nova on the south bank. This was the principal weakness in the Portuguese position since, if forced to retreat, they only had a single method of crossing. The Portuguese placed several artillery batteries on the heights of Serra do Pilar on the southern riverbank covering the bridge, comprising at least twenty cannon. Up to thirty merchant vessels, mostly British-owned and destined for markets in England, lay at the quaysides. With a strong northwest wind and restless ocean, these ships were at that time stranded in Porto as they could not put to sea.[3]

Many guerrillas and enthusiastic volunteers had flooded into Porto over the previous weeks as Soult's army approached and the Portuguese had a considerable number of men under arms. Oman recorded the presence of around 5,000 regulars including the 6th and 18th Line regiments (raised in Porto), 2 battalions from the south under General Vittoria, a battalion of the 21st Line (Valenza Regiment), elements of the 9th Line (Viana Regiment) and the remnants of the 2nd Battalion of the Lusitanian Legion, which had escaped the route at Braga. Some militia regiments were present but the standard of their training and weaponry varied enormously, while the rest of the force comprised guerrilla bands (more like bandits than soldiers) and a host of untrained volunteers lacking weaponry and discipline. While the Portuguese were able to field an impressive number of guns to defend the city, they were short of trained artillerymen, with Oman estimating the number of gunners at 1,000, supported by willing but poorly trained militiamen. This deficiency accounts for the poor performance of Allied artillery in the struggle that followed. French accounts place the total number of Portuguese defenders between 40,000 and 60,000 but Oman claimed 30,000 as a more realistic figure.[4]

Soult was undismayed by the large number of defenders, being well aware that these mostly comprised militia, which his army had overcome with relative ease at Chaves and Braga. Therefore, he dispatched an emissary to the bishop advising him to calm the passions of the populace and surrender, as these levies were unlikely to withstand a serious attack. He also reminded the bishop that for hundreds of years soldiers had claimed the right to sack a city or fortress that refused to capitulate as a reward for hazarding their lives during the assault. While he did not condone such behaviour, controlling men maddened by the rigours of storming a city was next to impossible and, if he accepted terms, Porto would be spared this dire fate. Le Noble summed up the gist of Soult's message thus, 'the French come not as enemies, but as the deliverers of Portugal from the yoke of the English. It was for the benefit of these foreigners alone that the Bishop would expose Oporto to the incalculable calamities attending a storm.'[5]

With anti-French feeling running so high, Soult sent a Portuguese major, taken prisoner at Braga, to carry his dispatch to the bishop. This officer met with such an angry reception from his compatriots that he felt compelled to deceive them, declaring that he actually carried an offer of French surrender as they were overawed by the unexpected strength of Porto's defences. It was either that or be shot on suspicion of being a collaborator. He was led into an audience with the bishop but, despite the truce, Portuguese gunners opened sporadic fire on the French forces deploying before them.

While negotiations continued, General Foy rode up to enemy picquets in the mistaken belief that they intended to surrender an outwork close to his position. He rode among them urging surrender but was pulled from his horse and captured. His companion, Major Roger, was shot down when he drew his sword and tried to cut his way out of the ensuing melee. Carried into Porto, Foy was mistaken for General Loison – notorious for his cruel repression of rebellion in the south the previous year. An angry mob gathered crying '*Matar Maneta*' (kill one-hand) but Foy, realising their error, raised both hands to show that he was not the one-handed Loison and was led into captivity.[6]

Placing generals Lima-Barreto and Parreiras in command, the bishop retired over the Douro to the Serra Convent and, from this vantage point, watched events as they unfolded the next day. He sent a defiant reply to Soult and correctly guessed that the northern defences would be stormed on 29 March. The people of the city anticipated a French assault that night or at dawn and were therefore in a highly agitated state. Church bells rang constantly throughout the night and regular false alarms of a French attack led to muskets and cannon being fired along the lines. Portuguese officers tried to calm their men but, with so many armed civilians and assorted militia under their command, enforcing discipline was extremely difficult. The chaotic situation was exacerbated by the onset of a heavy thunderstorm in the night, with the thunder frequently mistaken for the rumble of French cannon fire. By morning, an eerie calm had fallen over the city.

Once it was clear that the Portuguese would resist, Soult ordered the lines to be thoroughly reconnoitred and mounted probing attacks to test the defences, driving in some outposts. He also placed General Merle's division on the right of the French line in the hope that the Portuguese would interpret this as a sign that he intended to mount his main assault there. Portuguese gunners laid down a heavy cannonade against this division as they deployed but Merle was able to take advantage of numerous enclosures and the undulating nature of the land in the area to shield his men and suffered few casualties.

News now reached Soult that guerrillas surrounded Tuy and Vigo and communications with those towns were cut. II Corps was becoming increasingly isolated as Soult had feared but, before he could restore links and protect his rear, he knew he had to take Porto. He had not heard that, unbeknownst to Soult, Vigo had fallen on 28 March when the Royal Navy came to the insurgents' assistance, threatening the garrison with the guns of two frigates (HMS *Lively* and HMS *Venus*). Although the small port was fortified, Colonel Chalot had only one battalion to defend it from attacks mounted from both land and sea. He capitulated on the condition that his men would be held prisoner in England rather than Portugal.[7]

Soult's strategy succeeded on the 28th with the Portuguese transferring many units in anticipation of an attack on their left by Merle's division. He had actually decided to make his primary assault against the strongest Portuguese positions in the centre and hoped to induce the defenders to weaken this area by divisional scale attacks on each flank beforehand. He had a force of 16,000 men available for the assault but at least 3,000 of these were cavalry and therefore of little use in assaulting fortified positions. However, once the infantry had penetrated the defences, the cavalry would be invaluable for exploiting their success.

Accordingly, Soult placed Delaborde's division, supported by Franceschi's cavalry, to assail the northeastern front, Mermet's division and La Houssaye's dragoons to storm the centre and Merle's division to assault the western entrenchments.[8] The French did their utmost to conceal the deployment of Mermet's division, hoping to fool the enemy into thinking their forces opposing the central fortifications were weaker. Once the flank attacks were making progress, Mermet's division would overcome the redoubts in the centre, driving forward into the city to secure the bridge, effectively cutting the Portuguese defences in half.

The French were ready to attack well before dawn but that night's rainstorm had soaked the earth, which would lessen the effect of artillery.

When firing roundshot, cannon relied upon this solid shot bouncing numerous times along the ground when it struck, potentially hitting more than one target. Soft ground reduced this effect, with cannon balls sinking further into the earth, so Soult delayed the attack until 7.00 am, hoping the ground would dry out.

The assault began with an artillery bombardment of the Portuguese positions. Attacks then began on both flanks with the infantry moving forward so swiftly that the Portuguese gunners only had time to fire a couple of salvoes before the French were below their walls and attempting to break into the redoubts. Several positions on both flanks were overrun and, just as Soult had anticipated, Parreiras transferred men from the forts in the centre to reinforce each flank. Observing these movements, Soult ordered Mermet to begin his assault. Although the Portuguese put up fierce resistance, the forts in the centre were assailed with French infantry climbing through the gun embrasures and putting the bulk of their garrisons to the bayonet. A huge Portuguese flag flew from the most prominent of these redoubts and, when the tricolour was raised in its place, the defenders rapidly began to lose hope.

Having broken the enemy line, Soult sent two battalions to assail the Portuguese western positions from the rear and a further two battalions straight into the city towards the bridge. A number of fortified positions on the east side fell in quick succession as General Delaborde's men assaulted them, taking at least fifty cannon in the process. Seeing that all was lost, Parreiras fled over the bridge with his staff to report to the bishop, while General Vittoria retreated east along the Valongo road into the interior. Vittoria's men had suffered losses in the assault but Franceschi's cavalry declined to pursue them much beyond the edge of the city, allowing them to withdraw in good order.

On the western (left) flank, the Portuguese defenders suffered far worse. After ensuring that the cannon in his remaining redoubts were spiked, General Lima-Barreto ordered a full retreat. The defenders fled in disorder with some making for the safety of the St João fort while others hoped to cross the Douro. They were closely pursued and Lima-Barreto urged his men to surrender, realising that all was lost. Within sight of the approaching French, his own men shot him down as a traitor. Some of the fugitives tried to swim the Douro but French cavalry pursued them into the shallows and the majority were sabred, captured or drowned. Those that managed to gain the safety of the citadel's walls later accepted terms from the French and surrendered.[9]

Allied troops in the centre simply fled into the deceptive safety of Porto as the French overran their positions. While the improvised barricades blocking the streets held for a time, French infantry swiftly overcame them and pulled them aside, their defenders being dispirited by the rapid fall of the redoubts. With French cavalry and infantry forcing their way down the streets towards the river, Portuguese soldiers fled before them, joined by hundreds of townsfolk who were terrified at the sight of enemy soldiers entering their city.

Men, women and children were among the fugitives who now funnelled into the area before the bridge of boats, all desperate to cross and gain the safety of the south bank. Thousands of people jostled and pushed their way towards the quays and onto the bridge. Seeing the approach of the French, a Portuguese officer (who has never been named) ordered the drawbridge raised in the centre of the span (designed to allow boats to pass underneath) to prevent the French crossing. This left a gap of 40ft (12m) but, as terrified people pressed from behind, those at the front of the crowd could stop but not turn around. A scene of the utmost horror ensued as people were pushed into the river, which was deep, swollen and fast flowing after the rain. Panic ensued as many fell or were swept off the sides of the bridge as some pontoons began to sink under the weight of hundreds of people. Auguste Bigarré, an ADC on Soult's staff, entered Porto with a battalion of the 17th Line infantry and witnessed the tragedy unfold:

Imagine 12–15,000 souls crowded together on the bank of a river crossed by a bridge of boats, whose centre has been pushed under the water. Imagine that mass ... pressing forward to cross the bridge. Imagine those unfortunates being hurled into a gulf whose existence they only discovered at the last moment ... exterminated by ... Portuguese guns on the left bank of the Duero [sic] and the bayonets of the French at their heels ... Mercifully, this scene of carnage only lasted for one hour, but ... for eight days afterwards one saw husbands, fathers and brothers dredging the river … for their wives, their children, their parents and their friends.[10]

As many as 4,000 people may have perished during the disaster and this wretched episode is commemorated in Porto to this day.[11]

Soon the waters were covered with the struggling forms of drowning people as they were swept downriver. Further chaos ensued when a retreating Portuguese cavalry squadron panicked and rode into the crowd gathered before the bridge, trampling many people beneath their hooves. As two battalions of French infantry spearheading the assault approached, they initially fired into the struggling crowds but, seeing what was happening, ceased fire. Some infantrymen attempted to save people, pulling them from the water, while others pushed civilians back from the bridge along the quays with the butts of their muskets.

Observing the arrival of French units before the bridge, Portuguese artillery on the Serra Hill opened fire cutting down friend and foe on the north bank and adding to the confusion. It took the French half an hour to clear the approaches to the bridge and, once artillery was brought up, they established batteries and directed counter-fire against the Portuguese artillery on the south bank. Infantry from Mermet's division then fought their way across, using timber to cover the yawing gap left by the drawbridge. Once over the Douro, they assaulted the hill but the Portuguese artillery withdrew before being overrun, as Porto was clearly lost. The suburb of Villa Nova was swiftly captured but 200 militiamen continued to resist in the Bishop's Palace near the centre of Porto, firing at the French from its windows. This was eventually stormed and, once the palace gates were broken down, all the defenders were bayoneted. The city was in French hands by noon.

Some French soldiers now vented their fury upon the city and its inhabitants.[12] Although officers attempted to restore order, the city was sacked with acts of drunkenness, arson, theft, murder and rape committed well into the night. De Naylies witnessed some pillaging:

Here and there fighting was still going on in the streets, but a heavy hand was being used against anyone who was caught with arms in their hands. For some hours the city was then prey to all the horrors of an assault. I was fortunate enough to save a young girl who was about to become the victim of a number of drunken infantrymen ... Running up the stairs, sabre in hand, I threw myself upon these brigands, but I was knocked down by one of them. The blow drew blood, and I was only saved by the fact that in his drunken state he failed to take proper aim. Attracted by the noise, three dragoons then ran in and helped me to chase them away.[13]

Seeing that all was lost, the bishop fled south (eventually reaching Lisbon) and as Soult struggled to impose order on the city, he must have grimly recalled his warning to the prelate of what would occur if the city was stormed. Similar incidents have taken place throughout military history when a city or fortification refused to surrender and attacking soldiers got out of hand. Oman placed the sack of Porto in the context of its times, 'It is to the credit of Soult that he used every exertion to beat the soldiers off from their prey, and restored order long ere the following morning. It is to be wished that Wellington had been so lucky at Badajoz and San Sebastien.'[14]

Naturally, the Allies used the sack of Porto to their advantage, citing atrocities committed in the city in anti-French propaganda. The following extract appeared in the *Literary Panorama* (derived from Portuguese newspapers) and is a typical example:

Military Execution by the French at Oporto. – A captain of a vessel who left that unfortunate city ... gives the following recital ... about forty French prisoners fell into the hands of the populace, who barbarously put them to death. As soon as the Marshal was informed of this, he ordered bloody vengeance to be taken. In consequence, some thousands of the wretched inhabitants were bayonetted without distinction of age or sex. – After the rage of the French was in some measure satiated, and the bodies of the slaughtered had been exposed three days in the streets, the remains of some were permitted to be interred ... but the greater number of the dead bodies was cast into the river. Marshal Soult ... gave strict orders to the soldiers not to hurt any of the English, as they, he was pleased to declare, generally respected the laws of war.[15]

While this acknowledged that atrocities were provoked to a degree, the idea that thousands were bayoneted is an exaggeration. The article also alleges that the sack of Porto continued for days (while most sources agree that Soult had brought his troops under control that night) and claims that a daily payment of 16,000 *crusadoes* was exhorted from the inhabitants upon the threat of further atrocities. In the light of Soult's actions while occupying Porto (see Chapter 6) these allegations are unlikely to be true. However, even French newspapers admitted that the garrison of the Bishop's Palace was slaughtered to a man.[16]

Meanwhile, in Lisbon Cradock's position was gradually improving with forces returning from Cadiz and reinforcements expected from Britain. Yet, while his military strength was growing, the complexity of the political situation still placed him in a serious dilemma. London continued to send mixed messages about whether they wished to defend or abandon Portugal while the Regency government urged him to assume the offensive. Among their repeated requests were proposals to send reinforcements to Zezere (to protect the Beira and Alemtejo regions) or to Alcantara in order to shore up Cuesta's flank and block the southern progress of the French I Corps. At the beginning of March, Cradock's intelligence about enemy movements was patchy and John Frere sent unclear information about events in Spain.

Although opposition to the French was widespread among the people and the clergy, it is easy to see why the British Cabinet entertained doubts about successfully defending Portugal. The Prince Regent had left for Brazil, taking many of the country's elite and significant wealth to his new court. While the Regency government was doing its best, parts of the country were barely under their control, falling under the sway of local ordenanzas or in a state of mob rule. Furthermore, Porto's junta was virtually independent of Lisbon and enjoyed great influence in the north. The Portuguese army was in disarray with many of its best officers having defected to the French and its men poorly armed and supplied. The remaining aristocracy and gentry were appalled by the endemic violence and anarchy that had ensued and, fearful for their lives and property, quietly considered accepting French rule merely to see law and order re-established. Portugal appeared to be on the verge of collapse.

Faced with a bewildering array of demands and conflicting advice, Cradock was in an unenviable political dilemma. He believed French strategy focused on capturing Lisbon and that occupying Portuguese provinces was a secondary objective for Napoleon. With limited forces at his disposal, he thought concentrating his army at the capital would discourage the French from marching against it until they had amassed sufficient numbers for the task. Accordingly, he believed it madness to disperse his command in fortresses around the country until the size of his army increased, enabling him to send forces large enough to defend them adequately.[17] Members of the Regency government, such as the powerful Souza family, interpreted his obstinacy as a highly Anglo-centric, as it condoned yielding large areas of their country to invading armies without firing a shot. Unsurprisingly, Cradock soon made many enemies in Lisbon.

Beresford's progress in raising and training Portuguese troops lifted Cradock's hopes, along with the return of forces from Lisbon and the arrival of two artillery batteries from England. His army had around 16,000 men by mid-March and Cradock was confident of defending Lisbon and manning the sea forts along the Tejo. However, he was still short of horses and baggage animals. The lack of mules to equip the artillery and commissariat was so serious that he felt obliged to send military buyers on a mission to the Barbary Coast to procure beasts of burden.

From January 1809, Cradock had begun pulling British forces back to Lisbon from outlying regions, fully expecting an order to withdraw from Portugal. This included the bulk of the British soldiers in Almeida, leaving the garrison of Portugal's northeastern fortress on the frontier severely depleted. It was the most modern border fortress and, designed to repel invasions from Spain, was of far more use for the Allies in this conflict than the opposing Spanish fortress of Ciudad Rodrigo, built against Portuguese incursions.

Constructed around a fourteenth-century castle, Almeida's fortifications were added during the 1700s and designed to withstand artillery. They included the addition of numerous glacis to deflect shot over the outer walls and its system incorporated ravelins, 'bomb-proof' traverses and strong gatehouses. The fortress presented a low silhouette to help foil artillery and Almeida was built on a plateau that commands the surrounding area.

It was well supplied with guns, ammunition and stores originally destined for Moore's army. Previous garrisons ensured that dwellings were not built too close to the walls and fields of fire had been kept clear of obstructions. Essentially, Almeida was a serious obstacle to invading forces approaching from Spain and would have to be taken or cut off and besieged before an army could move further into Portugal.

Sir Robert Wilson, commanding the 1st battalion of the Lusitanian Legion, had been established in Almeida since January. Contrary to the wishes of the Bishop of Porto and Cradock, he not only reinforced the garrison but conducted aggressive forays over the border between January and March, establishing a forward base in Spain for this purpose. When Cradock instructed battalions of the 45th and 97th regiments to quit the fortress and join the main army at Lisbon, he knew that he had no power to order Wilson to do so since he remained under the bishop's nominal authority. Wilson conferred with his officers and all agreed that they should consider themselves in Portuguese service and abandoning Almeida at this point would be dishonourable, despite Cradock's advice.[18]

Yet, Wilson was in no way discouraged by the departure of the British infantry. He maintained Almeida with only two companies of infantry under Lieutenant Colonel Mayne, drawn from the legion and remaining Portuguese regular soldiers who had refused to leave. There were also artillerymen manning the fortresses guns and a squadron of cavalry but Wilson considered this small force an adequate garrison while he led raids over the frontier. Not only did elements of the legion venture as far as Ciudad Rodrigo (then under Spanish control) but they assailed French outposts around Lapisse's headquarters in Salamanca and beyond. Wilson acted with such aggression and confidence between January and the end of March that Lapisse, who had 9,000 men at Salamanca, assumed that the Anglo-Portuguese had a far larger garrison at Almeida.

According to Napoleon's instructions, Marshal Victor was supposed to be moving along the Guadiana Valley into southern Spain and would eventually send troops to support Soult's attempts to take Lisbon. It was also part of the plan to subdue the fortresses of Ciudad Rodrigo and Almeida before moving on the Portuguese town of Abrantes. On 28–9 March, General Cuesta attacked Victor's I Corps with an army of 24,000 men south of Medellín near the River Guadiana. Although the French had only 17,000–18,000 men, the Spanish were assaulting a prepared French position and were repulsed in a disastrous action that cost them almost 10,000 men.[19]

Despite this triumph, Victor felt unable to move beyond Mérida, which lies directly east of Badajoz. During this campaign, his command had suffered from guerrilla activity in a similar manner to Soult's experiences. Yet, the news that British and Portuguese regular troops were conducting large-scale raids in his rear troubled him. The Lusitanian Legion was mounting regular attacks on small garrisons and supply convoys and now occupied the Pass of Baños. Lapisse felt unable to do much more than establish a screen of outposts in the region of Ciudad Rodrigo, let alone take serious action against the fortress, and was clearly intimidated by this interference. By the end of March, Wilson contemplated a serious move against Alcantara hoping to sever communications between Victor and Lapisse entirely.

Opinions among historians differ about how effective Wilson's raids were in influencing Victor's decision to halt offensive operations. Historian Michael Glover believes that Wilson himself did not conform to this view but acknowledges that Parliament praised his efforts in 1810, stating that the disastrous effect of his actions on the French went far beyond what would normally be expected from a small command. Sir John Fortescue, while acknowledging Wilson's proficiency, thought that Lapisse's timidity was equally responsible, while modern historian René Chartrand thinks the Lusitanian Legion's effect on French operations is incontestable – the arrival of regular soldiers in his rear constituting far more of a threat than nuisance attacks by guerrillas.[20] Whatever the truth of the matter may be, Victor's refusal to move undoubtedly foiled the emperor's initial plan for the invasion of Portugal as Soult was left unsupported.

By 1 April, Cradock had received news of the fall of Porto and Cuesta's defeat at Medellín. He believed that, due the extent of Cuesta's defeat, any British move north would be compromised, as his right flank was exposed to an attack by the French I Corps and he risked the possibility of being caught between two French armies. Beresford advised that even sending token forces north would greatly boost morale in the country but Cradock was implacable, especially with Badajoz desperately requesting assistance. The fall of this large Spanish fortress on the Spanish–Portuguese border would be a major setback for the Allies and, in the wake of Medellín, there was little to prevent Victor moving south and besieging it.

Yet, the arrival of Major General Hill with five infantry battalions and some artillery on 4 April boosted Cradock's confidence to the extent that he finally took offensive action, marching forces north to Obidos, Caldas and Rio Mayor. An advanced corps pushed even further north but further movement was postponed when Lisbon received news that the horse-buying mission to the Barbary Coast had failed to procure sufficient numbers of baggage animals.

To Cradock's dismay, Horse Guards informed him on 18 April that General Wellesley was coming to replace him and had already embarked for Lisbon. Although he would receive the governorship of Gibraltar, this sideways move did not discourage Cradock from advising London of his view that Portugal was devoid of resources and its people were war weary. Nevertheless, he moved the main army north, reaching Leiria by 21 April where he contemplated taking offensive action, writing, 'As soon as our equipment is complete, and our supplies assured, and we have no anxiety about Marshal Victor, we shall advance to dislodge Soult.'[21] However, Wellesley disembarked on 22 April and was able to assume command two days later. Cradock later took ship for Gibraltar with his active military career effectively over.

By the end of March 1809, the French invasion of Portugal had met with mixed success. While Soult's army encountered great difficulties and was behind Napoleon's schedule, II Corps now controlled Portugal's second city. Indeed, the First Battle of Porto was a military triumph for the French. Historian Digby Smith records that 8,000 Portuguese had been killed with an indeterminate number wounded and 225 taken prisoner. At least 197 cannon and 20 colours were captured, such losses traditionally illustrating the extent of a victory. Napier puts the total of Portuguese casualties at 10,000, while Oman and Fortescue concur on the figure of 7,000–8,000, although these estimates include civilian losses. Most sources agree that the French suffered around 500 killed or wounded during the battle, although Smith places French casualties at 72 officers and 2,000 men.[22]

Admittedly, the fact that Portuguese forces largely comprised militia and ordenanza around a core of 5,000 regular soldiers lessens the impact of this victory somewhat. However, the loss of Porto was a severe blow to the Allied cause, provoking fears of a swift French descent on the capital. Yet Soult's position was far from secure:

> the Marshal was in reality almost as far from having completed the conquest of northern Portugal as the day when he first crossed the frontier. He had only secured for himself a new base of operation, to supersede Chaves and Braga. For the next month he could do no more than endeavour ineffectually to complete the subjugation of one single province.[23]

Even so, Soult now held a major city with docks, shipping and well-supplied storehouses seized largely intact.[24] Yet, he was isolated from Ney's VI Corps in Galicia and had not received dispatches for almost a month. Most of the garrisons he had established during his march were either threatened or retaken by the Allies and it was imperative that he restore his communications. He had heard nothing from Marshal Victor and felt the need to establish links with I Corps before marching on Lisbon. It seemed foolhardy to move south before consolidating his gains. Accordingly, he decided to halt at the Douro.

Chapter Five

A Change in Command

Sir Arthur Wellesley's campaigns in the Peninsula would prove so successful that he has come to be considered one of Britain's finest commanders, quite an accolade considering the military history of the British Isles. Aged 40, he was in his prime in 1809 but his prospects in early life had looked uncertain, even according to his own family, 'I don't know what I shall do with my awkward son Arthur,' complained Lady Mornington to her daughter-in-law, he was 'food for powder and nothing more'.[1] She believed he lacked ambition and, just like his father, only seemed interested in music and trivial distractions. She felt an army vocation was inferior to the career paths his brothers had chosen but even declared that he had little chance of succeeding as a soldier.

Born in 1769, Arthur was the son of Garret Wesley, first Earl of Mornington. While the Wesleys were an Anglo-Irish family of respected heritage, they were impoverished compared with families of similar status and their financial situation was dire when Lord Mornington died in 1781. When Arthur's elder brother Richard became head of the family he chose to revert to the former, more aristocratic spelling of the family's name, Wellesley. Arthur studied at Eton but, displaying little academic promise, was sent to France to finish his education at the Royal Academy of Equitation at Angers (Anjou). His family then bought him an officer's commission and he became an ensign on 7 March 1787, in the 73rd Highland Regiment, rising to the rank of lieutenant before the year was out.

As a Tory Member of Parliament, Richard Wellesley soon became a force in politics and assisted his brother's career both financially and through his influence in Parliament and at Horse Guards (British army headquarters). The army employed the purchase system, allowing officers to buy promotions when a vacancy arose if they had spent a specified time in their current rank. The Establishment assumed that most officers had private incomes and paid them a token wage, so selling and exchanging commissions was virtually their only means of profiting from their profession. The system was open to abuse since an officer was not obliged to serve with his regiment in a literal sense and long periods of absence were commonplace. However, the rank of general and above was only attainable by merit. The reason the Establishment tolerated this antiquated arrangement harked back to the civil wars of the seventeenth century, when Oliver Cromwell (and others) made common men officers based on their abilities alone. During this period King Charles I was executed and, for a brief time, England was a republic. Therefore, the authorities prized loyalty to the Crown above military talent and hesitated to create a professional officer class, enabling men of unproven loyalty to gain military power. Essentially, it was believed that wealthy men were unlikely rebels since they had a personal stake in the country and therefore favoured the Establishment. Revolutionary turmoil on the Continent reinforced these reactionary attitudes.

Contrary to expectations, Arthur made an excellent officer, famously burning his beloved violin in an act symbolising the end of his carefree youth. He took his profession far more seriously than many officers and in later life commented that he 'was not so young as not to know that since I had undertaken a profession I had better try to understand it'.[2] Accordingly, he read widely on military subjects, took an interest in every aspect of his duties and endeavoured to excel. He quickly gained a reputation as a dispassionate man with little time for leisure. Although he relaxed somewhat in private company, he only associated freely with those of his own class and could be extremely cold to those he considered below his station. He was a quintessential aristocratic gentleman who supported the Establishment and the old order.

Wellesley probably cultivated his austere image hoping to be taken seriously in his profession. While it won him few friends, the formal impression he presented usually ensured that his opinions were respected and, since he was clearly a competent officer, superiors came to rely upon him. Soon all traces of the happy-go-lucky young man he had once been disappeared and he came to be seen as a solemn man, dedicated to his career alone.

By 1793, he was a lieutenant colonel in the 33rd Regiment of Foot and was one of the few officers to emerge from the Duke of York's disastrous campaign in the Netherlands (1794–5) with his reputation enhanced. Wellesley also became an MP in Ireland and divided his time between politics and the army but set political aspirations aside when he left for India in 1797.

India made Wellesley's name in military circles and it was there that he learned valuable lessons that served him well in the Peninsula. However, many European soldiers were dismissive of those who won reputations serving in the colonies, believing that experience gained in fighting 'native' armies compared poorly with fighting modern armies in Europe. While Western military technologically outmatched some cultures, this was a misleading generalisation. For example, the Mahratta princes who Wellesley fought against in India raised a vast and effective army against the British, equipped with modern muskets, artillery and formidable cavalry, which had benefitted from being trained by European officers.

Wellesley participated in the siege of Seringapatam in 1799, which contributed to the fall of the city, and was highly successful in battlefield commands, notably at the battles of Assaye on 23 September 1803 and Argaum on 29 November 1803. He also became governor of Seringapatam (largely due to his brother's influence as Governor-General of India) which enabled him to hone his administrative and diplomatic skills.

The experience he gained campaigning in India would prove invaluable in the Peninsula. Knowing how much the climate affected movement and supply, Wellesley made a serious study of logistics, an area that most officers ignored. He took great care to ensure that enough bullocks (used as draught animals) and carts were available to convey the enormous amount of baggage armies required. Although transporting food, weaponry, tents and other baggage was important, water was an essential requirement for campaigning in India because of the climate. The weight and difficulty of transporting it in sufficient quantities had to be overcome on campaign. Indeed, for every fighting man at least three camp followers were required to tend to the army's needs. Operations on this scale demanded a high level of organisation but Wellesley's perseverance and dedication proved equal to the task.

Crucially, he also learned to avoid antagonising the local population in India who entertained mixed views regarding European intervention in their affairs. While many armies simply requisitioned what they wanted, Wellesley realised that ill-treating the populace led them to conceal supplies, mislead scouts, conduct acts of banditry or enlist with their enemies. To reduce these risks, he ordered that all supplies must be paid for (with money or promissory notes) and that soldiers under his command caught abusing the locals were to be severely punished.

Even more importantly, Wellesley developed the belief that swift offensive action against an enemy was the most effective way of winning a campaign. While he took care to ensure that important fortifications were garrisoned, his campaigns concentrated on finding and bringing the enemy to battle. He believed that defensive strategies were only acceptable when a force was vastly outnumbered as this approach usually resulted in long protracted wars. It was far better to strike quickly to damage or destroy the enemy's main army.

Wellesley became familiar with the problems a large army encountered moving swiftly through the Indian countryside, which was a serious undertaking given the logistical difficulties involved. Wellesley had to manoeuvre through or around extensive forestry, hills, mountains and rivers on the subcontinent, and rivers were a particular challenge as bridges capable of carrying heavy guns and wagons were rare. Furthermore, seasonal rains often raised river levels so high that spanning them required skilful engineering, strict discipline and (above all) careful judgement when timing a crossing. He gained great experience in fording or bridging rivers during campaigns where there was always a risk of enemy interference during such operations.

A famous example of Wellesley making an opposed crossing occurred at the Battle of Assaye. Having observed the strength of the enemy position, the forces of which outnumbered his army by at least three to one, he chose to cross the River Kaitna to attack the Mahratta's centre and left flank, to drive them into the town of Assaye and pin them against the Juah (a tributary of the Kaitna) lying in the enemy's rear. The Mahrattas would be forced to redeploy in a restricted position where their superiority in numbers would no longer be such an advantage and the flanks of Wellesley's army would be protected by the two rivers. This bold strategy depended on crossing the Kaitna in considerable force before the enemy could interfere and the army faced annihilation if it went wrong, as the river would block its line of retreat.[3]

There were no bridges and scouts informed him that fords did not exist in the area. With his knowledge of the Indian countryside, Wellesley noted that two villages lay close to each other on opposite banks of the Kaitna, correctly surmising that they would never have been built there 'without some habitual means of communication between them'.[4] Sending cavalry to reconnoitre, a ford was discovered precisely where he had predicted, and Sir Arthur ordered the army to cross there. While aware that the ford lay in full view of enemy guns, he judged there was time to cross the river before the enemy could prevent them. The Mahrattas levelled a heavy cannonade against troops, inflicting losses as they crossed, but Wellesley's estimate was accurate and the enemy was obliged to redeploy to meet this unexpected threat. Wellesley's bold move caught the Mahrattas off-guard, which had a great effect on the outcome of the battle, and he later claimed it as one of the finest actions of his career.[5]

As the youngest lieutenant general in the army, Wellesley was fortunate to gain command of the expedition to Spain in 1808, but, when the Spanish Galician Junta refused British assistance, the expedition was re-directed to liberate Portugal. After conferring with the Bishop of Portugal, Wellesley landed his army in Mondego Bay between 1 and 8 August, intending to march south to Lisbon.

Wellesley employed the methods he had learned in India, insisting that all supplies were paid for. He also made examples of looters as a deterrent and, on one occasion, 'Having satisfied himself as to the guilt of the soldiers ... turned round to the Provost-Marshal, and in that brief expression which ever characterised him, said, "In ten minutes report to me that these two men have been executed."'[6] General Junot saw the hanged men during a truce and inquired about the crimes they had committed. He was surprised to be informed that they had merely been caught plundering (despite having assaulted a Portuguese civilian while committing their crime) as such offences rarely merited the death penalty in the French army.

The first clash with a small French force under General Delaborde occurred at Roliça on 17 August, during which Sir Arthur developed a profound respect for the enemy despite his ultimate victory. Paradoxically, the far larger Battle of Vimeiro on 21 August proved to be far less of a challenge for Wellesley. Hoping to gain surprise by attacking swiftly, Junot assaulted the prepared British defensive position and delivered his attacks piecemeal. The outnumbered French were repulsed with relative ease and Junot's army suffered a clear defeat.

While the campaign was a military triumph up to this point, events then conspired to tarnish Wellesley's victory. In a move unparalleled in British military history, General Burrard assumed command at the end of the battle and was replaced by General Dalrymple shortly thereafter. Unsure of his ground, Burrard denied Wellesley permission to pursue the enemy, which may have resulted in a decisive victory. Political chicanery in the British Cabinet lay behind the decision to make two changes in command in only forty-eight hours and the disruption it caused undoubtedly contributed to the fiasco that ensued.

Dalrymple and Burrard were inexperienced in Portuguese affairs and overly keen to accept the terms the French proposed at the armistice. Although they achieved a complete French evacuation of the country, the Portuguese and the British Cabinet thought they granted concessions that were far too generous. These included the Royal Navy transporting Junot's army back to France with its arms, equipment and goods obtained (or looted) in Portugal. The Portuguese were enraged, London was dismayed by the news and the generals responsible for the Convention of Sintra were brought before an inquiry, the findings of which effectively ended the careers of Dalrymple and Burrard. Wellesley was lucky to emerge with only minor damage to his reputation.[7]

Although Castlereagh trusted Wellesley implicitly on military matters, until his exoneration by the inquiry, his support waned and Sir Arthur learned some painful lessons from the affair. Afterwards he pressed for Wellesley to be reappointed to command the army in Portugal, knowing that he was the best commander Britain could offer after Moore's death. He informed him privately of his appointment at the end of March and officially on 2 April 1809. When Sir Arthur set sail for Lisbon on 14 April, he accompanied a squadron bearing reinforcements that would raise British forces in Portugal to 30,000 men.

As Sir Arthur Wellesley stepped ashore at Lisbon on 22 April 1809, he was a very different man to the one who had left under a cloud the previous year. He knew this war would either make or break his career and he was no longer politically naive. Having direct experience of fighting the French in the Peninsula, he was confident of success on the battlefield but the scandal surrounding the inquiry taught him to be less trusting with his political masters.

It became evident that his political rivals were set to undermine him when, on 20 January 1809, Mr Whitbread MP rose in the House of Commons asking whether General Stuart kept his office as Under Secretary of State for the War Department even while serving abroad with the army. He also mentioned that this had been the case when Wellesley (Chief Secretary for Ireland at that time) went to Portugal in 1808. Reluctantly, Castlereagh confirmed that both officers had retained their government roles although they were unable to perform their actual duties while serving overseas.

Further questions were raised on 2 February when Sir Arthur was present in the House to answer Whitbread. Wellesley confirmed that the Duke (his superior) could have removed him had he chosen to and he 'was prepared to expect it would have been done, had his absence continued much longer. But from personal kindness to him, the noble duke certainly retained his name in that situation while he was abroad with the army …'.[8] He admitted that, during his two-month absence, he received a portion of his salary but, while he was not guilty of any impropriety, the Whigs had won a political point at his expense. The fact that Wellesley retained his office due to personal connections said much about the nature of the Establishment and gave radicals further cause to demand reforms. Consequently, Sir Arthur resigned his government position before embarking for Portugal in 1809.

While he already conducted himself with considerable reserve, Wellesley now decided to play his cards very close to his chest. Indeed, he regularly commented on the fact that junior officers felt free to criticise him in the newspapers, as their letters were uncensored at this time, a fact that the French gleefully took advantage of in order to gain military intelligence. Consequently, he was reluctant to share information with his officers to the extent that his staff complained that he kept them in the dark about his intentions until the last moment.

Indeed, Wellesley had little time for sentiment and sometimes could be tactless when dealing with officers or the rank and file. While he set high standards for himself and endeavoured to achieve them, he was correspondingly intolerant of those who failed to live up to his expectations, becoming notorious for delivering severe reprimands in tones of icy formality if his orders were not carried out to the letter. Although often compared to Napoleon, he never attempted to win his army's love as his most famous opponent did, managing them with a very firm hand on occasion. While usually fair in his rulings, this gained him grudging respect rather than winning the army's devotion.

Sir Arthur tried to treat his predecessor fairly, perhaps recalling the manner in which he had been superseded the previous year. At the time, he felt the sting of that unmerited humiliation keenly and resented how his replacement towards the end of a battle affected the campaign. He even wrote to Castlereagh offering to delay assuming command if it disrupted operations, the latter remarking on his 'very honourable feelings of disinclination to interfere with Sir John Cradock's command in Portugal, in the event of finding that officer engaged in active operations in the field'.[9] Castlereagh went on to say that if this proved to be the case, Wellesley should place himself under Cradock's command and await further orders. Having learned to be cautious, Sir Arthur took care to make this a verbal message rather than commit his offer to writing but it was a generous consideration nonetheless. He was well aware that he was assuming command just as Cradock was preparing to take the field against Soult, which would be resented. Nevertheless, Cradock handed over his responsibilities to Sir Arthur without complaint, appreciating the considerate way Wellesley handled the matter.[10]

One of Wellesley's main concerns was the creation of a new Portuguese army, which would essentially become part of the British army for the foreseeable future. Lieutenant General Beresford had been appointed to reorganise Portuguese forces and enlisted large numbers of men prior to Sir Arthur's arrival. He was promoted marshal in Portuguese service on 2 March and immediately began to recruit British officers who spoke Portuguese, one of whom recorded, 'Sir John Cradock has received me in the kindest and most gratifying manner ... He informs me that Marshal Beresford has asked for me to be Quarter Master General of the Portuguese Army, which he has just commenced the task or re-organizing ...'.[11] Wellesley took great interest in the restructuring of the Portuguese army, finding that he worked well with the new marshal, who shared his serious manner and no-nonsense approach.

The illegitimate son of an Anglo–Irish lord, William Carr Beresford had joined the army at the age of 17 and served in India, France, Corsica, Egypt, Africa, South America and Portugal. He lost an eye in a shooting accident early in his career but saw action at the siege of Toulon in 1792, taking part in the storming of the original Martello tower at Mortella Point in Corsica in 1794 among other engagements. While physically imposing and immensely strong (he wrested the lance from a French cavalryman who attacked him at Albuera in 1811), it was felt his real talents lay in administration and training. During his time as the governor of Madeira, he learned to speak fluent Portuguese and enjoyed some influence in Lisbon.

The task of re-organisation was challenging since the former Portuguese army had been old-fashioned and hidebound in tradition even before the disruption of 1807–8. Many officers were derided as *fidalgos*, meaning they owed their positions to influence at court rather than military competence, and corruption was rife. The Regency reluctantly granted Beresford complete authority and he immediately began placing elderly officers on half pay (effective retirement in this context) and cashiering those found guilty of misconduct. He also imposed discipline in the ranks, which included the shooting of deserters and other harsh punishments as required. His actions made him unpopular but Wellesley gave him his full support, knowing that only an honest but inflexible man, dedicated to the rulebook, would achieve results. He believed that the Portuguese officer class was crippled by indiscipline. 'Long habits of disregard of duty, and consequent laziness made it not only difficult but almost impossible to induce many senior officers to enter into any regular and continued attention to the duties of their situations, and neither reward nor punishment would induce them to bear up against the fatigue.'[12] Wellelsey wrote to Castlereagh on 7 April supporting Beresford's view that major restructuring was necessary and that only the appointment of British officers into the service would bring swift results. He justified this on the grounds that Portugal currently lacked suitable officer candidates since so many had left for Brazil after the departure of the Prince Regent. While the Regency lacked funds, the British army could afford to pay these men so it made sense to attract British officers to enlist in Portuguese service, the most common incentive offered being a promotion in rank.

Unsurprisingly, this arrangement was difficult for the Portuguese to accept. To spare national feelings, Beresford tried to appoint as many Portuguese officers as possible but stipulated that the officer immediately above and below them in rank had to be British or have extensive military experience. With so many appointments given to foreigners, Beresford's actions were resented at first but complaints lessened once his system produced good results.

The situation was different among the rank and file of the Portuguese army. While standards had suffered under the old system, the men were keen to fight the French and Beresford believed they would make fine soldiers once they gained more combat experience. Upon taking command, he discovered that there were only 30,000 men under arms and officially there should have been twice that number.[13] It would take time to make up for this shortfall but Wellesley stressed that training efficient soldiers was more important than amassing new recruits.

While specialist units such as engineers and a commissariat existed during this period, an army comprised three arms: cavalry, infantry and artillery. Cavalry was still considered the elite in European armies, as it was closely associated with the nobility who had been extremely effective during the medieval period. Yet, the cost of horses made them very expensive to deploy in significant numbers and the increasing accuracy and lethal nature of firearms had seen their use on the battlefield lessen. In 1809, the Portuguese cavalry was divided into 12 under strength regiments with only 590 men on paper. As a result of the lack of horses, it was rarely possible to put more than 300 mounted men in the field.[14]

If used well, cavalry attacks could have a devastating effect on enemy formations but the large target they presented to muskets and cannon meant they risked serious losses when used unwisely. While an advance was in progress, decisions had to be made swiftly in the saddle and doing this effectively required the kind of quick thinking that only came with experience as a commander. Cavalry excelled when fighting enemy cavalry but charges against infantry or artillery were best delivered against an opponents' flank, rear or when the attack was combined with other arms. Cavalry was most effective when pursuing a fleeing enemy as they were the fastest and most manoeuvrable unit on the battlefield, but they required good ground and aggressive action required careful timing to achieve this.

With the lack of horses in the region, Wellesley wanted light rather than heavy cavalry regiments (whose primary role was delivering charges in battle) and the British army believed light cavalry performed almost as well on the battlefield in any case. They also excelled at reconnaissance, foraging, guarding an army's flanks on the march, screening units from observation, providing a commander with intelligence and discouraging enemy cavalry from doing the same. Wellesley wanted as many Portuguese cavalry regiments as possible but knew that their expense would limit his allowance.

Infantry formed the core of all armies and in 1809, the Portuguese army consisted of twenty-four line regiments, each comprising two battalions except the 21st Regiment, which had suffered heavy casualties at Porto. They were armed with the smoothbore flintlock musket, which was the primary infantry weapon of the time. Firing a large calibre, spherical lead ball, it could kill or incapacitate with ease but the musket's weakness was accuracy. Although the projectile was potentially effective at over 200yd, an infantryman was unlikely to hit a man-sized target at much beyond 50yd. Therefore, it was best fired en masse, which explains the dense linear formations the infantry used during this period. Men standing or kneeling in line could deliver a heavy volume of fire against the enemy and increase the likelihood of inflicting losses. An infantryman might not hit the man he aimed at but his musket ball could well strike the soldier next to him with men placed shoulder to shoulder in formation. While some Continental armies deployed infantry in three ranks, usually with the first rank kneeling so the rear ranks could fire over their heads, the British used only two. Beresford intended that the Portuguese infantry would adopt this practice.

As single-shot weapons, muskets were slow and awkward to reload with a ramrod and paper cartridges and this was best carried out while standing. British infantry were some of the best drilled in the world at this time and one of the few armies that regularly practised with live ammunition, as many governments could not afford the expense. Despite this, firing more than three shots in a minute was a difficult feat to perform even for well-trained infantry, though Beresford hoped the Portuguese would be soon able to match this performance.

Rifles were becoming increasingly common and it was believed that as the Portuguese loved hunting, they would make excellent marksmen. Rifles easily outranged muskets and were capable of hitting targets at up to 300yd or more but were slower to load than the musket and the dense smoke produced by the gunpowder of the time limited their prolonged use in major engagements. During this period, rifle-armed units were generally used as sharpshooters and skirmishers and were particularly useful in opposing their French counterparts (usually armed with muskets), targeting officers and inflicting losses on the enemy before they were able to respond. Rifle regiments were regarded as elite units in the British army and the intention to raise similar cadres in Portuguese service would eventually be successful. By the end of 1809, Beresford had six Caçadore (hunter) battalions, which would soon justify their elite status during the conflict.[15]

For hand-to-hand fighting, muskets and rifles were equipped with detachable bayonets – a bladed stabbing weapon. After an initial exchange of fire, the advance of the side who had gained an upper hand in a firefight with levelled bayonets was often enough to persuade the enemy to retreat. Bayonets were a vital defence against cavalry, which could decimate infantry by exploiting gaps in their ranks if they became disordered. As a defence against this, infantry would form a square formation several ranks deep or more, presenting a wall of bayonets into which most horses would refuse to charge. While nearly invulnerable against cavalry, these squares presented a large target to enemy gunfire and if sufficiently weakened by this, cavalry could overcome them.

Artillery was the biggest killer on nineteenth-century battlefields. Although guns needed to be deployed with care and protected against cavalry, cannon had the longest range of any weapon on the battlefield and were capable of inflicting horrific losses on infantry and cavalry. Roundshot and shell were the two most common projectiles. As a solid iron ball, roundshot often caused instant death or horrific wounds (usually the loss of a limb). Ideally fired at a point just before the target, these cannon balls would ricochet over the ground potentially hitting multiple targets until their kinetic energy diminished. When targeting the dense infantry formations of the period, ten or more men might be killed or incapacitated by a single well-aimed shot. Roundshot was also effective against defensive structures and large-calibre artillery was vital for battering down fortifications.

While similar in appearance, shells were packed with gunpowder and ignited by fuses. Most were designed to explode shortly after impact and would shower the immediate area with fragments of their iron casing. Much depended on timing with the length of the fuse and, if a shell exploded above a unit of infantry or cavalry, it could be devastating. The British had developed a new shell, designed by Major Henry Shrapnel, intended to detonate above the target and shower it with musket balls contained within its casing. Portugal had seen the first major use of this weapon at Vimeiro in 1808, where it wrought considerable damage on French infantry attack columns.

Artillery also fired canister (or case shot) which consisted of a canister packed with musket balls that would break up after firing, scattering these projectiles in a manner similar to a shotgun's spread of shot. Better known by the naval term 'grapeshot', canister was a short-range projectile designed to be used when cavalry or infantry were attacking an artillery battery, the intention being to strike down multiple targets simultaneously.

The Portuguese artillery was divided into four regiments of differing strengths and could supply as many as ten field batteries in addition to manning the guns of fortresses and garrisons. While the Portuguese had a history of skilled gunnery, Beresford desperately needed more officers for this arm. As one of the most professional areas of soldiering, artillery officers had to be well versed in gunnery in order to deploy and use cannon effectively. With far more training required than for the cavalry and infantry, it was felt that good-quality artillery would be harder to produce quickly in comparison with the other arms.

Wellesley left Beresford in no doubt that he had little use for militia and ordenanza. Considering them ill-disciplined, he was reluctant to arm them with valued muskets and intended to confine their use to guarding garrisons or deploying them in open country to prevent the enemy foraging and to cut their communications. The 1808 campaign demonstrated that these enthusiastic but poorly trained volunteers stood little chance against French infantry on the battlefield if they faced them on equal terms. When Trant and Silveira later attempted to use militias in a normal combat role, they found that this was still the case.[16]

With the situation so confused in Portugal, morale in the army was low and uncertainty in the Regency government soured the soldiers' mood even further. Mixed messages received from London were also unhelpful and by the time the Cabinet had made up its mind to defend Portugal, three months had elapsed. Yet, rather than cajole the army, Beresford adopted a firm line, saying that their nation would be saved by skill at arms, steadfast courage and firm discipline. His proclamation to the army was blunt, leaving them in no doubt that (in his opinion) regular Portuguese troops had performed badly at Porto:

> The great city of Oporto ... defended by 24,000 men, with trenches and redoubts furnished with more than 200 pieces of artillery, fell an easy conquest to an enemy of little more than half the number of its garrison, notwithstanding the people and their defenders were loyal and brave, because that enemy had been able to produce, under the appearance of patriotism, disunion, and a general insubordination; the consequences of which must ever be most ruinous. The Marshal therefore hopes that the army will perceive that we ought always to distrust those who have been with the French or their partizans, and whatever reports they may propagate, as they are undoubtedly paid by the enemy to promote confusion and distress ...[17]

The marshal made a determined effort to eradicate French sympathisers from the army but took care to act lawfully, conducting civil trials and courts martial. It is possible that Beresford personally intervened in the apprehension of one suspect, who had acted as his host on one occasion, and most of those found guilty were publicly whipped, exiled or (in a few extreme cases) faced a firing squad.[18]

As an interesting aside, the famous poet William Wordsworth believed the fall of Porto was directly attributable to the scandalous Convention of Sintra between the British and the French in 1808. He believed it undermined Portuguese confidence in their allies, which resulted in despondency, inefficiency and self-doubt within their army. He held Dalrymple and Wellesley accountable for this but was reluctant to do more than hint at this in the tract he wrote upon the subject, fearing potential libel suits. Although he did confide these beliefs in a private letter to his editor, the events of

May 1809 made him even more reluctant to expound on this theory. In consequence, his accusations are often overlooked.[19]

While Beresford was a stern disciplinarian, he endeavoured to be fair and standards in the Portuguese army swiftly improved under his guidance. Yet, Sir Arthur still entertained reservations about the readiness of the Portuguese troops and distrusted their officers in particular. However, he believed Beresford's assurances that they were ready to prove themselves, albeit under the stipulation that they were initially brigaded with British regiments to learn by example.

Possessing some inside knowledge of Cabinet secrets through his contacts in the government, Sir Arthur knew that the Austrians planned an offensive in central Europe, which, regardless of whether it was successful or not, would undoubtedly divert reinforcements and supplies intended for the Peninsula. This would give the scattered Spanish armies time to recover and it was unlikely that Napoleon, obliged to fight on two fronts, would be able to send enough men to be certain of conquering Portugal that year.

With this in mind, Wellesley felt he had an opportunity to mount a pre-emptive strike against one of the armies moving towards Lisbon. With harsh terrain lying between them, Wellesley believed that I and II Corps were too far apart to assist each other. He also guessed that guerrilla actions were tying down significant numbers of French soldiers while Soult and Victor attempted to restore their communications and re-establish their supply lines. News that Ney's VI Corps faced a serious insurrection in the north also made it unlikely that Soult would receive support from that quarter.

He knew that he must strike quickly before the French could recover by blocking one French army with a portion of his army and defeating the other. While tentative communications with Cuesta's Spanish army had been restored, Sir Arthur believed that they currently lacked the strength to support him after their recent defeats. While attacking I Corp made military sense, since it would relieve pressure on Lisbon and Seville, Anglo-Spanish co-operation had never been easy and Wellesley's commissariat might not be up to the logistical task of transporting supplies so far inland.

There were also strong political reasons for relieving Porto first as Portuguese morale would undoubtedly improve if this major city was liberated, as well as the fact that the Douro Valley was one of the most fertile and prosperous regions of the country. Furthermore, the Royal Navy would be able to support the commissariat by bringing supplies ashore close to areas where fighting was likely to take place. Wellesley's letter to Mr Frere (British ambassador at Seville) on 24 April emphasised how confident he was of forcing Soult to quit Portugal:

> I think it probable that Soult will not remain in Portugal when I pass the Mondego: if he does, I shall attack him. If he should retire, I am convinced that it would be most advantageous for the common cause that we should remain on the defensive in the North of Portugal and act vigorously in co-operation with Cuesta against Victor.[20]

Wellesley spent five days in the capital conferring with the Regency government, ensuring that Beresford's commissariat was efficient and making his plans for the forthcoming campaign. It was during this time that the French traitor Argenton approached Wellesley and gave him useful intelligence about Soult's army (see Chapter 6). He suspected that his opponent contemplated a new offensive as French cavalry patrols had ventured as far south as Leiria. Swift action was therefore imperative and he left Lisbon on 29 April.

As he rode north, Sir Arthur must have speculated about the character and abilities of his adversary. It was highly unlikely that Soult would mount a reckless assault against him as Junot had done in the hope of securing a quick victory. The marshal was a commander similar to himself, pressing forward confidently when he had an advantage but knowing when to halt and wait if the result of an engagement was uncertain. He knew that Soult was no glory seeker and did not need to prove himself to the emperor, unlike his predecessor Junot in 1808. He was also patient enough to secure a good defensive position and await reinforcements, knowing that if the Allies failed to dislodge him, Victor could march on Lisbon while he tied down the Allied army. Time was a crucial factor for Wellesley in this campaign. During this period in the war, a long campaign favoured the French and Soult could afford to wait. If the two French armies restored their communications and made a combined effort against the Allied army, Wellesley was doomed. He could not afford a protracted campaign and needed to strike swiftly and decisively or face defeat.

Chapter Six

The Marshal Who Would be King

Portugal was in a state of turmoil and near anarchy prevailed in the countryside between April and May 1809. While the majority of Portuguese opposed the French, they distrusted the British after the furore of Sintra the previous year, suspecting their army might withdraw and leave them to fight alone. Those with land and property watched nervously to see which side would gain the upper hand before committing themselves. Disturbing rumours from the north frightened investors, such tales including the fall of Porto (to either side), false intelligence that General Sebastiani was leading an army to combine with Soult's forces, talk of Wellesley's defeat and speculation that the French intended to withdraw from the Peninsula altogether.

It is ironic, therefore, that one of the most bizarre incidents during the Second French Invasion of Portugal is supported by numerous sources testifying to the fact it took place. The events surrounding the Argenton Conspiracy revealed political divisions and treachery within the French army as well as allegations that Soult aspired to become King of Portugal. While the details of the plot sound more like fiction than reality, the fact that Wellesley and Napoleon took the matter seriously render this rare occurrence worthy of study.

Having decided to halt at Porto, Soult sent a division north (under General Heudelet) to relieve the garrisons left in his wake. Heudelet was ordered to secure the main coastal road thereby restoring links with VI Corps in Galicia. Relations between General Loison and Soult had deteriorated so the marshal dispatched him east with another division to seize the bridge over the Douro at Amarante. This would secure II Corp's left flank, but he also ordered him to seek intelligence concerning the whereabouts of Lapisse and Victor. Loison found General Silveira's force blocking his progress at the Tamega (a tributary of the Douro) and while he attempted to dislodge him, established his headquarters at Amarante. Meanwhile, Soult repaired the bridge of boats at Porto and sent elements of Mermet's infantry division over the Douro to create a defensive screen south of the city. Franceschi crossed the river with his cavalry and began to send out reconnaissance patrols towards Coimbra. His orders were to ascertain what opposition II Corps was likely to encounter but to fall back if seriously threatened.

Soult pondered his options carefully and later wrote in his memoirs that he felt it would have been madness to move further south before garrisoning Porto and restoring his communications. After all, his forces were now distributed over a large area and it made sense to halt until he had consolidated his position. He also thought it prudent to unite with Lapisse and Victor before marching upon Lisbon.[1] This strategy has drawn criticism from many quarters, including Portuguese historian Chagas, who saw this inaction as 'inexplicable. If he had marched immediately on Lisbon he would not have encountered any Portuguese troops capable of resisting him and Cradock's forces would probably have embarked immediately.'[2]

Yet, it was uncertain whether Soult could concentrate enough men for a move against Lisbon while he carried out these plans. Furthermore, even if he took the capital, was his force large enough to hold it? Unusually for a capital, Lisbon had few fortifications and no city wall. Outnumbered and isolated in 1808, Junot had quickly sought terms from the British, as defending Lisbon was not possible under such circumstances. Soult was wary of falling into a similar trap with only a single corps to defend the city. A concerted move against the capital in conjunction with the two corps massed somewhere along the Spanish frontier stood a far greater chance of success. Soult felt that it was better to wait and assemble enough forces to make the fall of Lisbon more likely.

Soult took up residence in the Palace of Carrancas on the western side of Porto. According to Oman, he had already begun calling himself Viceroy of Portugal in Chaves but contemplated aiming higher. Despite the obvious unpopularity of the French after recent fighting, Soult believed that many Portuguese would support a pro-French party in Porto if it were handled carefully. Foremost in his mind was the fact that he had enticed Swiss irregulars to lay down their arms and join with revolutionary France only ten years before. Providing the Portuguese with a strong figurehead to lead them out of their current difficulties might appeal to a population weary of conflict. For a month and a half he was so distracted by the political situation that he began to fail in his duties as a commander-in-chief, not even visiting Amarante (only a day's ride away) when it became clear that the situation there was deteriorating.[3]

While it has never been proved that Soult seriously intended to declare himself king, the evidence of numerous diarists certainly reveals that he made a serious effort to gain Portuguese support. Along with his staff, the marshal attended mass in Porto Cathedral and tried to appoint as many Portuguese officials as possible to govern the city for him. The marshal's staff issued promissory notes stating that those who had fled the city were safe to return, and a remarkable number did so without suffering repercussions for any role they had played during the fighting. Soult even made arrangements for raising a national guard (up to 6,000 strong) to help keep order within Porto and this display of trusting recent enemies made a serious impression in the city.

General Ricard (Soult's chief-of-staff) was directed to solicit Portuguese support and accordingly organised missions into the towns of northern Portugal (in addition to Porto) proposing that the emperor appoint a French ruler to restore order in the north. Some returned with thousands of signatures from Portuguese citizens endorsing French rule. He even managed to muster a delegation of thirty-six respected officials to declare openly their willingness to submit to Napoleon's rule and request that he provide a prince of his blood to govern Portugal in his stead.[4]

British propaganda habitually emphasised the harsh treatment that the Portuguese peasantry received at French hands. This was unsurprising as Napoleon's armies lived off the land rather than paying for supplies, which always led to tensions. News that Soult was trying a different policy proved unwelcome when it reached Lisbon, 'The enemy has … on this occasion, practised those arts which Frenchmen are so expert in – circulation proclamations and insidiously abandoning, for a moment, their usual system of terror, plunder, and desolation, *treating the inhabitants with feigned moderation and kindness*'.[5]

Soult replaced silver icons, candlesticks and other religious items stolen from churches during the sack of the city and made serious attempts to reconcile the clergy with the French cause. Although opposition to France was strong in the priesthood, some members going to the extent of denouncing Napoleon as the Antichrist, Ricard met with a degree of success. At least one priest, Father Veloso, joined the *anfrancesado* street orators haranguing the crowds gathered outside the Carranco Palace calling for a 'Kingdom of Northern Lusitania' to be created. Officials threw coins down to the crowds from balconies, which encouraged shouts of '*Viva o Roi Nicolao!*'[6] Ricard also had proclamations posted around the city openly proposing Soult be crowned king.

Through these and similar actions, Soult gained some popularity, particularly as many had 'lost confidence in English support; they were weary of anarchy, bloodshed and invasion, and would have welcomed a firm hand at the helm'.[7] Indeed, the virtual British monopoly over Porto's wine trade and the stifling effect that their naval blockade had on trade made them unpopular in some quarters. While Junot's tenure as a de facto viceroy for Napoleon had gained little support, Marshal Soult was a more attractive prospect:

> He was better informed and much more suitable for a political mission than Junot. He thought mainly of gaining the loyalty of the Portuguese. They were, of course, unlikely to get true liberty from a French dictatorship but many people were better disposed towards the illustrious power of Napoleon and his revolutionary code than the worn out 'old regime' of Portugal.[8]

While the prospect of French rule was repugnant to many Portuguese, pragmatism might quell their patriotic feelings if the Allies continued to lose territory. Furthermore, the people of northern Portugal hesitated to rely upon Britain and the tentative rule of the Regency government in Lisbon showed alarming signs of turning their nation into a satellite state of Brazil. At this time of massive social upheaval, Soult's alleged designs on the Crown were not as ridiculous as they first appeared.

Napoleon's own origins were humble but he had risen to rule a nation, deposed monarchs and dictated terms to the Russian tsar nonetheless. He had also crowned his own relations regardless of the Bonaparte family's lack of royal blood. Examples include Jérôme Bonaparte, who was created King of Westphalia, and Louis Bonaparte who was crowned King of Holland. The first was an idler and a spendthrift while the second was constantly at odds with his brother over his dynastic plan for Europe, so much so that Napoleon eventually deposed him. More important was the fact that successful soldiers had been created princes, dukes and counts for their services and Marshal Murat (the son of an innkeeper) was crowned King of Naples, so the emperor had already set a precedent in this regard.[9] While a brave and capable soldier, Murat possessed few talents off the battlefield other than a penchant for seducing beautiful women. Therefore, despite his marriage to one of Napoleon's sisters, many considered his elevation to royalty to be a joke made in poor taste.

Soult made a better candidate for kingship compared with many of the emperor's recent appointments, and Napoleon caused him great offence by creating Marshal Bernadotte Prince of Ponte Corvo after Austerlitz. Bernadotte delivered a lacklustre performance at the battle while Soult, who practically saved the day according to the emperor's own testimony, was denied a dukedom connected with the victory (see Chapter 2). Some now pondered the fact that the French had fought the Revolutionary Wars seeking to gain a meritocracy only to see their emperor bestow titles through nepotism and favouritism. Therefore, the prospect of King Soult of Portugal was not that outrageous. The pressing question was should Soult benignly wait to be offered the Crown as a reward for services rendered or seize it and seek his emperor's approval afterwards?

While Soult was preoccupied in attempting to win over the civil population, Wellesley assumed command and became equally busy making preparations for an offensive. He was unsurprised to hear that a French emissary wished to see him, thinking that the enemy sought a truce or negotiated settlement, but the news that this officer came surreptitiously and without official approval intrigued him.

Mr John Viana, the son of a Porto merchant, had already made approaches to Marshal Beresford at his headquarters at Aviero. Viana informed him that the handling of the war dismayed some French officers to the extent that they were prepared to co-operate with the British. Treachery was clearly afoot but Beresford reluctantly arranged for one of his staff to meet an agent who represented this group. A rendezvous was attempted on Lake Ovar but both parties missed each other in the darkness and, discovering that his boat had drifted close to French picquets, the officer returned to Beresford at Aviero.[10] Viana subsequently brought this emissary directly to Beresford who arranged a meeting with his commander-in-chief.

Major Douglas (Beresford's chief-of-staff) brought Captain Argenton of the 18th Dragoons to Wellesley at Coimbra, or possibly Lisbon (sources disagree on the location). A former Jacobin who now claimed to be a Royalist, Argenton styled himself the Sieur d'Argenton (possibly in an attempt to impress British officers). He informed Sir Arthur that II Corps was rife with discontent over the way the war was being fought, particularly regarding excesses during the 'People's War', as guerrilla warfare was called at that time. Soult's 'ludicrous' designs on the monarchy disillusioned many officers who had now lost confidence in him. Discontent was particularly strong in the elements of the corps transferred from Junot's former Army of Portugal, and he claimed to speak on behalf of several senior officers. The mood among the rank and file was mixed. While many were scathing about their marshal's statements, the French army were always disposed to grumble and often meant little by it. Certainly, there was discontent but whether these men would follow their officers into rebelling against their commander was questionable.

Wellesley listened calmly and dispassionately to Argenton's tale and was bemused to hear allegations that Soult meant to crown himself king, but even more intrigued when told that the conspirators wanted the British to persuade the Portuguese to support him in his design, arguing that it would provoke the army into mutiny. If the British were prepared to collude in this, he assured Sir Arthur that II Corps would abandon the invasion and return to France. Wellesley ended the meeting by refusing to commit himself until presented with a definite plan and declined to offer any assurances until this was done.

While Sir Arthur detested dealing with men who were prepared to betray their commander, he was too good a politician to pass up an opportunity that might spare lives and property. He was plainly sceptical, writing, 'I doubt whether it will be quite so easy as their emissary thinks to carry their intentions into execution ...'.[11] Beresford also disdained this cloak and dagger

In 1809 the French army under Napoleon I appeared invincible but this was about to change. Engraving by Denis Auguste Marie Raffet (1804–60).

Napoleon's need to overcome Great Britain's naval supremacy lay behind the French invasion of Portugal. Engraving from the *Leisure Hour*, 1868.

Marshal Jean de Dieu Soult, one of Napoleon's most experienced generals, was ordered to invade Portugal for a second time in 1809.

General Sir John Craddock faced the unenviable task of defending Portugal while the British and Portuguese were uncertain about how to respond to the French threat. Painting by Sir T. Lawrence.

General Sir Arthur Wellesley (later Duke of Wellington) decided to march north and stop Soult's invasion in its tracks rather than adopt a passive defence.

French soldiers risked a grisly fate if they fell into the hands of Portuguese or Spanish guerrillas. Painting by Francisco José de Goya y Lucientes.

Outraged by guerrilla attacks, the French often responded in kind and summary executions and atrocities were common during the Peninsular War. Painting by Francisco José de Goya y Lucientes.

The British government debated whether to continue the war after General Moore's death at Corunna and the evacuation of his army from Spain. Engraving by Rouget.

Napoleon underestimated the strength of resistance he would encounter in the Peninsula as the Portuguese and Spaniards had been whipped up into a fury by the clergy. Engraving by Rouget.

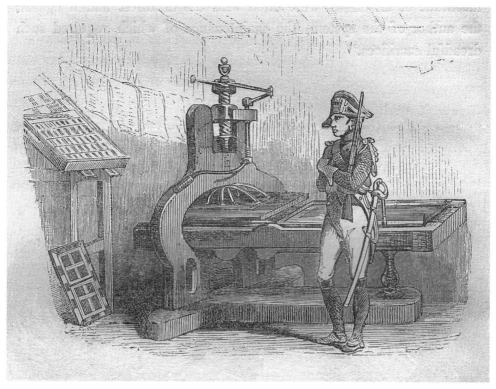

A sentry guards a printing press shut down by the French authorities. Press restrictions were commonplace during the Napoleonic Wars and all sides published extensive propaganda. Engraving by Rouget.

Faced with tough terrain and challenging weather conditions in the Peninsula, the elaborately uniformed armies became increasingly ragged and encountered difficulties in procuring supplies. Engraving by Leopold Beyer, 1813–15.

Once they crossed the frontier, Soult's II Corps were attacked repeatedly by Portuguese guerrillas and militia as they marched south.

A nineteenth-century engraving of Porto (Oporto), Portugal's second city, printed in the *Illustrated London News*.

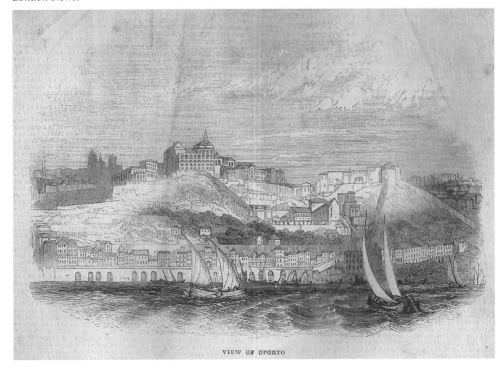

VIEW OF OPORTO

The bridge of boats over the Douro collapsed as the French assaulted Porto. Hundreds of Portuguese civilians were swept away and drowned. Engraving by Henri Félix Emmanuel Philippoteaux (1815–84).

Marshal Soult at the First Battle of Porto. Painting by Joseph Beaume (1796–1885).

An Allied landing supported by the Royal Navy was the kind of attack Soult predicted at Porto. The actual assault was quite different. *Landing troops in the Face of the Enemy* by M. Dubourg after J.A. Atkinson, *c.* 1820.

General Wellesley observes as his troops cross the River Douro.

General Baron Maximilien Foy was the first to learn that Allied troops were crossing the river. Engraving by Amédée Maulet (1810–35).

The 4th Light and 5th Line battalions counter-attack during desperate French attempts to push the Allies back into the river. Engraving by G. Browne.

The Bishop's Palace in Porto today. (*S. Hadaway*)

The Memorial to the Peninsular War in Porto. (*S. Hadaway*)

A detail from the Memorial to the Peninsular War in Porto showing Portuguese artillerymen dragging a gun. (*S. Hadaway*)

A plaque in Porto commemorating the lives lost on 29 March 1809 in the disaster on the river during the Portuguese retreat. (*S. Hadaway*)

A photograph of the Douro River which shows its width. (*S. Hadaway*)

The Bishop's Seminary where the Allies gained their foothold on the northern bank of the Douro. (*S. Hadaway*)

A view of the Douro with the Bishop's Seminary visible in the background under the bridge and the Serra Hill on the right. (*S. Hadaway*)

A view across the river with the modern bridge looking towards the Serra Hill where Wellesley placed his artillery to cover the attempted crossing. (*S. Hadaway*)

Constant skirmishing took place between French light infantry and Portuguese peasants and militia as Soult retreated through the hills and mountains.

Despite terrible losses, the British infantry stubbornly resisted French attacks at Albuera in 1811, causing Soult to comment, 'We had won the day but they did not know it and would not run away!'

Following Napoleon's final defeat, Soult ingratiated himself with succeeding governments and became a pillar of French society. From a painting by Pierre-Louis de Laval, engraved by T. Johnson.

affair and Napier wrote scathingly that the conspirators' political grievances did not justify treachery in the field as the lives of their countrymen were at stake.[12]

Nevertheless, Wellesley agreed to meet again when the campaign was well under way. He rode to meet Argenton at Martede (a village 10 miles north of Coimbra) on 6 May. Trust would be foolhardy in such an affair and Sir Arthur insisted that Argenton was brought to the meeting on byroads so that he would be unable to see Allied troop movements or estimate their numbers.

Argenton claimed to have conferred with high-ranking officers in Porto and Amarante, such as Loison and Delaborde, who he said were in favour of mutiny. Even those who supported Bonaparte were 'dissatisfied with Soult's conduct, particularly with an intention to declare himself king of Portugal; and they were determined, if he should take that step, to seize him and lead the army back into France'.[13] As Soult had not made a formal claim to the Crown, the conspirators hesitated to put their plot into action but they had three specific requests for Wellesley. First, that he make aggressive manoeuvres against II Corps (they recommended that he should attack at Vila Real) forcing the army to concentrate, which would also allow the conspirators to unite. Secondly, Argenton requested passports guaranteeing safe conduct to France for himself and two other officers, where they promised to contact other conspirators planning a *coup d'état* against Napoleon. Third, they wanted Wellesley to use his influence over the Portuguese to exaggerate the strength of Soult's popularity. This would make Soult feel secure enough to declare himself king, which would result in his arrest and replacement, or so they believed.[14]

Sir Arthur would not discuss his plans with Argenton and stressed that he was free to take whatever steps he pleased, whether Soult's officers turned upon him or not. However, he made his refusal to interfere in the Portuguese succession crystal clear, 'that in respect to his propositions, regarding the measures to be adopted by me to induce Soult to declare himself king of Portugal, they were quite out of the question; that I could not risk the loss of the confidence of the people of Portugal ...'.[15] Ultimately, Wellesley knew that discord in Soult's army would help his campaign but refused to assist the conspirators beyond giving Argenton the passports he requested. He also advised him to conceal these documents carefully as their discovery would result in his immediate arrest. Sir Arthur gained far more from the exchange than Argenton:

> The prudence of Wellington in dealing with people of this class is characteristically described by himself in allusion to this interview ... 'He gave me' (says Wellington) 'a good deal of information respecting the strength, the position, and the plans of the enemy, and of the detestation of Soult generally prevailing in the army ... and I *sent him back without his having seen any of our troops or knowing that we had such numbers collected here* ...'[16]

On 8 May, only days before Wellesley's attack on Porto, Argenton was arrested after attempting to persuade General Lefebvre, on whose staff he had once served, to join the conspiracy. This loyal officer immediately denounced him to Marshal Soult, informing him that Argenton had actually crossed enemy lines and conferred with Wellesley. Initially, the dragoon captain refused to name his associates but a promise to spare his life if he did so persuaded him to betray some conspirators. He accused Colonel Lafitte (his own commanding officer) and Colonel Donnadieu of the 47th Infantry, both of whom had played valiant roles in the First Battle of Porto. Both were arrested and, while Lafitte was permitted to return to his regiment due to lack of evidence, Donnadieu was imprisoned.

Soult was astounded that his own officers were plotting to overthrow him and became understandably paranoid upon hearing this shocking news. While he could rely on the loyalty of men like Heudelet and Franceschi, he knew his relations with some high-ranking officers were strained and he wrote to King Joseph voicing suspicions about Mermet, Loison, Lahoussaye and Quesnel. Although these allegations were never proved, the strange performance of Loison in particular over the following weeks gives some grounds for suspicion.[17] The unmasking of the Argenton Conspiracy at this point undoubtedly affected Soult's performance as a commander. Cut off from support and knowing that he would face an Allied attack within days, he was already contemplating a withdrawal and disloyalty within his own army must have dismayed him.

Napoleon was campaigning against the Austrians between April and July and it was not until 14 October 1809, when the Peace of Schönbrunn ended the conflict, that he heard detailed accounts of events in Portugal. While the campaign was in progress, he was disinclined to take the allegations against Soult seriously. As one of Soult's detractors claimed, 'Napoleon, who never liked to have made a mistake, seldom struck at those whom he had raised. In the present case he must either have the marshal shot or laugh at him; unluckily for himself, he took the latter course.'[18]

Indeed, the emperor and Marshal Berthier made light of the affair, referring to Soult as 'King Nicodemus' for a time, unaware that similar taunts would be shouted against Napoleon himself when he fell from power in 1814 (see Chapter 2). Yet, the emperor was concerned enough to send a stern reprimand, 'Berthier was told to write him a severely-worded warning and order him to stop making an ass of himself ... "I am enclosing some proclamations which you will recognise as the style of him born to rule well!" It was one of the neatest snubs ever administered ...'.[19]

At the end of the Danube campaign, Napoleon received Loison and Quesnel, who both expressed their dissatisfaction over Soult's actions in Portugal. Neither had served Soult well in Portugal and Loison's relations with his superior had been so acrimonious that he had ample motivation to pour poison in the emperor's ear, making much of Soult's alleged ambition to become king. As Madam d'Abrantes later wrote, 'when Loison arrived and related, with the venom of a serpent, the whole disastrous history of Soult's army, well knowing the effect the news produced upon him [Napoleon]; he turned pale and was seized with one of those nervous affections to which he was occasionally subject.'.[20]

Consequently, when Colonel Brun de Villeret (on Soult's staff) delivered his dispatches, he endured two stormy interviews with the emperor, who raged at him demanding that he confirm or deny the generals' claims. This time Napoleon wrote to Soult personally, stating that he was disappointed about his recent conduct and accusing him of allowing Ricard to go too far in the proclamations he posted around Porto. An extract from one had particularly annoyed the emperor: 'The Duke of Dalmatia would be asked to take the reins of government, to represent the sovereign, and to invest himself with all the attributes of supreme authority ...'.[21] Napoleon wrote that:

If you had claimed supreme power for yourself *proprio motu*, it would have been such a crime as to oblige me to consider you guilty of *lèse-majesté* and of a culpable attack on my authority. How could you have forgotten that the power you exercised over the Portuguese sprang from the command I entrusted you, and not from the play of passions and intrigue?[22]

One of the worst offences a subordinate could commit was to usurp power and, in a scornful line that clearly referred to the Argenton Conspiracy, Napoleon sneered, 'You have undermined your own authority; for it would be difficult to say, after this circular of yours, whether any Frenchman could be blamed for ceasing to obey your orders ...'.[23]

Yet, despite these stinging reproofs, the emperor then recalled Soult's loyal service in the past and declared that he had decided to overlook the matter. Indeed, he concluded his letter by conferring overall responsibility for the armies in Spain upon Soult, remarking that King Joseph's inexperience of warfare meant he would welcome his counsel. This certainly lessened the strength of the reprimand and Soult felt that Napoleon simply wanted to make a point and little had really changed between them, writing in his memoirs that, 'I understood my sovereign's letter perfectly and I never replied to it. I had no need to do so.'[24]

Perhaps the best insight into how the emperor felt about the affair was revealed when Jomini defended Soult after the infamous argument between him and Ney in Galicia following the invasion. When he recalled the affair, the emperor rounded upon him angrily saying, 'You have too much sense to believe stories. Soult had good reasons for acting as he did. He just had to build up a French party in Portugal.'[25] This strongly implies that Napoleon felt his earlier reprimands necessary because they were expected of him (as the incident became so notorious) rather than seeing the affair as a serious infraction on the marshal's part.

Whether Soult really intended to claim the Crown of Portugal continues to provoke debate among historians. Most contemporaries believed that he coveted a crown but disagreed over his motivations for doing so. Baron Marbot heard first-hand testimony from Pierre Soult, who claimed his brother was instructed by Napoleon to bring Portugal into the fold by any means necessary. Yet, he emphasised that Soult would only have accepted the Crown with Napoleon's approval. Even Marshal Jourdan, who was no friend to Soult, acknowledged that the marshal was acting out of political and strategic necessity rather than pure self-interest.[26]

Madame d'Abrantes definitely believed that Soult had designs on the throne. She had reason for bias since, as Junot's wife, her husband had become the de facto King of Portugal in 1807–8. Nevertheless, she possessed inside knowledge of military affairs and cited a quotation from a biography of Soult, published in Brussels under the pseudonym of Julien. This alleged that Napoleon had not only been aware of the marshal's ambitions but also encouraged him in a similar fashion to the way in which he had supported her husband's rule in Lisbon. Allegedly, Napoleon wrote the following lines to Soult, 'Monsieur le Maréchal, the Duke of Abrantes by my order, has declared that the house of Braganza had ceased to reign. Repeat the proclamation; and if for the preservation of Portugal it is necessary to give her a new dynasty, I shall see your's with pleasure.'[27]

While there is little evidence to support claims that this was Napoleon's intent, Madame d'Abrantes' opinion that the British actively tried to encourage Soult to proclaim himself king is more convincing, especially when read in combination with Wellesley's letters:

A member of the English parliament justly observed, that it was the policy of the English government to support, or even to incite the inclinations of Soult; to place in his hand and on his head the attributes he refers to in his circular to the generals of division, informing them that, the Emperor having enjoined him to retain Portugal at all hazards, he had at length determined on accepting the attributes of royalty.[28]

Thiébault went even further in his memoirs, to the extent of suggesting that Soult deliberately took advantage of Napoleon's preoccupation on the Danube to cover this outrageous attempt to seize power. This theory does not allow for the fact that II Corps were isolated in Portugal and received no dispatches from Paris or Madrid for one-and-a-half months. Therefore, it is unlikely that Soult heard much about affairs in central Europe at that time. Even Napoleon failed to acknowledge that Soult was isolated for almost two months and the campaign must be judged with that in mind. Clearly, Thiébault's grievances against Soult lay at the root of such allegations and Butler, his English-language biographer, purposefully omitted some of his more vitriolic passages.[29] Yet, the fact that so many seized upon this incident to castigate or ridicule Soult is revealing in itself.

Marshal Marmont believed that Soult recognised an opportunity in Portugal and took advantage of it for personal gain. Commenting on his memoirs in a review, the *United Service Magazine* summarised his opinion:

> Marmont represents him as *doué de tres peu d'esprit, fort passionné, à une ambition sans bornes*. He considers that his reputation for *finesse* is founded upon his habit of saying the contrary of what he thought, and that this cunning disappeared when his passions spoke, for then his intelligence was obscured so as to make him fall into incredible aberrations. Such was the case when he fancied becoming King of Portugal.[30]

Marmont also claimed that his fellow marshal was unpopular in the army and regularly the subject of scorn, the frequent notices he issued offering explanations of his conduct often drawing ridicule. However, the magazine's reviewer commented that, as Soult was far more successful than Marmont, jealousy might have prompted these remarks.

Historians view the allegations against Soult more dispassionately. Napier believed that the idea of Soult proclaiming himself king was erroneous and his reasoning that Argenton used such allegations to justify his treachery is credible.[31] Oman was less generous, commenting, 'Clever and cautious though the Marshal was, it is impossible to avoid the conclusion that he had for once allowed his ambition … to whirl him off into an enterprise that was worthy of the most hair-brained of adventurers'.[32] Oman also thought that Soult could easily have stopped excessive propaganda claims being made by his staff and his failure to do so revealed intentions far beyond creating a pro-French party in Porto.

Hayman gives a more modern view, suggesting that the bulk of the criticism Soult received stemmed from malicious tales put about by his enemies. Yet, he concedes that the marshal probably did intend to bring

Portugal into the First Empire by creating a new monarchy, qualifying this by pointing out that any French candidate for the throne was subject to Napoleon's approval.[33]

Unsurprisingly, Soult was reluctant to talk about his intentions in Porto after 1809. However, there is no doubt that 'vacant' thrones were sought after by Napoleon's generals once the emperor had set a precedent with Murat. Yet another example of this arose when Napoleon reluctantly endorsed Marshal Bernadotte's election as Crown Prince of Sweden the following year (he became King of Sweden in 1818). The situation in the Peninsula was different (as King Joseph's desperate attempts to placate his Spanish subjects revealed) since any French monarch would have to be maintained by force of arms. Ultimately, if Soult had claimed the Crown he would have needed Napoleon's support to keep it. With only a single French army corps under his command, it seems inconceivable that Soult would have considered this force strong enough to maintain power alone. Yet, to the end of his life Soult declined to reveal what his intentions had really been, writing ambiguously that, 'An army chief who is not ready to act on his own initiative is not worthy of command. Of course the Emperor could always disclaim any action I took afterwards.'[34]

Chapter Seven

The Bridge at Amarante

S ir Arthur Wellesley's campaign in northern Portugal is remarkable for the confidence, speed and aggression he displayed in trying to drive Soult's II Corps from the country. His willingness to take calculated risks was less evident in subsequent campaigns he fought in the Peninsula and the strategies he used would bring him praise and criticism in equal measure.

Sir Arthur's plan for the campaign was straightforward. He intended to advance directly on Porto with his main army, driving back elements of Soult's II Corps that had crossed the Douro before taking the city. Knowing that Silveira held a strategically important bridge on the Tamega, which posed a threat to Soult's left flank, he meant to detach a force under Beresford to reinforce him. If Porto fell as swiftly as hoped, Beresford and Silveira could cross the Douro and cut the French off if they attempted to retreat east towards Spain. Soult would have to move northwards but, if he crossed the Spanish frontier, Wellesley would be satisfied with liberating northern Portugal, abandoning pursuit and concentrating on the French threat from the east. He hoped that Soult would stand and fight while he had the advantage of superior numbers, as there was a chance of inflicting a serious defeat upon II Corps.

Fortescue estimated that the Allied forces in Portugal numbered about 50,000 men but only a fraction of this number were available for the campaign. In addition to those garrisoning fortresses, almost 16,000 Portuguese troops were inexperienced and undergoing basic training and therefore unavailable. Furthermore, while Sir Arthur judged a strike by I Corps over the frontier unlikely, he felt obliged to leave 12,000 men under Major General Mackenzie with instructions to hold the line of the Tejo if Victor attacked south of that river or the line of the River Zezere if I Corps approached Lisbon from a point further north.

The Allies possessed a sizeable artillery arm but most guns were committed to the defence of strongholds or were impractical for field operations. Horse teams for dragging cannon were in short supply and this meant that only thirty guns were immediately available. Wellesley had encountered the same difficulties as Cradock in procuring horses and mules and, until animals were shipped in from abroad, was compelled to rely upon ox-drawn carts to convey his baggage train. This form of transport, along with the poor roads and weather, would undoubtedly slow down Allied movements.

Wellesley was also handicapped by a lack of funds, the army's war chest containing little more than £10,000. London was slow in sending financial assistance and many Portuguese creditors were impatient to cash in their promissory notes, which did not improve Anglo-Portuguese relations. However, Wellesley's clear determination to march north after months of inactivity restored Portuguese confidence and bought London time to meet these debts.

Ultimately, Wellesley was able to concentrate an army of just over 18,000 men at Coimbra between 30 April and 4 May. A total of 16,000 British and 2,400 Portuguese troops were available for the campaign and Wellesley organised these into 1 cavalry division and 3 infantry divisions under generals Cotton, Sherbrooke, Paget and Hill.[1]

Morale was high but many believed that advancing on Soult instead of waiting for him to attack would allow Victor's I Corps to seize Lisbon in the absence of the main army. Indeed, it was possible that Sir Arthur's forces could be caught between two French armies. Aitchison, a junior officer in the 3rd Guards, loyally pointed out that Cradock had been preparing to march north and that Wellesley simply continued this strategy. He thought there was a strong possibility that Lisbon would fall:

Upon a reference to the map you will perceive that it is a very bold measure our marching against Soult, and that *its* success will in a great degree depend on the rapidity of our movement – not that I have the least doubt of victory if he accepts battle, but, as it is evidently in his interest, I suspect he will retire on our approach, in order to draw us to such a distance from Lisbon before he fights as to make it impossible for us, even if we be successful, to arrest the progress of Sebastiani and Victor, who are to advance along the banks of the Tagus [Tejo].[2]

During April and early May the strategic situation started to change. After Soult's halt at Porto, II Corps was dispersed over a wide area, Napier describing their position as being in the rough shape of a triangle with Porto at the apex. The other points extended to the Tamega (where Loison confronted Silveira) while Franceschi's cavalry had advanced as far as the River Vouga and Mermet's division had crossed the Douro in his support. Heudelet had also taken a sizable force north and Soult's communications relied upon the bridge of boats at Porto. Marching from the extremities of this triangle to Porto would probably take between three and five days, presenting the Allies with an opportunity of attacking Soult before he could concentrate his army.[3]

Heudelet attempted to relieve Tuy and Vigo, clear the Lima and Minho river valleys of insurgents and re-open the coastal road. General Botilho's force comprised almost entirely militia and ordenanza but tried to block French progress nonetheless, defending bridges across the Lima. He was swiftly defeated and withdrew back into the mountains leaving his only three guns to be captured in the action. Heudelet then seized the fortress of Valenza, which was easier to approach from the south, and the 200-strong garrison surrendered without a fight. He then relieved Tuy, where General Lamatiniére had been cut off for seven weeks, but discovered that Vigo had fallen. On 12 April, a link was made with General Maucune who had led a brigade south on Ney's orders to check on the condition of the garrisons at Tuy and Vigo. He informed Heudelet that there was no prospect of Ney sending reinforcements as La Romana's army was active once again and Galicia lay in the grip of a serious insurrection.

Guerrillas had already closed in behind Heudelet's division and Soult was obliged to send 3,000 men under Lahoussaye along the coastal road to determine how matters stood in the north. Partisans were increasingly becoming an annoyance for the French. Although the losses sustained through their raids and ambushes were usually small, they tied down large numbers of men when efforts were made to guard communication routes or attack them and (worst of all) they severed their communications. One

French officer made an astute analogy regarding their situation, 'The march of the 2nd Corps may be compared to the progress of a ship on the high seas: she cleaves the waves, but they close behind her, and in a few moments all trace of her passage has disappeared!'[4]

When informed of the situation, Soult realised that he had achieved all he could in the area, particularly as he anticipated an Allied attack in the near future and could not spare a division to pacify the north. Therefore, he ordered Valenza abandoned, as its fortifications were in poor repair, and approved Heudelet's decision to evacuate the garrison from Tuy. Garrisons were retained at Braga, Viana and Barcelos. Although guerrilla attacks on foraging parties and raids on the main road were still endemic, Heudelet was ordered to march his division back to Porto.[5]

One event that greatly assisted Wellesley's plans was the decision of Lapisse to move south. With a division only 9,000 strong, he had too few men to defend Salamanca and tackle the border fortresses, let alone march on Abrantes as Napoleon wished. That city was 200 miles from his position and he realised that guerrillas would harry him if he moved there. Furthermore, Wilson's actions between February and March 1809 had been so effective that he had no idea of Soult's whereabouts and communications with Victor's I Corps were only intermittent. Initially, Marshal Jourdan (writing on behalf of King Joseph) urged Lapisse to move towards Abrantes or at least to menace the Allied fortresses on the frontier. However, he reluctantly gave in to Victor's request that Lapisse march south and unite with his army as these objectives were beyond his practical reach.[6]

Lapisse then marched on Ciudad Rodrigo and called upon the fortress to surrender. Unsurprisingly, since the French lacked a siege train, the city governor made a defiant response but it had never been Lapisse's intention to besiege the city anyway. It was a ruse to circumnavigate Wilson's forces and, once they were distracted, he marched on Puerto de Parales. Travelling through the mountains to Alcantara, he was harried by partisans and elements of the Lusitanian Legion, but reached the town on 12 April. Here militia who defended the old Roman bridge leading to the town blocked the French path, but they were soon overcome. Alcantara was bombarded and cruelly sacked with many non-combatants killed and women raped.[7] The French were enraged after weeks of attacks by Spanish guerrillas and ferociously pillaged the town as a consequence. By 19 April, Lapisse had joined with Victor's I Corps at Mérida.

Lapisse marching south effectively isolated Soult's II Corps strategically. He had contravened Napoleon's instructions, which were admittedly impractical, and there was now no chance of a concerted effort against Lisbon by three separate French forces.[8] Wellesley received news of Lapisse's manoeuvre in early May along with letters intercepted from Soult, informing him that II Corps lay inactive as the marshal wished to unite with the other armies before taking offensive action. He knew that he would never have a better time to attack.

Meanwhile, Loison's operation to secure the French left flank encountered unexpected resistance from the Portuguese. Fresh from retaking Braga, General Silveira led his army south hoping to oust the French from Porto in a burst of confidence after his recent success. Although he commanded 9,000–10,000 men, only 2,000 of these were regular soldiers and the rest comprised militia. Loison initially withdrew over the Souza River on 12 April. Soult raised Loison's command to 6,000 and, when he advanced on 18 April, Silveira boldly marched out of the town of Amarante to confront him, suffering a predictable defeat as his force was hopelessly outmatched. Withdrawing into the town, the Portuguese swiftly retired over the bridge and Silveira contemplated a full retreat into the mountains to save his army.

However, Colonel Patrick (a British officer under Portuguese command) occupied a convent and houses near the bridge to cover the withdrawal. Commanding a battalion of the 12th Portuguese Line Regiment, Patrick put up stubborn resistance and broke the impetus of the French pursuit. This persuaded Silveira to deny the old Roman bridge to the enemy and he ordered an entrenchment dug across its far end, bolstered by a barricade comprising masonry and rows of wooden palisades (eventually three lines were built). As a further precaution, Portuguese sappers laid a mine under the left-hand arch of the structure to destroy it if necessary. The French attacked the following morning, and Patrick was mortally wounded as his battalion was driven from the buildings on the northern bank, although the troops manning the barriers repulsed the assault and drove it off with losses.

The bridge at Amarante had become strategically important since the other bridges at Mondin, Cavez and Canavezas spanning the river had been destroyed. The Tamega flowed through a rocky, steep-sided ravine and was in spate as a result of the snows melting in the mountains. During this season, it was too deep to ford and the French had to cross it to dislodge the Portuguese. Silveira now reinforced his position by digging entrenchments on the southern riverbank. A hill commanded the bridge and he camped his main force there and positioned an artillery battery near its summit to enfilade the bridge.

Soult considered that defeating Silveira was now paramount and raised Loison's force to 9,000 men, but numbers alone could not overcome the tactical difficulty of crossing the Tamega. Rather than use a trail of gunpowder to ignite the mine, which was vulnerable to accidental ignition or rainfall washing it away, the 'Portuguese mine was constructed with the muzzle of a loaded musket in the chamber [a wooden case enclosing the weapon], a string being tied to the trigger and passed over the trenches to secure the greatest precision for the explosion'.[9]

Using their spyglasses, French engineers had observed how the mine worked and despaired of capturing the structure intact as the Portuguese would almost certainly have time to destroy the bridge if they stormed it. Yet, the span was the only way of getting horses and guns across the Tamega quickly while its waters ran so high, so they dug a flying sap (a zigzagging trench designed to allow men to approach fortifications under fire) towards the end of the bridge to get their sappers closer. Their efforts drew heavy fire from the Portuguese battery over the river along with musketry from the barricades and the French suffered numerous casualties. As a result of the difficulties experienced by the engineers, Loison ordered a pontoon bridge constructed upriver. However, this drew heavy fire from the far bank and, since the Tamega proved deeper than the engineers expected, they abandoned the project. Ultimately, the French lost over 180 men during these operations.

While exasperated by the delay, Loison and Delaborde were sceptical when an engineer (Captain Bouchard) proposed a solution, having:

> devised a method of forcing the passage, so singularly bold, that all the generals, and especially Gen. Foy, were opposed to it. The plan was, however, transmitted to Oporto; and Soult sent Gen. Hulot, his first

aide-de-camp, to report if the project was feasible. Hulot approved of Brochard's [sic] proposal, and the latter commenced his operations[10]

The essence of the captain's scheme was to place his own counter-mine before the Portuguese barricades on the bridge and the resulting explosion should clear the bridge of impediments and sever the cord to the musket (by snapping or burning it). In the absence of a better plan, Bouchard's proposal was approved by Soult who desperately needed to capture the bridge.

Preparations were made for a night attack and on 2 May several companies of grenadiers quietly deployed on the edge of the town near the bridge to form the spearhead of an assault. Bouchard ordered twenty *tirailleurs* (sharpshooters) to take up positions along the riverbank and they opened intermittent aimed musket fire on the defenders, hoping to distract them but not to threaten the Portuguese enough that they would suspect an attack was imminent. Fog drifted in, helping to conceal French actions, and after the barricades had been harassed for over an hour, Bouchard sent men forward, 'a sapper, dressed in dark grey crawled out, pushing with his head a barrel of gunpowder which was enveloped in cloth to deaden the sound. Thus advancing, on that side of the bridge which was shaded by the parapet, he placed his barrel against an entrenchment covering the mine and retired'.[11] A couple of other sappers brought gunpowder up by the same means without suffering any mishap, but a fourth was shot and wounded by soldiers defending the barricades. He managed to crawl back in spite of his wound and the Portuguese probably mistook him for an observer sent forward to scout their positions. Bouchard judged that three barrels of gunpowder was sufficient and sent another man forward to lay a sausage (French army slang for a powder trail) up to the barrels before he crawled back undetected.

Bouchard fired the powder trail at 3.00 am and a large explosion rent the night sweeping away or badly damaging the barricades and killing many of the Portuguese infantrymen on the bridge. With a deep-throated roar of '*Vive l'Empereur!*', the grenadiers then charged the structure, dragging the remnants of the palisades aside and bayoneting any guards who resisted. Some Portuguese soldiers fired on the grenadiers but, after a brief clash, the survivors fled demoralised by the thunderous explosion and the unexpected assault. Bouchard ran onto the bridge with a company of sappers and, seeing that the musket's cord had been severed, doused the Portuguese mine with buckets of water to make sure it did not detonate.

Silveira was sleeping in a house he had commandeered nearby and was nearly taken prisoner as the French charged over the bridge to attack his headquarters. Only partially clothed, he leapt from a rear window and joined the fugitives as French infantry stormed the Portuguese camp. Other than sentries, few men were under arms and the French only met token resistance as they carried the hill, storming the artillery battery and firing into the tents. A few half-awake men tried to fight but the speed of the assault made resistance futile and most took to their heels. The battery was quickly silenced, only having time to fire a few salvoes at the oncoming infantry before being overrun.

The French lost only seven or eight men but inflicted hundreds of casualties on the Portuguese. They captured all 10 guns in the battery along with 5 flags and over 300 prisoners.[12] Loison sent cavalry out into the night to pursue the fugitives, who fled in total disorder, and Silveira had great difficulty rallying them. Nevertheless, he had occupied the attention of 9,000 French troops and prevented their advance from 20 April–2 May by holding the last bridge over the Tamega.

At this time, Soult had little intelligence about Allied intentions and despaired of reaching Lisbon without support. He considered crossing the Tamega and marching the army along the north bank of the Douro to Braganza, where he hoped to re-establish links with Lapisse. With this in mind, he ordered Loison to move against Mezamfrio and Pezo de Regoa. Although he had allowed Mermet to take his division over the Douro, he anticipated an Allied advance and this movement was designed to cover Franceschi's retreat rather than signifying intent to march south.[13]

Wellesley had heard about the Portuguese defeat on the Tamega on 3 May and modified his plans accordingly. D'Urban later wrote that the news of Silveira's retreat did not deter him from acting offensively; it merely made him more cautious.[14] He still intended to reinforce Silveira, who had fallen back to Lamego, but realised that he might have to confine his efforts to preventing the enemy crossing that river and abandon his more ambitious plan of cutting them off. He sent Beresford with Tilson's British infantry brigade along with five battalions of Portuguese infantry, two squadrons of the 14th Light Dragoons and two field batteries. This force comprised about 6,000 men but Beresford was to proceed by way of Vizeu and rendezvous with more Portuguese forces on the way.

The quality of the Portuguese troops now under arms was steadily improving and Warre, who was Anglo–Portuguese, wrote, 'The Portuguese troops immediately under the instruction of British officers are coming on very well. I could have wished we had been allowed more time, but even now have great hopes of some corps.'[15]

Beresford was ordered to continue with the original plan of cutting off the French retreat routes to the east if possible, but this depended on the condition of Silveira's forces and he was to make a careful assessment of their combined strength when he reached Lamego. Nevertheless, Sir Arthur allowed him a considerable degree of latitude, permitting him to advance as far as Vila Real if he crossed the Douro. Yet, he warned him, 'I should not like to see a British brigade, supported by 6,000 or 8,000 Portuguese troops, in *any but a very good post*, exposed to be attacked by the French army.'[16] After reaching Vizeu, Beresford marched north towards Lamego on 6 May.

As the Allied army continued north, reconnaissance reports persuaded Wellesley that there was a chance of trapping elements of Soult's army that had crossed the Douro. In addition to the cavalry sent across, it was possible that he could cut off Mermet's entire infantry division if he moved swiftly. Accordingly, Cotton advanced north towards Porto, driving back the French cavalry outposts with Stewart and Murray's brigades following in his wake. Meanwhile, Hill's division would embark on boats at Aveiro early on 9 May, sailing up the coastal lagoon to land at Ovar. They were to conceal their presence until Cotton engaged the French and then move to cut them off if they withdrew, trapping them against the main force as it marched north.

Wellesley believed that Hill's unconventional amphibious manoeuvre would probably surprise the French as Lake Ovar reached 20 miles beyond their cavalry outposts and its edge was largely unguarded. The British had learned this from Portuguese fishermen and virtually all the fishing vessels were in Allied hands and made available for the crossing. With luck, the French would retreat before Hill's force with their flank totally exposed to him, but even if Hill failed to block their withdrawal, Sir Arthur hoped he would be able to pursue them closely as they fell back on the Douro. One of the British divisions might be able to seize the bridge of boats if they pressed the rearguard's withdrawal closely enough or prevent the French from destroying the structure.

British cavalry crossed the Vouga on 9 May just before midnight and drove in French picquets at dawn, leading to skirmishing before Albergaria Nova. French reactions were confused at first as, although Franceschi had informed Soult that the British appeared to be concentrating in the Mondego Valley, he had not realised that their main army was so close. Nevertheless, he swiftly recovered from his surprise and withdrew to a stronger position. As Cotton brought the bulk of his force up, he wanted to attack as Franceschi only had around 1,200 cavalry to oppose him. However, the French had halted next to a wood where they deployed infantry and had a horse artillery battery in support. Therefore, he felt obliged to wait for infantry support.[17]

The small flotilla ferrying Hill's 1st brigade landed near Ovar at sunrise on 10 May. Sending scouts forward, Hill learned that Franceschi had engaged with Cotton but was unlikely to march across his front as predicted. Learning that three battalions of Mermet's infantry were only 6 miles away at Feira, he sent his boats back to Aviero with orders to bring Cameron's brigade back with them. Meanwhile, Hill prepared to advance on Feira but remained in position until his 2nd Brigade joined him.

With poor knowledge of the ground beyond the Vouga, the infantry were delayed and confusion set in as gun carriages broke while going over rough ground, holding up the advance of Stewart's brigade. Therefore, Trant's Portuguese troops were the first to reinforce Cotton but, having difficulty negotiating a ravine, Trant found his brigade confronting the French centre instead of their right flank, as intended. With the French already withdrawing, Cotton immediately sent the 16th Light Dragoons forward and a brief cavalry skirmish ensued with neither side sustaining serious losses. Franceschi retired on Oliveira de Azemis and, by conducting a forced night march, was able to fall back on the heights of Grijo where the bulk of Mermet's division was encamped.

As Wellesley led the main army over the Vouga, the French took up positions on the heights to fight a brief delaying action. They deployed across the road to Porto on this range of steep hills. A wood protected their right flank and Mermet posted infantry there. While a village and broken ground lay before their centre, the French left flank was less secure.

Sir Arthur had the advantage of numbers with 7,000 infantry against 4,000 under Mermet and 300 more cavalrymen (the British rarely had more cavalry than the French in the Peninsula). If the French did not disengage before the main army came up, they were likely to be overwhelmed. Wellesley ordered Hill to move along the road and led his command in a frontal assault against the heights. As Stewart's brigade pressed forward, they encountered serious resistance and Wellesley ordered a battalion of the 16th Portuguese to engage the French right while elements of the King's German Legion manoeuvred in an attempt to turn the weak French left.

Mermet soon became aware that he was about to be outflanked and pulled back before his force was heavily engaged. The ground beyond the heights assisted him in this as the farmland was tightly enclosed with stone walls and his infantry were able to fall back slowly and fire upon the British cavalry pressing their retreat without serious risk. However, the colonel of the 31st Light Infantry handled their withdrawal poorly and, observing this, General Charles Stewart requested Wellesley's permission to mount a serious attack.

Due to the enclosures, Stewart advanced with two squadrons of the 20th Light Dragoons and 16th Light Dragoons, which moved forward in single file along a narrow walled lane. The French 31st were already slightly disordered and the speed of this unconventional advance took them by surprise and panic ensued. As the infantry fled en masse, the British dragoons deployed into line once they passed the enclosures and ran down many fugitives, taking about 100 prisoners. Fortescue later wrote that 'if the swordsmanship of the British dragoons had been better, the regiment would have been cut to pieces ...'.[18]

Yet, the combat at Grijo was inconclusive with the Allies losing about 100 men and the French about twice that number. Mermet was able to retreat in good order and Wellesley knew there was no chance of preventing the enemy from re-crossing the Douro. As the cavalry followed up after the fight at Grijo, one hussar officer recorded some macabre sights on the journey that:

> showed us the horrors produced by a war of invasion. Beyond Grijon
> [sic] nine bodies of unfortunate Portuguese peasants were seen hanging

on trees by the side of the road, blackened in the sun. The common people naturally considering the enemy as *hors de la loi*, sought every means, open or otherwise, for their destruction. This brought on them that retaliation produced by the military ideas of a regular army, who conceived they had only a right to be opposed by *soldiers*, and not by the unclothed and unorganized population. These they considered as insurgents and brigands, and shot and hung, with as little compassion as we should a burglar.[19]

Soult learned that Wellesley was likely to advance on 8 May during Argenton's interrogation. With his troops still widely dispersed, he knew he was in a precarious position. Insurgents had closed in around him and his link with Ney was tenuous to say the least. His officers seemed to be turning against him and there was still no word from Victor or Lapisse. Indeed, he had not received a dispatch from the emperor for more than two months. While he made efforts to concentrate his forces in Porto, he made immediate preparations for a retreat through Tras-os-Montes. Nevertheless, he was determined to hold the line of the Douro for a time and ordered Loison to maintain his position at all costs as it protected his line of retreat. Loison was to defend Mezamfrio if possible but, if forced back, he must not yield the vital bridge at Amarante to the enemy or he would place the entire army in jeopardy. Soult sent some cannon and stores towards the Tamega with a view to withdrawal.

At this time, Soult had 11,000–12,000 men in Porto and guessed that Wellesley's most likely plan of attack was to attempt a crossing at the mouth of the Douro supported by the Royal Navy. Hill's amphibious assault at Ovar had only failed by a narrow margin and the French believed these boats could easily be utilised in such an operation. Accordingly, Soult positioned his forces to oppose an attack from that quarter and ordered his cavalry to patrol the lower reaches of the Douro and look for signs of Allied preparations. To protect the army against strikes further upriver, he ordered ferries destroyed and all riverboats brought to the north bank, moored there and placed under guard. Soult believed that it would be days before Wellesley was in a position to attack and a lot could change during that time.

Mermet's infantry streamed back over the bridge overnight and, late on 11 May, the last of Franceschi's cavalry retired across the Douro. Soult then ordered the bridge of boats destroyed. The bulk of Wellesley's army was encamped within a few miles of the river when a thunderous explosion shattered the night, awakening the tired soldiers sometime between 1.00 and 2.00 am on the morning of 12 May (accounts of the exact time vary). As the flames from the burning bridge reddened the night's sky, Wellesley realised that his army's only easy means of crossing the Douro had gone.

Chapter Eight

The Passage of the Douro

The Douro River was broad and deep. It flowed swiftly between scarp slopes and cliffs for much of its length and presented a daunting barrier to an army, especially if an enemy tried to dispute a crossing. With the bridge destroyed and riverboats placed under guard on the northern shore, Soult thought his army's position was secure. At the very least, he believed the Allies would have to sail a large flotilla of small boats up the coast to ferry troops across, allowing him time to prepare a defence.

There had been no dispatches from Loison for four days, which was disturbing, but Soult still intended to hold the city and predicted that he had two days' grace before Wellesley would attack. During that time he intended to cover the march of his divisions towards Amarante and Vila Real. General Lorges would then move his troops down from the north into Porto while Loison cleared the roads of partisans, allowing II Corps to march into Tras-os-Montes. Once he moved east, Soult hoped to discover the whereabouts of I Corps, potentially allowing him to return with a larger force.

Accounts disagree but Soult either retained his headquarters in the palace or relocated to a villa on the western side of the city. Both structures permitted a fine view of the river valley from Porto to the ocean and Soult predicted that Wellesley would attack across this estuary. He believed that the Allies would bring fishing vessels up the coast to carry troops, whose crossing would be covered by the guns of Royal Navy ships. He ordered Franceschi to patrol the 5 miles of riverbank between Porto and the sea with great care and deployed the bulk of his forces to oppose a crossing in this area, garrisoning the Castelo de São on the north bank and setting up artillery batteries along the Douro's lower reaches. It was a good defensive position, which would be difficult to overcome even with naval support, and Soult believed he could inflict significant losses on the enemy before retiring.

Soult knew the British vanguard had already reached Villa Nova but thought there was ample time to prepare and ordered the bulk of his wheeled transport conveying wounded and reserve ammunition sent east. In the meantime, he instructed outposts along the estuary to keep watch for British sails on the horizon, thinking that the arrival of a Royal Navy squadron would undoubtedly precede an Allied attack. Soult planned the withdrawal carefully and stayed up into the early hours dictating dispatches and instructing his staff. Complaining of sickness, he went to bed safe in the knowledge that the British were unlikely to attack that day once they saw the strength of his position.[1]

When Wellesley arrived south of the city, he immediately climbed the Serra Hill to view the area, which rose 150ft (45m) above the river. From this vantage point, he observed clouds of dust from the northeast raised by a large body of men and horses moving along the Vallongo Road. Upon closer examination, he judged this force comprised at least two large infantry columns escorting a long wagon train. These were troops of Mermet's division accompanying wagons (laden with sick and wounded soldiers) and the reserve artillery moving towards Amarante. Wellesley took this as evidence that Soult was withdrawing and altered his plans accordingly.

Although confidence in Wellesley's leadership remained high, many Allied officers believed Soult could defy their army with impunity with the barrier of the Douro between them unless they attacked with overwhelming force. Crossing in the face of the enemy would probably result in heavy losses and the only other option was to move upriver to cross (outflanking the city) and bombard Porto to persuade the French to leave. Yet, Wellesley was loath to bombard an Allied city occupied by civilians. Most believed he would only attempt to cross the Douro if Beresford and Silveira were successful upriver, threatening Soult's position from the east. Ensign Aitchison expressed typical reservations about an opposed crossing:

Oporto defended by the French will not surrender so soon as when defended by the Portuguese – nay, Soult will make a desperate resistance, there is every reason to believe, and if we have not been fortunate to secure the passage of the Douro at Lamego we shall make but little impression for some time.[2]

Such doubts were well founded according to conventional military thought but Wellesley (aware that all defensive positions had weaknesses) ordered a thorough reconnaissance along the river nonetheless.

While the general and his staff scanned the northern bank intensely, only patrols and guard posts could be seen along the riverbank and no large formations of men were visible in Porto itself. The guard posts were widely distributed and only small patrols were observed on the far bank and even then just at irregular intervals. The only real signs of movement were the troops moving along the Vallongo Road and the city itself seemed remarkably quiet considering it was mid-morning.

There was one prominent feature directly across the river from Wellesley's position, the bishop's seminary (a training college for priests). This large two-storey white building lay at the edge of the city and was hemmed in by a high garden wall extending down to the river on both sides of the structure. The main entrance in this wall was an iron gate on the north side and the enclosure was big enough to contain two infantry battalions. The gate opened onto a lane that led toward the Vallongo Road.[3]

While Sir Arthur pondered his options, scouts brought him intelligence that the ferry at Barca d'Avintas (3 miles upriver) could now be used. Although the French had scuttled the ferryboat, the villagers were so concerned at the effect this boat's loss would have on their livelihoods that they dragged it from the river and swiftly repaired it. Colonel John Waters, one of Wellelsey's 'exploring officers' chosen for his skill in reconnaissance, brought even more inspiring news. Riding along the south bank opposite the city, he met a Portuguese civilian who made his living as a barber in Porto (no accounts name this individual). In the hope of preventing the French from confiscating or destroying his skiff, he had rowed it over the river and concealed it in a thicket on the south bank. He was prepared to take the colonel across and, to Waters' delight, told him that he also knew of four large wine barges lying unguarded on the north bank.

Waters also encountered the Prior of Amarante in that vicinity. He brought local men to offer their assistance in procuring the barges and the party crossed the Douro in the barber's skiff. Waters located the barges and, although they were heavy and unwieldy in untrained hands, judged them capable of holding about thirty men each. To his surprise, he also learned that the seminary was unguarded. Consequently, Waters instructed his party to sail or row the wine barges back across the Douro as quickly as possible. Although Waters took care to ensure the barges crossed individually in an effort to conceal the move, it is remarkable that the manoeuvre escaped the enemy's notice.[4]

By this time, several Portuguese notables (including priests from the convent) had joined Wellesley and his staff. They were eager to see the French ousted from Porto and Sir Arthur questioned them closely about the city. He was particularly interested in what they could tell him about the great river that lay before him. The Douro was fast flowing at this time of year and he wished to know how quickly heavily laden boats could cross it this close to the ocean. Even more importantly, he wished to know how visible this part of the river was to French forces positioned downriver.

Wellesley had an opening and decided to seize it. If he could ferry enough men over the river and take possession of the seminary, they might be able to defend this foothold until reinforced. Meanwhile, he would send a force upriver to cross at Barca d'Avintas and cut the enemy off from the east. The success of this operation depended on how quickly the infantry could get across in significant numbers, whether they could seize the seminary before the French became aware of what was going on and if they could withstand counter-attacks until reinforced. It was a bold and risky enterprise.

He ordered three artillery batteries (about eighteen cannon) brought up and positioned on the hill, and these were to be loaded but kept out of sight. On Wellesley's command, they would be wheeled out onto the terrace before the convent and brought into action. This artillery was well placed to cover the barges as they crossed but they could also command the approaches to the seminary across the river, with the exception of its northern side.

Wellesley also ordered General John Murray to take a brigade comprising two squadrons of the 14th Light Dragoons, a squadron of the 20th Light Dragoons, the 1st and 2nd battalions of the Kings German Legion (Hanoverian troops) and two guns to move upriver and cross using the ferry at Barca d'Avintas. He hoped that Murray would be able to sever the French line of retreat to the east but, if this proved impractical, he would be able to attack Porto from the northeast.

Assessing the river with a practised eye, Wellesley estimated that the chances of success were high but knew there were many factors that might disrupt the operation. Much depended on maintaining the element of surprise, which would be difficult in broad daylight, as the French were unlikely to remain oblivious for much longer. If he was successful, he might catch Soult in the act of departure and secure an unexpectedly swift victory. Yet, failure could result in severe losses and it was clear that some of the staff were nervous about the risks he was running. With an outward appearance of calm, Sir Arthur turned to an aide at around 10.00 am and remarked nonchalantly, 'Well, let the men cross.'[5]

The operation began shortly after 10.00 am when a battalion of the 3rd Foot (Buffs) started to cross. The barges could only hold a company each and it is likely that they rowed over one at a time, hoping to remain unobserved for as long as possible. The first company to land (one subaltern and twenty-nine men) immediately ran up the steep bank towards the seminary. Gaining the courtyard, they closed the gate and took up defensive positions along the north wall. The second company to land entered the seminary, confirmed it was unoccupied, and adopted firing positions at the windows facing the city.

Frantic work began to construct banquettes out of barrels and any wood that lay to hand in the area to allow men to fire over the high garden wall. They also knocked loopholes in the walls of the seminary to enable them to fire muskets out of the building against the inevitable counter-attack. Wellesley and his staff watched quietly as more boats slowly rowed over the river. The tension must have been unbearable, 'For the best part of an hour the Commander-in-chief must have been fully aware that his daring move might end only in the annihilation of two or three companies of a good old regiment, and a check that would appear as the righteous retribution for recklessness.'[6] It was not until the third boat crossed, carrying General Paget, that the alarm was raised. Sentries fired warning shots and drums beat to arms in Porto as the French finally realised what was going on.

Officers under Mermet's command reported to him that a crossing seemed to be in progress but he scoffed at the idea that the Allies would attempt such a manoeuvre in broad daylight and continued his march towards Amarante. General Foy was riding along heights near the river when he spotted a vessel filled with redcoats crossing at around 10.30 am. He immediately sent an aide-de-camp to alert Marshal Soult and ordered the nearest battalion (of the 17th Légère) to stand to arms.[7]

Soult was eating breakfast with his staff when the aide brought news that the British were on the river. Thunderstruck, he immediately issued orders to his staff and sent instructions that Foy must hold the northeast sector of Porto at all costs, allowing him time to bring the main army back into the city. He guessed that the Allies could only have secured a tenuous foothold and hoped to drive them back into the Douro.

Although it was imperative to mount a swift counter-attack, Foy knew that a rushed assault against a well-defended position would be foolhardy and likely to be repulsed with heavy casualties. His preparations took almost an hour and he began by placing an artillery battery on heights near the Chapel of Bom Fin, about 700yd north of the seminary. Foy also ordered guns brought up near the river to fire upon the barges ferrying Allied troops over the river. Luckily for the French, the 17th Légère was a light infantry regiment (well suited to street fighting) and could provide accurate sustained fire to cover a major assault on the seminary. The 17th provided the bulk of the troops for the first French attack.

Foy sent in the first assault at about 11.30 am, an hour-and-a-half after the Allies had begun to cross the Douro. By this time, the British garrison had risen to just under battalion strength. The French mounted infantry attacks on the north and west sides of the building and skirmishers were rushed forward to take up position in the streets and buildings near to the seminary, opening a close-range fire against the garrison. Infantry advanced in columns against both sides of the building and guns were rapidly brought up near the river.

As the attack began, British cannon were swiftly wheeled forward onto the convent terrace and opened fire on French troops assaulting the western side of the seminary. Just as French horse teams stopped and began unhitching their guns, 'The first shot fired, a round of shrapnel from the 5½-inch howitzer of Lane's battery, burst just over the leading French gun on the further bank, as it was in the act of unlimbering, dismounted the piece, and by an extraordinary chance, killed or wounded every man and horse attached to it.'[8] Although French artillerymen stubbornly tried to position their guns to respond to this cannonade, their bravery was in vain, as the British levelled a devastating fire against them. The guns on the Serra Hill dominated the position, raking the French batteries with roundshot and shrapnel shells, dismounting some cannon and forcing the gunners back from their cannon to take refuge in nearby houses. The battery near the chapel was too far away so there was little chance of the French interfering with the crossing if the British could sustain this rate of fire. Wellesley ordered his officers to redouble their efforts and get as many men as possible over the river while they possessed this advantage.

With the French batteries silenced, the artillery trained their guns on the infantry assaulting the western wall. The British artillery could fire straight into the flank of these soldiers marching in formation, allowing them to strike down more men. The grazing (ricochet) effect of roundshot as it struck the ground meant that it not only hit the intended area but regularly bounced further into the formation striking down numerous targets with a single shot. Shrapnel shells also burst above the French, showering them with musket balls and casing. Combined with the musketry fired from the seminary walls and windows, the western attack was beaten off with heavy losses.

Meanwhile, the French delivered a ferocious assault on the north side of the building. The seminary and other structures obscured the view of the British guns on the Serra Hill so they could do little against this assault and the French artillery near the chapel was also handicapped by buildings blocking the line of sight. Although the French artillery directed fire against the building and its circuit wall to prepare the way for the assault, the guns inflicted little damage before they were obliged to cease firing for fear of hitting their own men as the infantry approached the walls.

As the main attack advanced against the seminary, the garden wall seemed to disappear in a wall of smoke as muskets fired through loopholes, over the wall or from the windows above. Scores of French infantrymen were shot down as they pressed forward. Ensign Bunbury of the 3rd Foot was:

posted at the iron gateway of the courtyard with orders to let in any of our men [meaning reinforcements coming up from the river], but to exclude their pursuers. These, however entered the garden, and endeavoured ... to get between us and the river so as to prevent the passage of more troops coming to our assistance.[9]

Although some French entered the courtyard they were rapidly hunted down by the redcoats and shot or bayoneted. Martial spirit among the Buffs ran so high that Bunbury even recalled mounting sallies out into the streets beyond the wall each time the French fell back. He gave a good description of the manner in which the French spurred themselves on to attack the position, 'The advancing French made a great noise when marching, every small party having a drummer thumping away with all his might, and against these poor devils of drummers our fire was principally directed. We shot several, and our opponents did not seem to get on well without them.'[10]

General Paget was directing the defence from the roof of the building when a French sharpshooter supporting the assault shot him through the arm. It was a serious wound and Paget was obliged to let General Hill assume command. The fighting was hardest for the defenders in the courtyard but the Buffs were well protected firing through loopholes, which exposed little more than a defender's face, or over the wall with only their heads and shoulders exposed to enemy fire. In many instances, three or more soldiers manned a single loophole working as a team. One soldier would fire through it while his comrades loaded and passed muskets to him in turn. This meant that a rapid, almost continuous, fire was maintained and the small apertures they fired through meant that French were unlikely to hit them unless they got very close.

While valiant attempts were made to get up to the wall and gate, the attack was beaten off after a sustained firefight. By this time, the Buffs were being reinforced by elements of the 48th and 66th regiments as Wellesley tried to get men across the Douro as swiftly as possible.

General Delaborde now arrived and committed the 70th Ligne to a second assault, which still included elements of the 17th. This attack was far larger and General Hill later termed it 'the *serious* attack' in his memoirs.[11] Although the French suffered severely from musketry fired from the seminary, they made it to the garden wall and attempted to break down the iron gate. Yet, this withstood their efforts and those trying to scale the wall were swiftly shot or bayoneted by the defenders. All attempts at another assault on the western side of the seminary came under such heavy cannon fire from over the river that the French confined their efforts to the north side.

As the fighting intensified, Wellesley looked in vain through his spyglass for signs of Murray's force moving to cut the enemy's line of retreat to the northeast. In fairness, Murray had not had enough time to march upriver and get significant numbers of troops over the river. Nevertheless, the situation was becoming critical and Napier wrote, 'Sir Arthur was only prevented [from] crossing in person by the interference of those about him and the confidence he had in Hill'.[12]

Soult was desperate to crush the foothold the enemy had gained on the north bank and ordered General Reynaud to march his brigade from its position guarding Porto's docks to join Delaborde. Seeing that the French were leaving the area unguarded, some bold citizens rushed down to the quays and began sailing or rowing all the boats they could find across the Douro. Others waved handkerchiefs and beckoned to the redcoats on the far bank that they could see from the rooftops. They hoped to attract their attention and encourage them to cross. Observing this, Wellesley sent an aide ordering General Stewart to move his brigade close to the shore and attempt to cross when enough boats had been assembled. While this operation was underway, Sherbrooke's Guards brigade came up behind Stewart's hoping to cross soon afterwards.

Jubilant Portuguese citizens greeted the 29th (Worcester Regiment), the first battalion to land near the docks. People cheered as they marched through the streets and the soldiers encountered some difficulty at first with the crowds and baggage discarded by the French during their hasty departure along this route. Hearing the fighting around the seminary, they headed towards the clouds of dust and smoke that indicated where the struggle was taking place. Surgeon Guthrie of the 29th Foot persuaded a Portuguese boatman to ferry his horse over the river and was probably the only mounted British officer on the north bank as he rode to accompany his regiment. Finding his way blocked by abandoned French wagons and stores, he fell behind and encountered Sir J.M. Doyle leading the 17th Portuguese Regiment through the streets. Offering to show him the way the British had marched, they came up behind the 29th which promptly turned about and presented muskets thinking this blue-jacketed Portuguese regiment was French as none of their officers were mounted:

Words were useless, but with a quickness of perception and decision which saved many lives, he tore open the blue great coat which covered his red one, and held it back, which at once caused the whole regiment, almost in the very act of firing upon them, to call out, 'The Doctor and the Portuguese!'[13]

Incidents of 'friendly fire' regularly occurred during the Napoleonic period because of confusion caused by different uniforms that sometimes failed to conform to stereotypical national colours. In the chaotic scenes in and around Porto with the city crowded with civilians and impeded by the baggage of a fleeing army, such errors were even more likely to occur. Both regiments were duly grateful to Guthrie for his actions, the 29th often acknowledging that he 'was by this time as much a soldier as a doctor ...'.[14]

The 29th soon encountered elements of Reynaud's brigade, which was now marching towards the Vallongo Road. The battalion swiftly deployed and began to fire on them but the French did not contest the issue for long and soon retreated, allowing the 29th to seize an artillery battery and some well-laden wagons they had abandoned. Once again, Guthrie played an important role:

seeing a gun in a lane to the left which the train attached could not drag through it, and the drivers and artillerymen dismounting to run away on foot, rode down, being the only mounted officer present, and took possession: but what to do with it was the question. He therefore cut the traces of the headmost mule, (a very fine one) brought her off as a trophy, and then sent a sergeant and a file of men to take charge of the gun, until he could report its capture to Sir J. Sherbrooke, who was mightily amused at the doctor's capturing a gun by himself.[15]

Soult was preparing to mount a third assault on the seminary but saw large numbers of troops marching up from the new landings downriver, which would threaten the flank and rear of his deployment. The Allies already had a foothold on the northern bank and he would not overwhelm it before these new forces came up to interfere with his operation. He had been completely outmanoeuvred and, judging any further attempt to hold the city hopeless, ordered a general retreat.

Portuguese official Don Miguel Persira Forjaz later wrote to Wellesley stating that the French left 'artillery, ammunition, 8 carts and many prisoners [behind] while retreating in utter confusion ... The Duke of Dalmatia and Ricard, Delaborde ... and General Quesnel fled half an hour after that important action'.[16] The fighting during the Second Battle of Porto lasted roughly three hours within the city itself. By the time of the second French assault on the seminary, the garrison had risen to over 1,000 men. This force suffered only 77 casualties during French attempts to dislodge them, while Foy recorded that the 17th Légère sustained 177 casualties and estimated that the 70th suffered far more than that during the second assault.[17]

While the garrison of the seminary was not yet strong enough for offensive action, elements of Stewart's and the Guards brigades advanced and pressed the French withdrawal. The rearguard Soult left to delay them was swiftly overcome and forced to retreat allowing the 29th to take numerous prisoners, 'They made no fight, every man seemed running for his life, throwing away their knapsacks and arms, so we had only the trouble of making many prisoners every instant, all begging for quarter and surrendering with great good humour.'[18]

It was no wonder that some French were keen to surrender under the protection of regular soldiers. While the locals enthusiastically cheered the British troops, shouting '*Viva!*' from the rooftops as they filed through the streets, they also had scores to settle with the French and the liberation of Porto turned ugly as French wounded abandoned in the retreat were set upon and had their throats cut. General Sherbrooke felt obliged to detach some companies from his force to guard the hospitals to protect the wounded and sick French from being massacred.

By this time, Murray's brigade had crossed the Douro at Barca d'Avintas. Wellesley had observed his progress and was hoping that he would be able to prevent the French retreating further east long enough for him to fall upon their rear. There was a chance here to inflict a decisive defeat upon Soult's army.

Murray received criticism from some quarters for his tardiness but it took a little time to transfer his entire force (including cavalry) to the north bank using only a single vessel. Once across, he marched north and was astonished to see the entire French army marching across his front in a state of some disorder. Although he had not been swift enough to block their retreat, he was ideally placed to harass their withdrawal. A suitably aggressive move on his part might inflict significant casualties and have a catastrophic effect on French morale after their rude ejection from Porto.

The ground in front was rocky, partially wooded and sloped down towards the Vallongo Road, along which the French were retreating about 2 miles from Murray's position. Fortescue believed that he should have advanced his 500–600 riflemen into this area where they could have sniped at the withdrawing French and, with cavalry poised to defend their flanks, the enemy would have had little chance of dislodging them. Yet, Murray seems to have hesitated and confined his efforts to bringing up his entire force before making any offensive moves. Admittedly, Soult's force vastly outnumbered his own.[19]

As the French withdrew, General Charles Stewart rode up carrying a dispatch from Wellesley. Appalled at Murray's inaction, he took command of the 14th Light Dragoons and advanced against the retreating French. As a result of the number of infantry battalions deployed before him, the nature of the slope and enclosures, the 14th had to advance in columns of threes. The dust raised by their progress meant that they were soon spotted and Soult ordered the rearguard to halt and face them.

As Stewart approached the French rearguard, he was still obliged to advance in a narrow formation due to the enclosures. Nevertheless, he mounted a charge and Captain Hawker of the 14th recalled what happened next:

A strong body was drawn up in close column, with bayonets ready to receive us to their front. On each side of the road was a stone wall, bordered outwardly with trees. On our left ... numbers of the French were posted with their pieces resting on the wall, which flanked the road, ready to give us a running fire as we passed. This could not be effectual as our men (in threes) were close to the muzzles of their muskets, and barely out of reach of a *coup de sabre*. In a few seconds the ground was covered with our men and horses. Notwithstanding this we penetrated the battalion ... the men of which, relying on their bayonets, did not give way till we were close upon them, when they fled in confusion. For some time the contest was kept up hand to hand.[20]

As the infantry broke formation many were cut down as they fled. It was rare for cavalry to inflict serious losses if infantry remained steady, presenting a row of bayonets that intimidated the horses, but horsemen gained a marked advantage in a melee if they panicked. It took some time for French officers to restore order and halt the rout. French commissary Pierre le Noble recorded that:

General Foy had been wounded, and General Delaborde thrown from his horse and badly bruised. Three hundred of our men had been killed or taken prisoner. The battery of light artillery, which covered the retreat, had had all the horses of its first piece shot down in a narrow street in the suburbs, and had had to be abandoned for want of any way to get the men past the obstruction. In the few moments in which an effort was made to clear the way eight men were shot dead.[21]

Delaborde was briefly taken prisoner but managed to escape in the chaos and Foy, nursing a deep sabre wound, acknowledged that the charge had been incredibly effective calling it '*Une charge incroyable*'.[22] Yet, the dragoons suffered considerable losses, were unable to press home their advantage and retired with their captives. Fortescue believed that Stewart's action, while brave, was ultimately reckless with such a small force and it violated military custom for a staff officer to seize command from regimental officers without good reason. While Napier condemned Murray for not supporting Stewart, Fortescue believed that the 14th had advanced too far for this and that the general's main fault lay in not attacking earlier.[23]

The impact of the French occupation of Porto had not been as bad as that suffered by some Portuguese cities. Soult went to some pains to treat the Portuguese decently and seems to have curbed the worst excesses after the city first fell to his army. However, Lieutenant Wood of the 82nd Foot had been billeted in the city before the First Battle of Porto and was shocked by what he saw when he returned to the house he had stayed in:

the destruction occasioned in this beautiful residence was truly pitiable ... fine balustrades broken; the chandeliers and mirrors were shattered to pieces; all portable furniture had been taken away and the remainder either wantonly burned or otherwise destroyed; the choice pictures were defaced, and the walls more resembled a French barrack than the abode of a Portuguese *fidalgo* from the obscene paintings that were daubed upon them.[24]

Nevertheless, Soult's occupation was not generally oppressive and the city would have suffered far more damage had he chosen to defend it for longer as street fighting almost inevitably led to civilian casualties and widespread destruction.

The French left behind considerable plunder during their retreat. Captain Bowles later wrote about what his brigade discovered discarded in the streets and houses by the enemy:

They left us a good number of horses, baggage, knapsacks, &c., the examination of the latter provided very amusing and profitable occupation for our men, as they were literally crammed with every species of plunder, the produce of the jewellers' and other shops at Oporto. Sacramental cups and plates beat flat to fit the shape of the back, rings of every description. Trinkets were certainly cheaper in our camp the next morning than I ever knew them before, and both horses and mules were to be had on very reasonable terms. I got two very good ones for a dollar each.[25]

While French soldiers had undoubtedly indulged in acts of pillage, very little of this recaptured property was returned to its rightful owners. Despite this, the Portuguese were ecstatic at the defeat of II Corps and its expulsion from their city. Celebrations continued into the night as the French were unlikely to return in the near future and the British were welcomed as liberators.

Although Wellesley was denied a total victory, forcing the passage of the Douro was undoubtedly a triumph. Fortescue estimated French losses at 300 casualties in Porto itself and 300 prisoners taken in direct action there. A further 1,000 prisoners were taken and were lying in military hospitals awaiting evacuation. Oman believed that their number was closer to 1,500 and added that 6 field pieces were captured during the fighting, with more cannon mounted in the forts undoubtedly falling into Allied hands. The

British recorded losing 23 killed and 95 men and 3 officers wounded along with 2 missing during the Second Battle of Porto.[26] These were remarkably small losses for an operation involving an opposed river crossing.

In a typically dispassionate and straightforward dispatch, Wellesley acknowledged that the army had performed well:

> The Commander of the Forces congratulates the troops upon the success which has attended their operations for the last four days, upon which they have traversed above 80 miles of most difficult country, in which they have carried some formidable positions, have beaten the enemy repeatedly, and have ended by forcing the passage of the Douro, and defending the position they had so boldly taken up, with numbers far inferior to those with which they were attacked.[27]

Yet, the campaign was far from over and Wellesley knew that he must deny Soult a chance to regroup in the hills and prevent him from combining his force with another French army if possible.

Although Porto was liberated and its people ecstatic at the end of the French occupation, Forjaz wrote about the grim aftermath as they counted those soldiers and civilians slain in the days after the battle:

> Right now people are engaged in burying the dead. In hospitals where there were great quantities of sick … [the people] watched me enter [the city] yesterday in front of the troops in order to examine them. They began to cry with crossed hands over the slaughter and this and other things aroused my compassion. – This letter was written in the countryside between horrifying piles of French corpses.[28]

Every good soldier knows that in the period following a victory, the enemy's retreat must be pressed hard, denying them a chance to recover. This was often the time when the most damage could be inflicted upon the enemy that was likely to be confused and vulnerable. Murray's brigade followed the French withdrawal in the wake of the 14th Light Dragoons' action but only desultory skirmishing took place and Sir Arthur ordered a halt that evening after riding to the forward positions in person. Realising that the enemy had eluded him, he knew that his men were tired following the gruelling 80-mile march from Coimbra and a hard fight afterwards.[29] He decided to concentrate his forces by ferrying the rest of his troops, artillery and baggage across the river, which continued throughout the night, but gave orders that the pursuit would be resumed the following day.

Chapter Nine

Harried Through the Mountains

A lthough Soult had suffered a defeat, he still believed his line of retreat was secure. He had been taken by surprise and ejected from the city far earlier than anticipated but losses could have been worse and II Corps remained intact. If he moved east and linked with I Corps, French fortunes might recover and the loss of Porto would merely postpone an advance on Lisbon. Yet, he was blissfully unaware of recent events upriver that were about to place his army in a desperate situation.

General Loison had mismanaged affairs from the outset, which must have been apparent to Soult. Even though his headquarters were only a day's ride from Porto, Soult confined his efforts to sending reinforcements (mostly artillery) and aides with tersely worded orders to Loison's force. This was partly due to Soult's preoccupation with the political situation and the need to prepare his withdrawal and move to the east.[1] Feeling snubbed and unappreciated by his commander-in-chief, Loison fell into a state of lethargy, sending almost no intelligence back to Porto and insisting that further reinforcements and supplies were required before progress could be made.

Meanwhile, Beresford picked up Wilson's small detachment at Vizeu on 8 May and joined Silveira at Lamego on 10 May. The British received news of Silveira's defeat at Coimbra and Beresford feared that the French would have crossed the Douro in force, obliging him to adopt a defensive strategy. To Beresford's relief, Silveira informed him that the French remained in the region of Amarante, displaying few signs of moving further south. There were over 11,000 men under Beresford's command. With the exception of Tilson's brigade and the 14th Light Dragoons, these were mostly untested Portuguese troops but Beresford had great confidence in them and decided to take the offensive.

Giving Silveira the vanguard, Beresford ordered him to cross the Douro by the bridge of Peso da Regoa, which was still in Portuguese hands and protected by entrenchments on the northern side. French scouts soon spotted the manoeuvre and Loison advanced against them having anticipated a counter-attack. Loison's force was strong in infantry and he had General Marisy's 1st Brigade of dragoons in support, comprising about 6,500 men. Observing more troops massed on the south bank of the river, the French attacked swiftly hoping to deny the Allies a bridgehead on the north bank.

With his position bolstered by the entrenchments and assured of reinforcement as Beresford came up with the main force, Silveira stood firm and fought off a strong infantry attack. Loison later claimed that he lost only eighty men in the action (including a colonel), but Oman believed this figure was an understatement. Seeing that the force on the other bank was almost double his own, Loison retired on Mezamfrio but was closely pursued by Silveira's troops who fell upon the rearguard each time it tried to make a stand. The French retreat continued the next day and Loison halted at Amarante but allowed the bridge to be captured.

Beresford already had cause for some satisfaction as he brought up the rest of his force to join Silveira on 11 May as Loison had little chance of retaking the bridge with a larger force opposing him. The French were now denied the opportunity to retreat east along the line of the Douro towards Vila Real but the route to Chaves still lay open to them. In all likelihood, a stalemate would now ensue as the bridge was easily defensible from the French side of the Tamega and Beresford was loath to attack it, knowing he would lose many men if he did so.

Loison had already let Soult down and Oman commented, 'It was a military crime of the highest magnitude that he had neither informed his chief of the check at Peso de Regoa on the tenth nor of his retreat to Amarante on the eleventh.'[2] Had he done so, Soult would at least have known that his route east into Tras-os-Montes was denied to him and altered his plans since roads to the north remained open to him. Yet, Loison now exacerbated the situation by abandoning Amarante and falling back towards Guimaraens on 12 May. Although outnumbered, his defensive position was strong and it was a strange decision, especially as it went against Soult's orders.

Colonel Tholosé arrived on 12 May bearing dispatches from Soult just as Loison was in the process of withdrawing and he begged him to hold the town as its loss would totally compromise II Corps's retreat. Loison was feared for his ruthlessness but also renowned for bravery so his insistence upon falling back from a defensible position is mystifying. Casting a baleful eye on the dismayed colonel, he bluntly refused to halt the operation but declined to offer his reasons for doing so. This adds some credence to allegations that Loison was involved in the conspiracy against Soult since refusing to follow orders was totally out of character.[3]

Soult received the terrible news early in the morning of 13 May shortly after crossing the Rio Souza. It was raining heavily and the troops were tired, wet and bedraggled as they trudged along poorly made roads. Soult had just suffered a fall from his horse near the riverbank, aggravating his old wound from Genoa, and was in a foul mood. His staff was already despondent because of the retreat but news of Loison's withdrawal appalled them. The bridge at Amarante was the only structure capable of withstanding the passage of guns and heavy equipment over the Tamega and it was unlikely that they could storm it before Wellesley's army fell upon their rear and trapped them with the river at their backs.

Some officers advised surrender as the army had advanced too far east to redirect the march north. Soult could probably have done this and evaded pursuit if Loison had informed him earlier. It seemed that at least two-thirds of Soult's army were condemned to destruction or capture as their route east was blocked and they were caught between Wellesley's and Beresford's forces. A lesser man might have given up at this point but Soult was determined to save what he could of his army and demonstrated the qualities that made him a great commander. Scorning calls to ask for terms from the Allies, he declared that he would fall back through the mountains and extricate the army from its predicament.

French cavalry had brought in a Spanish pedlar they captured travelling through the region. He knew the area well and through either fear of the French, a dislike of the Portuguese or the offer of money he, 'offered to guide the Marshal by a track leading over the Sierra de Catalina to Guimaraens'.[4] This narrow trail ran along the Souza before winding up into the mountains.

While treacherous in places, it was wide enough to lead horses and mules in single file but taking wagons or guns along this track was out of the question.

Soult knew that the enemy would soon be upon him and there was no time to disassemble guns or wagons to carry them through the hills. If the army moved fast, he might save his cavalry and infantry but a forced retreat over the mountains was a horrific prospect nonetheless. It was time to make some difficult decisions and Soult reluctantly ordered that all heavy equipment and baggage had to be discarded. Nothing could be left for the Allies to capture. Wagons and caissons were set on fire and the supplies and gunpowder they carried cast out into the driving rain to spoil. He refused to allow his cannon to fall into enemy hands, to be used against them or displayed as trophies, demonstrating the extent of the Allied victory. Cannon were spiked or placed muzzle-to-muzzle and fired, bursting their barrels and rendering them useless.

While the cavalry retained their mounts as long as possible, mules, donkeys and other beasts of burden were now shot to deny their use to the enemy. Sick and wounded men who could walk were told to follow the retreat if they could but those whose wounds obliged them to travel by cart were abandoned. This dismayed the army since they knew that vengeful peasants would descend upon them once they left to slaughter them. The wounded were given muskets but everyone knew that leaving them behind was a virtual death sentence.

There was also no question of carrying Soult's military treasury due to its weight. Rather than allow the British to seize this plunder, Soult ordered the strongboxes opened and placed at the roadside as the troops marched past. If any soldier wished, he could fill his pockets with as many coins as possible. Yet, the veterans of the army declined to do so knowing that this would weigh them down and that food and drink would be far more use in the mountains than money they might never live to spend. As the French toiled up the trail into the mean hills before the mountains, many swiftly discovered the truth of this and cast down their money by the roadside. In later years, Portuguese peasants would recall picking up numerous coins along the route of the French retreat.

On 13 May, as Wellesley was organising the pursuit, Captain Argenton came to his headquarters. He sheepishly admitted that the general's own papers had sealed his fate as he was carrying them at the time of his arrest, despite Sir Arthur's advice. During the retreat through the mountains, he escaped the gendarmes guarding him on a narrow trail, possibly with the connivance of Colonel Lafitte. Despite the failure of the plot, he insisted that the scheme had merely suffered a setback and announced his intention to return to France to renew his efforts against Napoleon's regime. Wellesley knew that there were underground societies which conspired against Napoleon but wisely handed responsibility for further action to the British government. Having no wish to engage further intrigues, he placed Argenton on a ship bound for England as soon as possible.[5]

On the surface, Wellesley's involvement in this wild enterprise appears strange as it contrasts with his reputation for level-headedness. It is quite possible that he dealt with it tentatively after his unfortunate political entanglements the previous year over the Convention of Sintra. To his credit, he adopted a non-committal stance throughout his dealings with Argenton, giving little away while gaining valuable military intelligence for the Allied cause. Ultimately, his decision to send Argenton back to London was very wise.

After spending a short time in England, Argenton returned to France disguised and travelling under an assumed name in the hope of bringing his wife out of the country. Alarmed by the conspiracy, Napoleon ordered Fouché (Minister of Police) to investigate allegations made against some officers but was appalled to hear that Argenton had returned:

> I send you a letter, the subject of which is important. If this Dessort really is that wretch Argenton, whose documents I sent you, let him be brought to Paris, with irons on his feet and hands. This business is worthy of all your anxiety. I conclude all his papers have been seized. It is inconceivable that he should have dared to come to Paris.[6]

Fouché's agents soon located and unmasked Argenton who was tried by court martial, found guilty of treason and executed by firing squad shortly thereafter.

Meanwhile, Sir Arthur received a flurry of reports as he reorganised his army in Porto. In the belief that Soult had fallen back in good order on

Amarante, he intended to pursue but it would be a careful advance as he considered the French army a formidable force. Had he known that Beresford had taken the town, he would have acted more quickly but, becoming aware of Soult's predicament, he decided to renew the pursuit as swiftly as possible and press the enemy hard. Despite the weather, intelligence quickly arrived in Porto with the local peasantry keen to see the despoilers of their lands defeated and punished. Wellesley soon heard rumours that the French had taken drastic measures to hasten their retreat:

> At Esperada they destroyed a number of tumbrels, tents and powder. The balls they threw away, and may be found in some pits. This happened between nine and twelve this morning. The whole of the army then took the road to Basto, from whence the road branches off to Braga and Guimaraens. This, however, is from report, as the informer had made his escape before they marched.[7]

Although unsure whether such reports were reliable, Wellesley guessed from the tone of most intelligence that Soult had suffered some kind of reverse. Perhaps he had clashed with Beresford or encountered a serious obstruction on the road east. Therefore, he decided to mount an immediate and aggressive pursuit, sending Murray in the vanguard with extra cavalry towards Peñafiel on 13 May. He hoped to re-establish communications with Beresford and order him to march along the Tamega to intercept Soult at Chaves. On 14 May, Wellesley marched the main army north towards the River Minho in two columns. The right-hand column marched on Braga while the left advanced over the Ponte d'Ave towards Barcelos. There might still be an opportunity to destroy an entire French Corps and Wellesley meant to take full advantage of it.

Despite the dreadful weather that had descended upon them, morale among the British troops was high as their officers made a point of informing them that the enemy were trapped. Their optimism was infectious and the news of impending victory sent back to Britain was somewhat premature:

> The accounts from Portugal are highly favourable. Marshal Soult is unquestionably reduced to a most perilous situation. He seems to be

hemmed in on all sides, and it is highly probable that the Duke of Dalmatia, to whom Buonaparte consigned the task of 'driving the English into the sea at Corunna', will be conveyed as a prisoner to England. The dispatches are understood to contain overtures on the part of Soult to capitulate on certain conditions, which were rejected. The age of *Conventions* is past, and the surrender, we have every reason to hope, will be absolute ...[8]

By 14 May, Beresford had not managed to re-establish links with Wellesley but had grounds to suspect that Porto had fallen. From Amarante he sent out aggressive patrols to gain intelligence and one brought in a French commissary, who informed him that Soult had evacuated the city. D'Urban wrote that his commander now anticipated Wellesley's orders and tried to cut the French off:

The probable retreat is Chaves. The Marshal [Beresford] sent an Aide-de-Camp to break the Bridge at Ruivães and gave orders for Silveira with his Division and the 4th Chasseurs to proceed to Chaves. The Brigades of Baccellar and de Souza to march for Chaves ... The British and the Cavalry to march at 3 to-morrow morning, the whole to arrive on the 16th. Orders sent to Sir R. Wilson, now at Lamego, to march to Chaves.[9]

Only a brave officer risked Sir Arthur's wrath by taking the initiative in this fashion. The news that Wellesley had indeed entered Porto was confirmed on 15 May but it was fortunate for the Allies that Beresford chose this course of action. When Wellesley reached Braga on the 15th, Beresford was at Chaves and Silveira was moving towards Salamonde and the passes at Ruivães and Melagaço. In all probability, Soult would be trapped and forced to surrender his entire army.

After a difficult journey, Soult reached Guimaraens where his meeting with Loison must have been stormy and peppered with recriminations on both sides. Lorge's dragoons joined them here, having escaped from Braga as Allied troops approached. Through his determination not to give up and good fortune, Soult had united his army and evaded pursuit for the present. He believed Wellesley would reach Braga before him and knew he had little chance of winning a pitched battle with his army demoralised, outnumbered and lacking artillery. Some officers, Loison being conspicuous among them, advised him to seek terms but Soult opted to head for the Spanish frontier. He would retreat further into the mountains where the terrain would handicap his pursuers, since they were slowed by artillery and wagons. Before leaving Guimaraens, he ordered the two divisions that had just united with him to destroy their guns and wheeled transport.

Soult's vanguard reached Carvalho d'Este late on the evening of 14 May. The sight of the position where his army had been victorious only weeks before restored the spirit of his men slightly and the marshal set about re-organising his army. He took command of the rearguard personally to demonstrate his confidence that their withdrawal would be successful. Still suspicious that some officers opposed him, he took care to divide those he suspected and placed General Loison in the vanguard. This was an adroit move as Loison was hated by the Portuguese and therefore had an incentive to force his way through the mountains rather than be taken alive by his enemies. As Napier observed, 'Maneta dared not surrender.'[10]

As the French marched north, it was cold and heavy rain continued to fall upon them. They had been defeated, outmanoeuvred, forced to quit the country and the best the French could now hope for was warm billets and meagre supplies in Spain if they made it over the frontier. With guerrillas occasionally sniping at them from the crags above, their mood turned ugly and Soult's benevolent attitude towards the peasantry became a dim memory, 'But if Soult's own advance on Oporto had been characterised by exceptional humanity, in his retreat he rivalled the cruelties of Loison. The pursuers could track him by the smoke of burning villages, and the peasantry were mercilessly butchered. The inhuman outrages were as savagely avenged.'[11]

Once the French reached Salamonde, Soult had a choice of routes to take before he could reach Montalgre. Scouts reported that the bridge at Ruivães was destroyed and around 1,200 Portuguese infantry, equipped with artillery, had taken up position to block that road. Therefore, he was obliged to take the second route that ran over two narrow mountain bridges – the Ponte Nova and the Saltador. Both spanned deep gorges containing mountain rivers and were in Portuguese possession. Fortunately for the

French, these troops were mostly militia and armed peasants, yet all it would take for them to block their last line of retreat was to destroy one of these spans, trapping Soult's army in the mountains.

The progress of II Corps was shadowed by guerrillas who prowled along the goat tracks above them seeking opportunities to sweep down from the hills to kill stragglers. Shots frequently rang out as they sniped from the heights above. Most were armed with shotguns or muskets and this harassment was more a nuisance than a serious problem but a few had hunting rifles and, striking from a distance out of range of French muskets, were able to pick off men without fear of retaliation. The only way the French could prevent this was to send companies of light infantry up into the high ground to drive them away. Yet, if they were firmly ensconced along high cliffs, they were difficult to dislodge or able to fall back swiftly only to return later. Men were lost in such skirmishes and these actions slowed the retreat down. With Allied forces converging to block their progress, the last thing Soult could afford was to slow his march, so the French largely endured this treatment without responding.

The mountain tracks were slippery and wet as it had not stopped raining for days and cold, stormy weather set in as the French marched on. By 14 May, Soult knew that the British were close behind them and, unless the bridges were captured swiftly, they would fall upon the rearguard. The Portuguese had been reluctant to destroy the bridges as they were difficult to construct and expensive to replace in such isolated areas. Suggestions by Beresford's aide that they blow them up with gunpowder outraged local militiamen since they suspected their government would be slow to pay to have them rebuilt. They relied upon these spans to transport livestock and losing them would ruin their livelihoods so they angrily refused to burn or blow up the Ponte Nova and merely ripped up the wooden planks forming its roadway. This left two large beams spanning the gorge but, at roughly 3ft (1m) wide, the bridge could still be crossed.

After consulting with his staff, Soult chose Major Dulong of the 31st Légère for this daunting task. Dulong had distinguished himself at the Battle of Eylau in 1807 and was under provisional command of his regiment at that time. He had already come to Soult's attention for the part he played in storming the Ponte de Lima and seemed the ideal officer to lead this kind of desperate attack. The marshal stressed the vital importance of seizing the bridge with the enemy coming up quickly behind them, remarking:

> 'I haven chosen you from the whole army to seize the Ponte Nuovo [*sic*], which has been cut by the enemy, right now. You will seek to gain surprise: the weather favours you (the rain fell in torrents). You'll meet him with the bayonet; you will succeed or perish. If you succeed, say so, but send no other report as your silence will suffice. Take 100 chosen men from wherever you want, this should be enough for you but 25 dragoons can also join you …'[12]

The same source recorded that the militia attempted to cut the beams but abandoned the task because of heavy rain and fatigue. Dulong chose to rest his men and attack under cover of darkness. Some shots were exchanged over the gorge but the ordenanza soon tired of this and settled down for the night. They posted sentries but did not expect the French to assault across the narrow remnants of the bridge. Most believed they would mount an assault in the morning or turn back as their position was difficult to approach.

When he judged the time right, Dulong silently crept forward with his chosen men, having selected fifty grenadiers to crawl across each beam. As the grenadiers edged across, one of them slipped from the damp surface into the darkness but the roar of the Cavado flowing below them muffled his scream. Accounts differ but some suggest that the storming party knifed or bayoneted sentries near the bridge once they were across with the sound of the river once again covering their cries.

Once enough men had crossed, Dulong formed a double line and led a bayonet charge against the Portuguese trenches and huts behind them where many slept. It was still raining and, knowing that muskets were prone to misfiring in the wet, the grenadiers probably did not load their firelocks and relied on their bayonets. They gained complete surprise and Napier recorded that most of the militia were mercilessly bayoneted and the rest fled into the darkness after a brief fight, fearing that the entire French army was upon them. Yet, some accounts challenge this and suggest that the action was a one-sided slaughter:

as for the resistance of the Portuguese, they made none; not a shot was fired. There was a small party of peasantry on the spot, who had been placed there by Lord Beresford's aide-de-camp: these – who had been selected from the few that would remain after hearing of the approach of the French army – had all, without any precaution, fallen asleep. In this situation they were surprised; and, with the exception of one man who got off badly wounded, and gave the alarm in Ruivaens just in time for the English aide-de-camp to escape, they were all massacred. The Portuguese made no resistance whatever; a circumstance easily accounted for, as they were merely peasantry, and armed as they could best provide themselves for the occasion.[13]

Once Dulong had enough men across to secure the position, the French hastily set about repairing the bridge and by 8.00 am on 16 May were crossing in force. Once across, the Duke of Dalmatia kissed Dulong and said, 'Thank you on behalf of France, good Major, you have saved the army; If I ever occupy a page in history, your name will be entered in next to mine; but be prepared the day is perhaps not yet over for you.'[14] Dulong was awarded the *Légion d'Honneur* for his courage that day.

The rearguard had already spotted British cavalry approaching and Soult knew that he could not afford the luxury of waiting for the cover of night to assault the next bridge. In any case, there was no chance of surprising its defenders and the bridge had to be captured before Wellesley brought up his main army behind them. The narrow road and tiny Ponte Nova bridge slowed the army's progress so there was no time to lose.

The Saltador bridge (its name means 'leaper' in Portuguese) spanned a deep ravine, through which the Miserella River flowed. Once again, the peasantry had refused to destroy this bridge but they manned rocks and trenches on the far side and had blocked the single-arched stone structure with an abbatis (either a specially constructed spiked wooden barrier or piled thorn bushes in this case). The force opposing the French entirely comprised ordenanza, but they were firmly entrenched and keen to fight. It was a narrow bridge (only three men abreast could walk across it) but the French had no choice but to storm it in the face of the enemy. As he had already implied, Soult hoped Dulong would lead this second assault but was not prepared to order him as he had already proved himself that day. He was gratified when the major stepped forward and volunteered to lead this second 'forlorn hope'.

The French had no choice but to mount a frontal attack in broad daylight. Dulong ordered *tirailleurs* to take up position on their side of the gorge and lay down aimed musketry against the Portuguese to cover his charge. As they rushed forward, the assault party came under heavy musket fire as they approached the bridge. The main problem was that the abbatis blocking the span had to be wrenched aside by the first attackers or the assault would stall and the men pressing behind them shot to pieces as they massed in front of the barrier. Dulong led two assaults:

> The enemy had crowded trees, masses of rock, and other obstacles ... already frustrated several attacks, and showed their joy by shouting and insults. The fate of the French army was again compromised as they must conquer or put down their arms. At the head of the grenadiers of the 32nd and the Legion du Midi, Major Dulong repeatedly attacked the enemy; but he was constantly repulsed.[15]

Yet, there was no turning back with Wellesley's army pressing their retreat. Dulong regrouped his men for a third assault and elements of the 15th Légère joined the storming party. Knowing that they faced certain death or capture if they failed, the French then mounted a ferocious attack. Many were shot down on the bridge but they hauled the abbatis aside, allowing their main body to charge across and rush the Portuguese positions on the other side. Leading from the front, the major fell near the bridge but the attack continued with the grenadiers setting upon the ordenanza in the rocks and ousting them out of their positions.

For the most part, the ordenanza did not stand to contest their positions in the rocks, either fleeing back along the track or clambering up narrow goat trails into the high ground above. Some were shot as they took flight and voltigeurs were sent up to chase them away. Nevertheless, while the majority fled, the light infantry found some sharpshooters difficult to dislodge from the cliffs above and they continued to snipe at the French as they crossed.

Behind them, the French could already hear heavy gunfire as the British attacked their rearguard during the final stages of the fight for the bridge – the Saltador had fallen just in time for Soult. Dulong lay badly wounded, having been shot through the head, and was not expected to survive and Soult expressed deep remorse at this gallant soldier's demise. Through necessity, many wounded were abandoned but most fell into British rather than guerrilla hands. Yet the 15th Légère, seriously impressed by Dulong's bravery, refused to leave him and General Heudelet personally ensured that he was placed on a stretcher and taken with them.[16]

Wellesley left Braga on the 15th and his vanguard fell upon the French rearguard at Salamonde on the morning of 16 May. Soult had positioned his troops carefully in the hills before the mountains. His infantry were placed with their right flank guarded by a ravine and their left flank protected by a steep hill. General Sherbrooke initially attacked with light infantry in an attempt to turn their left flank. The weakness of the French position was that they lacked cannon. Initially, only a few light guns could be brought up (two 3-pound cannon, according to Fortescue) as the vanguard had relied upon speed to catch up with the enemy, but they were able to fire upon the French lines without fear of retaliation. Due to their small calibre, they only inflicted a small number of casualties so the French engaged in a brief firefight before falling back. The 3rd Foot Guards took part in the clash and one officer recalled, 'Our eight companies in front immediately attacked and drove them from the village, but the road unfortunately being on the side of mountain and extremely narrow did not admit the brigade to come up before the enemy had formed …'.[17]

Harassed by cavalry all the way, the rearguard withdrew to the Ponte Nova. Before the bridge, a battalion formed to repel cavalry while the rest fell back over the bridge. By this time, more cannon had arrived and these targeted the infantry before the bridge, inflicting some losses. Frustrated at their inability to reply without artillery, this battalion did not stand for long and fled over the bridge. Observing this, British dragoons rode forward, cutting down scores of fugitives. Panic ensued and in the struggle to get across, many men fell or were unintentionally pushed into the defile and perished in the waters below. After this clash, the British sent back their prisoners and continued to pursue Soult's army. Yet, now they were over the bridge, the French were able to quicken their pace and the narrow mountain road slowed their pursuers, especially as they had to manhandle cannon along the rough mountain track while the French did not have this difficulty.

General Silveira reached Montalegre on 16 May, but immediately placed his men in billets rather than continuing their flanking march through the relentless rain. Beresford also encountered difficulties and one of his aides carrying dispatches was slowed by the appalling weather, which meant Silveira did not receive orders to cut the enemy off at Vila de Rey soon enough to block Soult's retreat.

Wellelsey knew that as II Corps had managed to force its way over the bridges it would now outpace him in the mountains. Writing to Castlereagh, he explained why this was so:

I hope your Lordship will believe that no measure which I could take was omitted to intercept the enemy's retreat. It is obvious, however, that if an army throws away all its cannon, equipments, and baggage, and everything which can strengthen it, and can enable it to act together as a body ... it must be able to march by roads through which it cannot be followed, with any prospect of being overtaken, by an army which has not made the same sacrifices.[18]

Soult's men had retreated over difficult terrain and were tired, wet and hungry but knew the end was in sight. Nevertheless, the infantry suffered terribly as cavalryman Joseph de Naylies recalled. Their shoes were tattered or destroyed after marching along rock-strewn roads and tracks and many had not eaten anything but parched maize for days. They were exhausted and, even though facing the near certainty of murder at the hands of local peasants, some despaired and sank down by the roadside to await their fate. Seeing that morale among his infantry was almost at breaking point:

the Marshal ordered each regiment of cavalry to transport fifty wounded infantrymen, these men being put on our horses which we then led on foot ... Laden with their knapsacks and with their muskets balanced across the saddle bow in front of them ... in any other circumstances, they would have been very amusing to us, but their pale and defeated faces, and their naked and bloody feet meant that we felt no other sentiment than pity ...[19]

The Allied troops were in a similar state as they had left their tents and provisions far behind in order to catch the French. As Lord Gough commented, 'The men were without a shoe to their feet – the result of their forced marching with incessant rain that welled the rivulets into rivers.'[20] Even though Wellesley punished looting harshly, the men had been pushed to their limit as Sergeant Cooper of the 7th Foot admitted, 'No sooner was the day's march ended than the men turned out to steal pigs, poultry, wine, etc.'[21]

Ensign Aitchison of the Guards was present during the final stages of the pursuit and wrote of the difficulty of coming to grips with the enemy as they retired along narrow tracks in the hills. It was often a matter of brief clashes between small numbers of men, as large bodies of soldiers could not deploy in these cramped conditions. Nevertheless, the British overtook many who fell behind:

> From the 16th a great number of stragglers were made prisoner, several were found on the roads dying of hunger and fatigue and many were dead who had been shot by the peasantry – so closely had we followed them that they had not time to dress the animals they killed, and on the 18th in the morning they shot a great number of horses and hamstrung all their mules to prevent their accelerating our march. They burnt the villages as they proceeded.[22]

D'Urban recorded that the French were pushed out of Ginzo de Lima on 19 May. The woods around the town were cleared by the 60th Foot (riflemen). They then received a dispatch from Wellesley calling off the pursuit saying that, 'he has ceased the pursuit for want of bread and was anxious to return to the Tagus. Of course pursuit alone was useless.'[23] By this d'Urban meant that merely chasing the enemy was unlikely to force a confrontation or cut off their line of retreat. A cavalry patrol under Colonel Talbot of the 14th Dragoons advanced beyond Alariz and took fifty-four prisoners, but these were probably stragglers the cavalry overtook rather than participants in a serious skirmish. Talbot observed seeing formed bodies of French infantry near Orense but this was the last action during the retreat.

Wellesley came close to cutting off an entire French army but various factors prevented him doing so. In a letter to his brother, he wrote:

> We should have taken Soult & his whole Army if Silveira could have reached Milgapey one hour sooner; or if the Capn. of Militia of Montalegre would have allowed the Peasantry to break the Bridge at Milgapey, which they wished to do; & we should have taken the Rear Guard on the 16th if we had only a quarter of an hour more daylight. The Light Infantry of the Guards pursued towards Ruivaens instead of towards Milgapey in the dark. But as it is the chase out of Portugal is a Pendant for the retreat to Corunna.[24]

However, I Corps still threatened Portugal's eastern frontier and Wellesley thought it prudent to return and protect Lisbon against another invasion. He believed Soult's army would take some time to recover and that he had achieved his main objective of liberating northern Portugal.

Sir Arthur was pleased with the results of the campaign and the Allied army's performance. In a remarkably swift campaign, he had ousted the French from a strong position in Portugal's second city and then forced II Corps back over the frontier. While avoiding destruction, II Corps suffered serious casualties (in return for small Allied losses) and limped back into Spain with its troops in a battered state having left its baggage and artillery behind. The Allied army had certainly proved itself, which would reassure the Portuguese and confirm Wellesley as commander-in-chief.

Historians estimate French total losses in Portugal at between 4,000 and 6,000 men, along with 25–35 cannon and all of II Corp's stores and baggage. Oman gives very specific figures for Soult's losses in Portugal, citing sources such as Le Noble's memoirs among others. Soult recorded the return of 19,713 men after reaching Galicia, having begun the invasion with 22,000, joined by a further 3,500 when II Corps reached Tuy. Oman estimated that the French probably left 5,700 men behind them in Portugal. Of these, about 1,000 fell in the early fighting, while 700 sick and wounded were captured at Chaves. He believes that as many as 1,500 were taken prisoner in Porto's hospitals and roughly 400 unwounded prisoners were taken in the fighting there. Over 2,000 fell on the retreat between Baltar and Orense, 13–19 May 1809 and possibly as many as 4,000. He concluded that II Corps lost almost a sixth of its total strength during this campaign. In contrast, Allied losses were placed at 300 casualties during the engagements between 11 and 12 May and, even considering those killed in the pursuit, total Allied losses did not amount to much more than 500 men. He commented that, 'There is hardly a campaign in history in which so much was accomplished at so small a cost'.[25]

Once the army crossed the frontier into Spain, de Naylies expressed his heartfelt relief at putting this dreadful mountain campaign behind them:

At the village of Santiago de Rubias we entered Galicia. Hope stirred once again in our hearts on setting foot on Spanish soil: we hoped that we would soon be back in touch with the other army corps, and that we would all receive news from France, news of which we had been deprived for more than seven months.[26]

Soult reached Orense on 19 May, finding northern Spain in the grip of armed insurrection, which was hardly a safe environment for II Corps to recuperate and seek supplies in. They received a poor welcome after their long trial, as the soldiers of Ney's VI Corps regarded the survivors with contempt and were reluctant to provide them with equipment or provisions. During Soult's absence, Vigo had fallen to the British and the French garrison at Lugo were under siege. Ney had failed in his attempts to defeat General La Romana's army and was in poor humour when the two marshals met at Lugo.

Corunna's storehouses held enough stores to re-supply II Corps but Ney prevaricated and was openly scornful when he learned that Soult had lost his artillery and entire baggage train. Napoleon's preference for Soult over Ney during the pursuit of Moore still rankled and he felt smug when his rival only won a partial victory at Corunna, which the British considered a French defeat. Now he could barely conceal his delight at Soult's humiliation, which led to a heated exchange of recriminations. The quick-tempered Ney came close to challenging his rival to a duel over the matter and was only prevented from doing so with difficulty. The problem was Ney feared, with some cause, that Soult would try to take command of French operations in Galicia.[27]

This was no way for senior officers to behave but even Soult's enemies conceded that Ney was at fault here. Thiébault, who heard the tale from General Delaborde who witnessed this infamous episode, disapproved of his unprofessional attitude:

> He ended with a statement that is painful to record. Marshal Ney ... possessed more artillery than he needed; enough indeed to be an embarrassment from its disproportion to the number of his troops and their requirements. Marshal Soult asked if he could spare him some batteries – a request which there were a score of reasons not merely to comply with but to anticipate. Ney did not let him have a single gun.[28]

Many who witnessed the altercation were shocked that the feuding marshals failed to put their differences aside for the sake of France. In the absence of recent orders from the emperor, they eventually agreed to divide responsibilities for the subjugation of Galicia between their respective corps. Under the so-called 'Convention of Lugo', Ney agreed to re-equip and provision II Corps from the stores, munitions and captured ordinance at Corunna. He also undertook to retake Vigo as soon as possible. Once II Corps was ready to fight, they would combine their efforts to corner and defeat La Romana's army.[29] It was shameful that two senior officers had to resort to this kind of agreement in order to resolve their dispute. In the event, Soult went back on the agreement, marching II Corps out of Galicia heading for Leon and never providing an official excuse for his actions.[30] While Napoleon actively fostered competitive spirit between his marshals, the enmity this created made co-operation between the armies in Spain very difficult. With hindsight, the emperor probably realised that he had pushed things too far and, when a subordinate questioned why he tolerated such disputes, he responded, 'Do you think it is an easy matter to control a Soult or a Ney?'[31]

After the abortive second invasion of Portugal, taunts against Soult in the French army grew worse. Soult's derisive nickname of 'Nicolas' probably originated in VI Corps and, when they heard tales about his pretensions to royalty in Porto, a song entitled 'Roi Nicolas' was swiftly composed and spread from Madrid to Paris with great speed.[32] Despite the rift between his marshals, Napoleon appointed Soult supreme commander over three corps (his own and those of marshals Ney and Mortier). Ney's fear that Soult would take control of events in northern Spain was therefore confirmed but, as the pair tried to avoid each other after the incident at Lugo, Ney was often left to his own devices.

Chapter Ten

Fortune Favours the Bold

Wellesley's campaign had been an overwhelming success witnessing the defeat of a vaunted French commander, the mauling and repulse of an entire French army and the frustration of Napoleon's Second Invasion of Portugal. This provided firm evidence of strong British commitment to the Peninsular War and was a propaganda gift for the British government as it assured the Portuguese of the strength of the alliance. Yet, the Wellesley family were unpopular in some quarters and their political opponents felt the campaign should have been fought in a different manner.

Initially, the news of Marshal Soult's defeat was welcomed in England and the Hyde Park and Tower of London guns were fired to celebrate a victory. Yet as more details emerged, hopes that it was a decisive victory were soon dashed:

> Mr. Stewart spoke to me about the news; of which he said (and really I think, after reading the Gazette, that he was right) that he saw nothing in it to fire the guns about – though *any* success against this Soult must be very pleasing – as retaliation for his half-triumph over the English army in having pursued them to Corunna – and still more for his execrable treatment of the people of Oporto ...[1]

Admittedly, the Second Battle of Porto was not a victory on a grand scale but at least the military were convinced it was worthwhile. It had been a difficult campaign conducted in foul weather and the lack of supplies made the pursuit particularly arduous, but Wellesley's leadership had impressed participants. They had achieved the objective of liberating northern Portugal but, just as importantly, suffered remarkably few casualties in the process. Aitchison's summary may have praised Wellesley to excess but many in the British army shared his sentiments:

The more you consider this campaign the more you will admire the genius who could plan it and the manner in which it has been executed. In the short space of ten days one of the greatest generals in Europe has been driven from a post he occupied six weeks, naturally strong, and pursued for 200 miles through a country hitherto supposed impassable for an army and which might have everywhere been defended by a handful of men. It has immortalised the hero of Vimeiro and it has proved that even in rapidity of movement no soldiers can equal the British.[2]

The French army was renowned for its marching speed and, although they ultimately evaded pursuit, came close to being trapped by British and Portuguese forces. Therefore, Aitchison had made a legitimate point, particularly when the fact that the French were unencumbered by artillery and baggage during their retreat is taken into account.

The French army tried to minimize the scale of Soult's defeat and disparage Wellesley's achievements. Napoleon ordered a Bulletin of the French Army issued in Paris on 22 June 1809 emphasising Soult's earlier success occupying the northern provinces and seizing Portugal's second city during the First Battle of Porto. Yet, it claimed that Soult was vastly outnumbered on the Douro and the affair amounted to little more than a skirmish:

the only action which took place was with our rear-guard at Oporto, the English having found means to convey on the right bank of the Minho about 1000 infantry and 50 horse. They have swelled this trifling engagement into a battle, the pompous relation of which (in no point of view a military one) has no other end than to deceive the people of London, and perhaps the Ministers themselves, in order to pay them for the immense sums of money which this expedition must have cost the British Treasury.[3]

While the number of casualties suffered was slight compared with many Napoleonic battles (casualties often amounting to well over 4,000 men on each side), they did not consider the number of wounded taken prisoner in

Porto's hospitals, or the propaganda triumph the Allies gained by retaking the city. However, the most important repercussion of the Second Battle of Porto was that Soult was forced into a flying retreat and came very close to losing his entire army. In addition, the Bulletin trivialised both the reasons for his ignominious withdrawal and provided a dishonest account of II Corps's losses:

> But a numerous corps of English and Portuguese having compelled General Loison to evacuate Amarante, the Duke found it necessary to pass through the defiles of Salamonde, and, in order to gain two marches of the enemy, to sacrifice a few pieces of cannon and their caissons, which he ordered to be destroyed, and the remains of which could prove of no use to the English.[4]

Yet, few would expect a nation at war to announce the true scale of a reverse in their official bulletins but the reaction to news of Wellesley's triumph in London is more perplexing.

When reports of a victory abroad reached England, it was traditional for the officer bearing the dispatch to receive an instant promotion. Although it depended on the scale of the triumph, the monarch often recommended that the House of Commons pass a vote of thanks for the victory, giving full credit to the army's commander and the achievements of his men. When Wellesley's dispatch was received, the officer who carried it did not receive a promotion and no vote of thanks was forthcoming, strongly implying that the Establishment entertained serious reservations about the way in which Wellesley had achieved this victory.

The trouble was that Britain maintained a small professional army quite unlike the vast, conscript-based armies put into the field by the French and other Continental powers. As a result of this, the Establishment demanded that the army be treated very carefully and while Wellesley had achieved much without suffering significant casualties, some critics deemed him reckless by sending men over the Douro piecemeal in an operation that could easily have met with disaster if the enemy had detected it sooner. In later life, Wellington complained that his enemies had far more freedom to take risks in warfare:

[Napoleon] had one prodigious advantage – he had no responsibility – he could do whatever he pleased; and no man has ever lost more armies than he did. Now with me the loss of every man told. I could not risk so much; I knew that if I ever lost five hundred men without the clearest necessity, I should be brought upon my knees to the bar of the House of Commons.[5]

Therefore, the primary lesson Wellesley learned from his early campaigns was that Britain had only one army to send him and he resolved to take great care of it. After 1809, he never acted with quite the same level of aggression during an offensive. This is not to say that Wellesley became cautious from that point onwards. A good commander always had to be prepared to take calculated risks since, as the military theorist Karl von Clausewitz astutely commented, 'No human activity is so continuously or universally bound up with chance'.[6] Nevertheless, there is a big difference between the campaigns he fought at the beginning of the war compared with later on in the conflict.

The fact that Soult's army had not been conclusively defeated led some to question the relevance of Wellesley's northern campaign:

When Parliament met, the Whigs made a series of determined attempts to turn out the Government. Rarely, if ever, has any Cabinet been subjected to such rhetorical vituperation. Henceforth, the Peninsular War ceased to obtain national support, and was carried on by the Tories alone in the face of the bitterest opposition. The methods of attack adopted by the Whigs were very varied. In the first place they minimised Wellesley's successes; some denied that he had obtained any. Grey dismissed the passage of the Douro as 'nothing more than an affair of a rear-guard'.[7]

As Lord Grey was widely respected, his dismissive attitude towards the battle was damaging and it is likely that the decision to deny Wellesley the traditional accolades for victory lay behind this and similar objections made in Parliament. Interestingly, this reference to the Passage of the Douro as a skirmish with the French rearguard bore a striking similarity with the language used in the French army Bulletin describing Soult's campaign.

While Wellesley always planned his operations precisely, he was well aware that he had taken advantage of an excellent opportunity on the Douro and success in operations of that nature owed something to luck. Nevertheless, it was a calculated risk and, in military circles, success was the criteria that pardoned all sins. Porto and its aftermath were undeniable triumphs of British arms but he was dismayed by some comments, writing in a private letter that 'I have received your letter of the 10th June, from which I imagine that you apprehended that I have got myself into some scrape. I don't think that the Govt. have treated me very well, in having allowed some reports to be circulated to which they appear to me to have given currency …'.[8] Certainly, the idea that he had merely cut off the French rearguard was grossly unfair as the bulk of Soult's army lay in defensive positions in and around Porto and were completely outmanoeuvred when the attack took place.

In July 1809, Wellesley won a resounding victory at Talavera, for which he received numerous honours including a peerage. Yet, the newly created Baron Douro of Wellesley and Viscount Wellington of Talavera encountered serious criticism regarding his actions in the aftermath of this battle. Parliament received a King's Message suggesting that an annuity of £2,000 be granted to Wellington along with a Vote of Thanks for his triumph, but Mr Howard MP opposed the motion on the grounds that 'the battle of Talavera was followed by none of the consequences of victory, and rather displayed ill-judged rashness on the part of Lord Wellington, than deliberate and skilful valour'.[9] These were strong words and Mr Calcraft MP added allegations that Wellington had lost almost a quarter of his army and then retreated, leaving his wounded to fall into enemy hands. Strategic necessity lay behind Wellington's decisions but Calcraft also raised the Passage of the Douro once again:

He allowed that the action on the Douro was a brilliant affair; but even in that there was room for much criticism. – On the whole, he did not think that any ground existed for the vote proposed. If Lord Wellington should survive the scrapes into which he was constantly bringing his army, he might one day be entitled to distinction and rewards. If he had destroyed the French armies under Soult and Ney, what more could he have expected than what was now proposed to be done to him?[10]

Calcraft thought it unfortunate that the Lords had already confirmed Wellesley's new titles and insinuated that the general's dispatches were deliberately misleading and designed to make the House believe his achievements were greater than they actually were.

Tory Members of Parliament rose to defend the motion but, even though Talavera had been a clear victory, it had a rough ride through the Commons before it was passed. In Wellington's defence, Mr Robinson MP argued that, 'He denied the insinuation, that the language in Lord Wellington's dispatches was exaggerated or inflated.'[11] He also took the opportunity to point out the gains that the Passage of the Douro had made possible, since it forced a French army to retreat into an area where it could not carry its heavy equipment. Mr Lyttleton MP also believed that Calcraft 'went too far in saying Lord Wellington might in time become an excellent officer' and proceeded to remind the House of some of his military achievements.[12]

General Craufurd MP also rose to defend Wellesley:

With respect to the operation on the Douro, Lord Wellington had most judiciously pressed upon Soult, for the purpose of forcing him to fight on very disadvantageous terms, or to retreat with great loss, and his retreat was actually attended with the loss of his baggage, cannon, etc and 5 or 6,000 men. His hon. Friend (Mr Calcraft) was under a complete mistake as to the real objective of the operation.[13]

Although many spoke on his behalf, Wellesley ultimately received a poor political accolade for frustrating the Second Invasion of Portugal in 1809.

Historians provide a more objective view of the commanders' performances during the campaign being less concerned with the political bias of Wellesley's and Soult's contemporaries. Most agree that Wellesley's bold move paid off and his detractors were merely looking to find fault in what was undoubtedly a notable success. As Fortescue wrote:

It has long been customary for the carpers at Wellesley's fame to reproach him with excessive caution; yet here in the first week of his campaign, in which the slightest mishap would have spelled professional ruin and evoked a storm of national indignation, he bearded so formidable an antagonist as Soult with the calm, phlegmatic order, 'Well, let the men cross.'[14]

In contrast, he believed that Soult had been negligent at Porto, allowing himself to be totally outmanoeuvred. Although he conceded that the marshal's ill-health that night contributed to poor command decisions, he cited arrogance as the main cause of French humiliation, 'the truth was that he despised his enemy, as indeed did every one of his brethren and the great Emperor himself, until convinced by the bitter experience of the error. There is no greater danger for an army than to be the spoiled children of victory.'[15]

Oman was slightly more generous regarding Soult's performance during the Second Battle of Porto but only to the extent of acknowledging that others shared the blame. He wrote that General Quesnel (Governor of Porto) and General Foy, whose 1st Brigade was tasked with the defence of the eastern suburbs, were at fault for failing to detect the crossing earlier.[16] Oman believed the French were generally guilty of complacency before the engagement.

Yet, Soult had taken extensive measures to protect his position by securing all crossing points and boats on the Douro to deny the enemy an easy passage. Considering that he had to cover the estuary, where he anticipated the main attack would occur, along with a considerable length of the river, it was not possible for his defensive forces to be strong at all points. As contemporary military theorist Jomini wrote in relation to guarding coastlines and riverbanks, 'I can only advise the party on the defensive not to divide his forces too much by attempting to cover every point.'[17] In the same vein, he counselled concentrating the forces available at predicted landing sites and recommended setting up a signalling system to warn the commander of incursions. Soult had adopted this course and, to a degree, suffered from bad luck when Wellesley's audacious crossing secured a firm foothold on the northern bank. He did all in his power to crush this but overreacted to the extent that he left the docks unguarded, allowing the townspeople to assist the Allies to cross at other points, thus making defeat inevitable.

Fortescue believed that Wellesley's previous experience of assessing the chances of making successful river crossings contributed to his success on the Douro, commenting on 'one of Wellesley's most remarkable gifts – the astonishing eye for ground, which enabled him to realise in a moment that the passage, granted certain conditions, was actually feasible'.[18] At Assaye Wellesley had also crossed a river in the face of the enemy and outmanoeuvred them. It bears serious comparison to the crossing of the Douro, as both were confident, audacious operations that could have gone awry. Nevertheless, these calculated risks paid off spectacularly and it is a military truism that 'success pardons all sins'. Wellesley's expertise in this area certainly influenced his decision to attempt a crossing at the Douro, which may have seemed spontaneous but was undoubtedly founded on experience and good judgement.

In Soult's defence, it is worth noting that his command was seriously undermined by treachery before and after Porto fell to the French. Any general faced with a plot like the Argenton Conspiracy would have felt his position compromised and Soult's confidence must have waned when he learned of this betrayal. Junior commanders also let him down and these factors must be considered when accounting for Soult's failures, 'In forcing the Douro and the recapture of Oporto, Wellesley was greatly helped by the carelessness and overconfidence of Soult and the unaccountable behaviour of Loison, but this cannot detract from the greatness of his achievement or his genius in profiting from his opponents' errors.'[19] Indeed, Wellesley only narrowly failed to trap II Corps by blocking their retreat from the city. Murray is usually blamed for this as a result of the slow progress of his flanking force (see Chapter 8) and undoubted hesitance to attack the retreating French when the opportunity presented itself. However, Oman concedes that Wellesley rarely followed up a victory as well as he should have and that his main fault as a battle commander was an over reliance on infantry and reluctance to use his cavalry arm to the full effect. The small number of cavalry the British army was permitted throughout the Peninsular War only partially excuses this shortcoming.[20]

Nevertheless, it is difficult to see how Wellesley could have conducted his pursuit any more effectively and the total destruction of capture of II Corps was mainly thwarted by valiant French efforts to seize the bridges in their path, the appalling weather and the impressive marching speed of the French. Furthermore, Beresford and Silveira's slowness to cut Soult off near the Misarella on the 17 May contributed to the Allies' failure to inflict a decisive defeat and these factors were largely out of Wellesley's control. Yet, in fairness, Allied troops were exhausted after marching through appalling conditions with few provisions and the weather contributed to Silveira getting lost and slowed their pace. Ultimately, Wellesley cleared northern Portugal of enemy troops and was still able to return to the south swiftly enough to counter the threat in the east posed by Victor's I Corps. Soult was dealt a severe blow that II Corps took two months to recover from. Oman went as far as to conclude, 'As to Wellesley, it is not too much to say that the Oporto campaign is one of his strongest titles to fame.'[21]

An insight into how Wellesley viewed the Passage of the Douro is gained by his family's reaction to his successive promotions and advancement in the peerage. The College of Heralds sought his brother William's advice about a suitable title and he selected Duke of Wellington, while Arthur was in the Peninsula at the time. He chose Wellington as it was the name of a town in Somerset not far from Welleslie and seemed appropriate. However, Lady Wellesley was unimpressed by the new honour and remarked that it failed to commemorate any of her husband's achievements. She preferred his previous title associated with the Passage of the Douro and argued that their son should retain it, 'My little boy's name is Baron Douro. They wanted to change his title and raise his rank, but I roared and screamed. The passage of the Douro, the most brilliant and least bloody of all his father's achievements, shall not be forgotten, and he shall keep the name.'[22]

Wellington was consulted over this arrangement and, despite the criticism the action attracted at the time, must have thought highly of the engagement to allow it to be associated with his eldest son. Indeed, when William suggested that Viscount Douro sounded like an odd title for his son to use in later life, Wellington objected and pointed out that his Portuguese soldiers nicknamed him 'Douro' in the Peninsula and consequently he felt rather attached to it.[23] Significantly, the Wellesley family retain the title to this day.

Once the political furore over Wellesley's style of command during the Regency period came to an end, the army were able to assess the Passage of the Douro more dispassionately. While some aspects remained controversial, it undoubtedly provided a textbook example of how to conduct a river crossing in the face of an enemy. With Wellesley gaining the advantage of surprise, it was only seriously opposed once the Allies had gained a foothold on the north bank and the sheer audacity and overwhelming success of the plan remains impressive.

On 12 May 1937 the Coronation of King George VI took place, an event accompanied by great pageantry and celebration. The British army played a significant role in the festivities and one great event was the Coronation Tattoo held at Rushmoor, Aldershot between 10 and 19 June that year. Foreign observers were impressed with New York City's *Brooklyn Daily Eagle* commenting, 'The British army will present at Aldershot next June the greatest military pageant ever staged – the Coronation Tattoo proclaiming allegiance to and affection for the new King. Incidentally, military authorities confidently hope that this last word in flag-waving will give needed stimulation to recruiting.'[24]

According to tradition, a battle from the past was re-enacted at tattoos and the Passage of the Douro was chosen on this occasion. As the *Illustrated London News* commented, the army were, 'Re-enacting a Peninsular battle with almost exactly the original number of men: artillery in action in the episode representing the Passage of the Douro, in 1809, during Wellington's advance from Lisbon – The British and French troops in the picturesque uniforms of the period.'[25]

Although the claim that the exact number of troops involved was an exaggeration, the display was certainly going to be conducted on a massive scale. A later publication revealed more precise figures of the troop numbers to be used, 'three cavalry regiments, a Field Brigade, R.A., and three infantry battalions participated, wearing the uniform of Wellington's day'.[26]

The Coronation Tattoo was a spectacular success and many commentators remarked on how impressive the re-enactment had been and how it recalled the splendour of former days. Even a sudden rainstorm failed to spoil the occasion for most spectators. Nevertheless, the lone and somewhat petulant voice of Mr Thorne MP was raised in the House of Commons, inquiring whether the Secretary of State:

'can give the House any information in connection with the damage done by the thunderstorm on Thursday last at the Aldershot tattoo to the Coldstream Guards' scarlet tunics and costumes; and who will pay for the damage done?' Reply: 'No particular damage was done, and no expense falls upon the soldier or the public.'[27]

Considering his troops were constantly exposed to the elements during the Peninsular War, Wellington would probably have been wryly amused by this comment had he been alive to hear it in 1937.

The fact that the authorities selected this small but spectacularly successful engagement on this significant social occasion spoke volumes. The difficulties of staging a river crossing in a realistic fashion must also have raised questions concerning the expense and practicality of the re-enactment, but these were addressed and overcome. Certainly, there were larger, more decisive battles to portray from history but the British army made a point of commemorating its finest achievements at a coronation and clearly included the Passage of the Douro among them.

For years afterwards, military analysts and historians referred to the event in books and journals and it is odd that the Passage of the Douro has become so obscure today. Perhaps the lack of a decisive and bloody battle during the campaign along with the fact that greater events (such as the Battle of Talavera) happened shortly afterwards go some way towards explaining this. It is also sad that this operation, which cost far fewer lives than most battles of the period, is often overlooked since it had a significant strategic impact on the course of the Peninsular War.

While Soult has been criticised by historians for being outmanoeuvred and defeated on the Douro, most acknowledge that he recovered swiftly from the reverse by conducting a masterly retreat. A lesser general would almost certainly have surrendered, especially when faced with a commander like Wellesley. Saint-Chamans rarely had a good word for Soult but conceded that, 'He rediscovered his greatness' during the retreat through the mountains and elaborated by saying that the Duke of Dalmatia was 'always at the front or the rear of the column, using resources that no one else would have done'.[28]

British historians praise Soult's performance, acknowledging that while he jettisoned his guns and baggage to speed his march and lost up to 6,000 men during the campaign, his losses would have been far worse but for his actions during the retreat. As Innes Shand concluded, 'Yet that he saved so much was infinitely to his credit as a general, for on the Souza river he was in far more desperate case than Dupont at Baylen or Junot after Vimeiro.'[29]

Some historians draw comparisons between Sir John Moore's retreat to Corunna and Soult's flight through the mountains. Significantly, many British historians consider Moore's retreat a triumph as he successfully fought off his pursuers allowing his army to embark. Therefore, it can be claimed that Soult has been denied sufficient credit for saving his army but successful withdrawals rarely gain the kind of praise awarded to victorious battles. However, Fortescue remained unconvinced that the two retreats were that similar:

Many comparisons have been instituted between his retreat to Orense and that of Moore to Coruña, which latter was held at the time to be fully avenged by the Marshal's discomfiture. But there was a broad difference between the two, that the British were rather mutinous from disappointment of their wish to fight than demoralised by failure. Soult's troops were disheartened and even cowed. Both armies degenerated in great measure into mobs, but Moore's was a fighting retreat, whereas Soult's was a flying mob.[30]

Considering the accounts written about the retreat, this summary seems unfair. Soult's army must have retained serious discipline in order to withstand guerrilla attacks and fend off the British rearguard. Otherwise, the men would probably have scattered or surrendered, which they certainly would have done had they been a disorganised rabble. Furthermore, II Corps came close to being trapped in the mountains and only saved themselves by concerted efforts to seize and secure the Ponte Nova and Saltador bridges. An armed mob could hardly have won through at those points during the withdrawal, as organisation and courage were required. Nevertheless, Fortescue's point that Soult was only forced into retreat because of his shortcomings at Porto is more difficult to refute.

Oman was more generous towards Soult and draws several parallels between his and Moore's retreats. Yet, he correctly points out that Moore had a far greater distance to march (roughly twice as far as Soult) and that Moore's retreat took twenty days compared with the nine days it took for Soult to reach safety in Galicia. However, this is partly balanced by the fact that Soult had far more difficult terrain to cover. While both retreats took place in abysmal weather, Moore enjoyed better roads and was largely marching through open country. Soult's army trudged over hilly and mountainous terrain using roads that were little more than mule tracks and the army were regularly obliged to march in single file. Moore was also pursued more closely and constantly had to turn and fight off the French vanguard, but Soult was really only pressed during the final days of his retreat.[31] Ultimately, both armies suffered enormous privations and Soult's successful evasion of the Allied pursuit has notable similarities with Moore's experience.

Despite the military reverses Soult had suffered from 12 May onwards, he largely escaped censure from the emperor. This may have been partially due to the misfortunes Napoleon suffered during the same month. On 21–2 May 1809, he faced his first serious defeat at the Battle of Aspern-Essling against an Austrian army under the Archduke Charles. Crucially, this encounter involved an attempted river crossing and provided a rare example of Napoleon being surprised by an unexpected attack.

Hoping to catch the Austrians unawares, Napoleon attempted to cross the Danube River while it was in spate but unwisely relied upon a single line of advance (and possible retreat) over two pontoon bridges to move his army to the Isle of Lobau and then to the Marchfeld Plain beyond. The Archduke waited until a third of the enemy army had crossed the river before mounting a ferocious series of attacks that came close to destroying the French forces trying to establish a bridgehead in the villages of Aspern and Essling. Simultaneously, the Austrians floated heavy objects downstream, severing the pontoon bridges, trapping those who had crossed and denying them supplies and reinforcements. Only the Archduke's reluctance to inflict vast numbers of casualties prevented him from destroying a large portion of the French army, which was obliged to retire back over the Danube.[32]

Although Napoleon ultimately won the campaign with his last truly decisive victory at Wagram on 5–6 July 1809, Aspern-Essling was a rare humiliation, requiring skilled propaganda to downplay it in France. Although fought on a far greater scale than the Passage of the Douro, it bore some resemblance to that action as Napoleon attempted an operation similar to Wellesley's ambitious manoeuvre over the Douro only to be firmly repulsed with loss. Perhaps wishing to avoid unfavourable comparisons, the emperor treated Soult's defeat at Porto as a minor rearguard action, understating his losses in men and equipment and praising his skill during the retreat.

Indeed, Napoleon's confidence in Soult was such that he promoted him over the other marshals in Spain even in the immediate aftermath of his humiliations in Portugal, although this decision was made prior to II Corps's re-emergence in Galicia after the debacle. While the emperor criticised his alleged designs on the Crown of Portugal and handling of the Argenton Conspiracy (see Chapter 6), Soult's military failings at Porto were largely overlooked.

Both Wellington and Soult continued to wield great influence during the Napoleonic Wars but the career of the former eclipsed his rival, seeing the duke become one of the giants of the period. From 1809–14 Wellington enjoyed incredible military success in Portugal and Spain. In 1810, he brought the third and final French invasion of Portugal to a shuddering halt when Marshal Massena's army found their way to Lisbon blocked by the Lines of Torres Vedras he had constructed to defend the capital. Having pursued the French from Portugal, he then set about besieging the major fortresses on both sides of the frontier and Portugal was virtually secure against further invasions once these were taken.

In 1812 Wellington took the offensive, inflicting a major defeat on the French at Salamanca. This demonstrated his ability as an attacking general, whereas previous victories (such as Busaco 1810 and Fuentes de Oñoro 1811) saw him labelled unfairly as a purely defensive general. However, he never displayed quite the aggressive spirit that he had shown in his earlier Indian and Portuguese campaigns and went to great pains to preserve the small army that Parliament had entrusted to him. Indeed, he was always prepared to conduct strategic withdrawals if victory was in doubt and return when the situation was more favourable.

Meanwhile, Soult remained in the Peninsula, eventually seeing almost six years service there. Wellington's decision to withdraw after his victory at Talavera in 1809 was partially due to the approach of armies under Soult and Ney, although a number of factors influenced that decision too. Soult's defeat of the Spaniards at Ocaña later in the same year also helped restore his reputation and he became King Joseph's chief-of-staff (replacing Jourdan), although he found his dealings with Napoleon's brother very trying at times.

In 1810, Soult invaded the Spanish province of Andalusia, eventually taking the cities of Seville, Olivença and Badajoz. The latter was particularly important as this fortress city guarded the Spanish frontier and the Allies were unlikely to invade Spain without securing it first. Furthermore, Soult was well placed to march over the border to seize Elvas, which the Portuguese had fortified to oppose Badajoz. Taking this city would have allowed Soult to invade southern Portugal but was disinclined to do so in support of the Third French Invasion of Portugal under Marshal Massena in 1810. Once again, rivalry between the marshals helped thwart French attempts to make a concerted effort against Lisbon.

On 16 May 1811, Soult fought the British under Marshal Beresford. The Battle of Albuera proved to be one of the bloodiest of the war as well as controversial. While Soult's casualties numbered 8,000, Beresford's army suffered 6,000 and both sides had grounds to claim victory. Indeed, Beresford was on the verge of retreating but was saved by the firm action of subordinate commanders and the stubborn resilience of his infantry. Exasperated by their tenacity towards the end of the battle, Soult supposedly snarled, 'The enemy was completely beaten. We had won the day but they did not know it and would not run away!'[33] While the French withdrew, leaving Badajoz exposed to a potential siege, Wellington was aghast, commenting frostily when he read a report of the battle, 'This won't do. Write me down a victory.'[34]

After Albuera, Soult moved south and invested Cadiz. It was during this time that he gained an unsavoury reputation for looting works of art and other treasures. Among the items he carried back to France was the much-admired *The Assumption of the Virgin* by Murillo, which he 'liberated' from Spanish hands. This work eventually came into possession of the Louvre.[35] However, he was forced to lift the siege of Cadiz that had been invested for almost two years as a result of Wellington's success at Salamanca.

Compelled to withdraw and link forces with Marshal Suchet in an attempt to drive the Allies back, the French recaptured Madrid and Wellington retreated towards the Portuguese frontier. Nevertheless, the situation in the Peninsula looked bleak for the French and Soult was glad to be recalled to Paris in 1813. Following the death of Marshal Bessières, Napoleon needed a general of Soult's calibre and gave him command of the Imperial Guard. He fought at Bautzen where the emperor was desperately trying to fend off superior Allied forces bent on invading France. While it was considered a French victory, they were unable to exploit this and other successes because of a crippling lack of cavalry. The loss of thousands of men, horses and equipment during the catastrophic Russian campaign of 1812 was a clear sign that the French were losing the war.

The Battle of Vittoria in 1813 saw Wellington finally break the back of French power in Spain and he was promoted Field Marshal of the British Army. Knowing that Soult had faced Wellington before, Napoleon sent him to defend the line of the Pyrenees, as an invasion of France from the south was imminent. This campaign in the mountains proved to be an arduous one for both sides and the defensive skill and tenacity that Soult and his army displayed won them profound respect from the British army. At one point, Wellington even caught a glimpse of his adversary:

> The Duke was making a reconnaissance near Pampeluna, when a noted spy told him he would show him Soult. The Duke saw Soult so plainly on that occasion through the glass, that he afterwards recognized him when they met at Paris. Soult was writing on his hat, and, when he had finished, he gave what he had written to an aide-de-camp, and sent him off in a particular direction, indicating the direction by pointing. The Duke guessed where the attack was to be made, from thus seeing the point to which the A. D. C. was despatched, and his surmise proved correct ...'[36]

Yet, Soult could expect little in the way of support since French armies were outnumbered and fighting defensively on all fronts. While Napoleon did his best to fend off the many armies that had invaded France, they converged on Paris and his regime was doomed. Ultimately, Soult retreated and Wellington led his army onto French soil, winning a final victory at Toulouse in 1814. Shortly afterwards, news of Napoleon's abdication (which unfortunately took place before the battle) ended the war.

Following the end of the Great War against France, Wellington hoped to resume his political career in earnest but Napoleon's return from exile in 1815 saw him placed in command of the British army in the Netherlands for one final campaign. While Napoleon made a stunning comeback, virtually unparalleled in modern history, he was finally defeated at the Battle of Waterloo on 18 June. Here the Duke of Wellington, commanding an Anglo-Dutch army in combination with the Prussian army under Marshal Blücher, inflicted a crushing defeat upon the French. Indeed, it was one of the most decisive battles ever fought.

Soult's performance at Waterloo was controversial. Having sworn loyalty to the Bourbons after the restoration of Louis XVIII, he defected to his old master upon Napoleon's return and was appointed the emperor's chief-of-staff for his final campaign. While Soult had ample experience, it was sixteen years since he had last performed this role for Massena at Genoa. It is worth noting that, in Spain, he acted more as a military advisor to King Joseph rather than a true chief-of-staff.

Although Napoleon's offensive began well, there was confusion among the staff from the outset and Soult is implicated in many of the debacles that occurred on the French side. These include the belated start of III Corps on its march to Charleroi, the farcical misunderstanding that led to d'Erlon's Corps marching between the Quatre Bras and Ligny (ultimately failing to arrive at either battlefield) and several poorly composed written orders to Marshal Grouchy. Soult's inability to co-operate with Ney also contributed to communication problems. Yet, the most serious criticism concerned ambiguous orders sent to Grouchy, tasked with pursuing the Prussians after the Battle of Ligny and preventing them from combining with Wellington's army. His failure to achieve this is often cited as the main reason for Napoleon's defeat at Waterloo, although many factors were significant, but poorly written orders undoubtedly played a part. Whether the fault lay with Soult for poor staff work or Napoleon's complacency is still open to debate.

Ultimately, the responsibility for French errors during the Hundred Days Campaign rests with numerous officers up to and including the emperor himself but few French soldiers emerged from the campaign with their reputations enhanced. Indeed, the performance of both Napoleon and Soult was lacklustre in comparison with their former glories and some doubt whether Soult was truly committed to the Bonapartist cause – a charge levelled at many senior officers who were weary of war and wished to retire in comfort. However, it is notable that while Napoleon used the poor performance of subordinate commanders to excuse his defeat (notably Ney and Grouchy), Soult was one of the few that Napoleon failed to blame for his downfall.[37]

During the final stages of the battle, when Napoleon's attempts to rally his army failed, he declared that he would enter the fray and die with his Old Guard as they struggled to fall back (ultimately fighting a famous last stand). Upon hearing this, Soult remarked to his despondent emperor, 'Oh! Sire, the enemy has already been fortunate enough' and grasped the emperor's bridle leading him to safety with the assistance of General Gourguard.[38]

Wellington's reputation as one of the world's greatest generals was now assured. His return to diplomacy and politics gained great momentum from the reputation he acquired at Waterloo but, in an act of stunning insensitivity to the French, he was made British ambassador in Paris. Unsurprisingly, he was unpopular with the French and an attempt was made to assassinate him, but he efficiently fulfilled his duties there nonetheless. He rose to hold ministerial office in England and eventually became prime minister from 1828–30. However, his ability as a politician failed to match his military competence and Wellington's popularity waned because of his opposition to political reform. Obliged to agree to an extension of the franchise, he even fought a duel of honour over the issue of Catholic emancipation in 1829, despite being a serving prime minister. Yet, his reactionary nature and outspokenness continued to provoke strong feeling and the nickname 'the Iron Duke' was actually applied to Wellington because of the iron shutters he used to protect his windows from stones cast at his London residence (Apsley House) rather than from any military connotation.

He continued to act as Commander-in-Chief of the British Army for a long period and, even after relinquishing the office, wielded great influence as the army still held him in great respect. Indeed, his devotion to duty and moral code led the early Victorians to consider Wellington as a role model and statues and monuments were raised to commemorate his achievements during as well as after his lifetime. He died at Walmer Castle on 14 September 1852 while still holding the office of Lord Warden of the Cinque Ports and received a state funeral, a privilege usually reserved for royalty.

In contrast, Soult was lucky to escape from France alive after the traumatic events of 1815. He was re-organising the remnants of the Army of the North after Waterloo when the Convention of St-Cloud saw the French Army decommissioned and his military services spurned. The Convention of Paris made with the Allies that July officially brought the war to the end and King Louis XVIII was restored. Despite an official amnesty, the Bourbons removed most of Napoleon's supporters from official posts and some were imprisoned or executed. The period became known as the 'White Terror' with many Bonapartists hunted down and murdered and Soult narrowly avoided a lynching. This took place in southern France where a Royalist mob accused him of being a Bonapartist and sacrificing French lives unnecessarily at Toulouse in 1814.[39]

Soult was proscribed by the new regime and, fearing imprisonment or worse, chose to leave France, taking up residence at his wife's home in Düsseldorf. It was not until 1818 that the measures taken against Napoleon's erstwhile supporters were relaxed and Soult returned to France the following year. His rank of marshal was restored in 1820 and, gradually regaining favour with the Bourbons, he was created a Peer of the Realm in 1827. However, it was not until the Revolution of 1830 that he regained prominence in the army and politics, becoming President of the Council of Ministers, 1832–4, Minister of Foreign Affairs in 1839 and enjoying two periods as Minister for War from 1830–4 and 1840–4.

Soult was a born survivor, which won him few admirers, one historian commenting that he 'was a thorough-going opportunist who was equally content to serve any form of government whether Republican, Consular, Imperial, Legitimist or Orleanist'.[40] Yet, he had lived through turbulent times and was not the only prominent man to switch allegiance when the political tide changed. While not above acting in his own interests, he had stayed consistently loyal to Napoleon until 1814 and, if his commitment in 1815 was questionable, the unexpected return of the emperor placed him in a very difficult position. Soult was a realist and tried to reconcile himself with the Bourbons after Waterloo but this did not stop him from writing the following lines his memoirs, which he began in Germany, 'Napoleon afforded France a protective authority, giving her safeguards which calmed down evil passions and ended the wicked forces of the Revolution. He provided for our armies not only the leadership of which he had given such excellent proofs but also limitless self-confidence.'[41] Considering that this was written in the immediate aftermath of Waterloo, it can be argued that he was still a Bonapartist at heart, but was forced to accept the inevitable after Napoleon's downfall. After 1815, the chances of Napoleon making a second return were virtually non-existent.

At the age of 71, Soult had long been a part of the Establishment and attended the ceremonies welcoming the return of Napoleon's remains from St Helena in 1840. He was promoted Marshal-General of France on 26 September 1847, the only previous recipients of this supreme distinction being Turenne, Saxe and Villars. While some questioned whether he deserved this great honour reserved for the finest commanders, all acknowledged that he had gained vast experience during his career. He retired the same year and died at Soultberg (a house he had built near his family's village of St-Amans) on 26 November 1851. Soult was one of the most prominent generals in Napoleon's Marshalate. If he lacked the spectacular brilliance of Davout, Suchet or Massena as a battlefield commander, he was an able tactician and strategist, excelled in logistics and was one of the emperor's most dependable generals. Upon his death, France mourned him as a military hero who had risen from humble origins to stand among the elite of their nation.

Although Soult encountered and spoke to Wellington in 1814 while acting as Minister of War for King Louis XVIII, their most memorable meeting was at Queen Victoria's Coronation in 1838. King Louis Philippe and the French government believed that the Tories would rapidly oust the Whig administration and selected Soult as their special envoy as he already knew Wellington, likely to be among the senior ministers in the next government. Yet, it would be another two years before the Tories returned to power under the leadership of Sir Robert Peel.

Soult was warmly received in the English capital and, when his carriage drew up outside Westminster Abbey, his appearance was greeted with even more cheers and applause than the arrival of the Great Duke. Londoners knew and appreciated the fact that he had been an honourable enemy when fighting the British and treated him accordingly. It was no surprise when:

> the main responsibility for looking after the veteran fell upon the Duke of Wellington. Characteristically, the Duke confided to George Seymour beforehand that he hoped that Soult's arrival would not coincide with the anniversary of one of his defeats. 'Indeed he would be puzzled to find a day in the present season when he would not have a disagreeable recollection!'[42]

At this time, the French were extremely interested in British commercial practices, the success of which far exceeded their own. Indeed, the beginning of the Industrial Revolution in England played a significant part in Napoleon's defeat as French industry lagged far behind their enemy's manufacturing capability. Therefore, Soult made a tour of England including the north and the Midlands. This was unusual as it was rare for the English royal family to visit these regions and virtually unheard of for a foreign dignitary to do so.[43] The fact that Soult made the effort to see British industry for himself speaks volumes about his business sense and acumen as he intended to pass on his observations to French industry on his return to France.

Yet, the meeting with his former adversary was undoubtedly foremost in Soult's mind when he arrived in London. The pair tried their best to outmanoeuvre each other in the Peninsula and had faced each other in battle on more than one occasion. When Wellington finally found Soult, he 'stole up behind the Marshal, saying, "I've got you at last!"'[44] As an aristocrat, Wellington would often act coolly towards those of a lesser social standing to himself but on this occasion his reserve melted and they were soon discussing old campaigns with warmth and enthusiasm. Those around them commented that the pair seemed more like old comrades than former adversaries. Of all their encounters during the wars, Wellington's first words when he tapped Soult on the shoulder had probably made both of them recall that fateful day in May 1809 when his troops crossed the Douro and pursued Soult into the mountains.

Notes

Chapter 1

1. Philip J. Haythornthwaite, *The Napoleonic Source Book* (London, Guild Publishing, 1990), p. 258. The Portuguese had this number of ships in active service during 1795 and the situation was similar in 1807–8. The Braganças did not take the entire Portuguese fleet when they fled to Brazil during the First French Invasion as a number of frigates and smaller ships lay in dock undergoing repairs. The French captured these vessels.

2. Arthur John Butler (ed. and trans.), *The Memoirs of Baron Thiébault*, 2 vols (London, Smith, Elder & Co., 1896), Vol. 2, p. 199. Dom João specifically ordered his subjects not to resist the French knowing that, even if they defeated this invasion, other military incursions would undoubtedly follow.

3. Ibid., p. 199.

4. David Buttery, *Wellington Against Junot – The First Invasion of Portugal 1807–1808* (Barnsley, Pen & Sword Books Ltd, 2011), p. 54.

5. Michael Glover, *Legacy of Glory – The Bonaparte Kingdom of Spain 1808–1813* (London, Leo Cooper, 1972), p. 14. Beauharnais wrote this in a letter to Talleyrand (then Grand Chamberlain of the Empire) on 12 July 1807. Beauharnais was the empress's brother and a strong supporter of Prince Ferdinand in his efforts to oust Godoy and wrest the crown from his father King Carlos IV.

6. William Norman Hargreaves-Mawdsley (ed.), *Spain Under the Bourbons 1700–1833* (London, Macmillan, 1973), p. 212. This edict was signed by Napoleon in the royal palace at Bayonne on 25 May 1808 and published in the *Gaceta de Madrid* on 3 June 1808.

7. Glover, *Legacy of Glory*, p. 43. Joseph's gloomy predictions eventually proved correct and, as Delderfield perceptively commented, 'The longer he wore the crown of the Bourbons the more it oppressed him. With less ambition but more prescience than his terrible brother he had foreseen that it would not be easy to win the loyalty of Spanish peasants, their proud grandees and their implacable priests', R.F. Delderfield, *Imperial Sunset – The Fall of Napoleon, 1813–14* (London, Hodder & Stoughton, 1968), p. 16.

8. David Gates, *The Spanish Ulcer* (London, George Allen & Unwin, 1986), p. 9. Here Gates is using a quotation from Maurice Girod de l'Ain, *Vie militaire du général Foy. Ouvrage accompagné de deux portraits en héliogravure, six cartes et trois fac-simile d'autographes* (Paris, E. Plon, Nourrit et Cie, 1900), p. 111.

9. Michael Glover, *Britannia Sickens – the Convention of Cintra* (London, Leo Cooper, 1970), see especially Chapter Ten, pp. 178–98. See also, Buttery, *Wellington Against Junot*, pp. 134–48. The aftermath of Vimeiro witnessed the highly unusual episode of a commander being replaced towards the end of a battle with General Burrard controversially forbidding Wellesley to pursue the retreating French army. General

Dalrymple subsequently arrived to assume command, resulting in the unprecedented event (for the British army) of two changes in command within only forty-eight hours. This was as a result of political manoeuvring in London and Wellesley's replacement as Commander-in-Chief at a crucial moment was poorly received by the military. The enemy took full advantage of Dalrymple's recent arrival and unfamiliarity with the campaign during peace talks and won extremely favourable terms, which Wellesley reluctantly endorsed. The Portuguese were angered by these overly generous concessions, as were many in Britain. At the inquiry in London, Wellesley's signature on the Convention came close to damning him. Eventually Dalrymple became the government's scapegoat for the fiasco but, considering that the Cabinet had placed the generals concerned in a very difficult predicament, this seems unfair.

10. *Gentleman's Magazine*, Vol. LXXIX (London, John Nichols and Son, 1809), p. 170. See also Major General Sir William Napier, *History of the War in the Peninsula and in the South of France*, 6 vols (London, Frederick Warne and Co., 1851), Vol. I, p. 361.

11. *Edinburgh Review or Critical Journal for April 1809–July 1809*, Vol. XIV (Edinburgh, D. Willison & London, Constable, Hunter, Park and Hunter, 1809), p. 244. The journal was reviewing the narrative of Charles Richard Vaughan (a fellow of All Souls College, Oxford) who was present during the siege and was hosted by Palafox himself.

12. Raymond Rudorff, *War to the Death – the Sieges of Saragossa 1808–1809* (London, W. & J. Mackay Ltd, 1974), pp. 117–18. Augustina Zaragoza (also known as Augustina Aragon as her surname was unknown) fought in the First Siege and reputedly prevented the Portillo Gate from being captured at a crucial moment. As her lover fell, she fired a cannon loaded with case shot into the advancing French, inspiring the other defenders (who were falling back) to return. This story was often repeated in Allied propaganda with portraits of Augustina painted and tales of her deeds printed in the newspapers. Lord Byron even dedicated three verses of *Childe Harold's Pilgrimage* to Augustina, romanticising her exploits, *The Complete Poetical Works of Lord Byron*, 3 vols (London, George Routledge and Sons, 1886), Vol. 1, first canto, verses LIV, LV and LV1, p. 271.

13. *Annual Register* (London, W. Bell and Co. and Harding & Wright, 1811), p. 740.

14. Ibid. The decree was signed by the Marquis of Astorga, Vice President, Martin de Garay in the Royal Al-cazan of Seville on 7 February 1809.

15. Antoine-Henri, Baron de Jomini, *The Art of War* (New York, Dover Publication Inc., 2007, first edn 1862), p. 29.

16. Butler (ed. and trans.), *The Memoirs of Baron Thiébault*, Vol. 2, p. 196.

17. Luís António de Oliveira Ramos, 'Os afrancesados do Porto', *Revista de história* (Universidade do Porto – Faculdade de Letras, 1980), Vol. 3, pp. 115–25.

18. Christopher Hibbert, *Corunna* (London, B.T. Batsford Ltd, 1961), p. 92.

19. J.W. Fortescue, *A History of the British Army* 13 vols (London, Macmillan and Co. Ltd, 1912–20), Vol. 7, p. 354.

20. Hibbert, *Corunna*, p. 117.

21. Fortescue, *A History of the British Army*, Vol. 7, pp. 29–30. Although the Duke of York had not proved an able commander on active service, Fortescue believed him a competent administrator and a great loss to Horse Guards and the army, calling him 'the best Commander-in-Chief that has ever ruled the army', p. 31.

22. *The Times*, 26 January 1809, p. 4. *The Times* devoted considerable column space to discussing the battle and printed letters that were highly critical of Moore's campaign

such as 'The fact must not be disguised,' wrote a correspondent to the paper, expressing a general opinion, 'that we have suffered a shameful disaster.', Hibbert, *Corunna*, p. 197.

23. *The Times*, 24 January 1809, p. 4. A lengthy passage was translated from *Le Moniteur* and printed by *The Times* to illustrate the French reaction to the end of the campaign.

24. *Cobbett's Parliamentary Debates*, Vol. 12, 19 Jan–7 March 1809 (London, T.C. Hansard, 1809), p. 145.

25. Ibid., Vol. 12, p. 141. Numerous historians agree with this line of reasoning. Napier began his great six-volume work on the Peninsula partly with the aim of vindicating Moore's reputation – see Philip Haythornthwaite, *Corunna 1809 – Sir John Moore's Fighting Retreat* (Oxford, Osprey Publishing Ltd, 2001), p. 91. Napier commented that Moore's withdrawal was the only feasible course left open to him under the circumstances and therefore 'an honourable retreat in which the retiring general loses no trophies in fight, sustains every charge without being broken and finally, after a severe action, re-embarks his army in the face of a superior enemy without being seriously molested', Napier, *History of the War in the Peninsula*, Vol. 1, p. 354.

26. Fortescue, *A History of the British Army*, Vol. 7, p. 29. Although many Whigs actively opposed the war with France, General Moore had enjoyed considerable support from the Opposition as a result of his unpopularity in government circles and the fact he owed his position largely to his abilities rather than patronage.

27. *Cobbett's Parliamentary Debates*, Vol. 12, p. 324. Lord Erskine also wanted to see the precise figures for expenditure on the wagon train, horses and artillery laid before the House of Commons.

28. Ibid.

29. Fortescue, *A History of the British Army*, Vol. 7, p. 125. Sir Arthur's reasoning was based on the logic that, while the French could amass large armies, maintaining them long enough to mount a successful invasion in countryside with few supplies for provisions and inadequate means of communication would be immensely difficult.

30. Fortescue, *A History of the British Army*, Vol. 7, p. 44. Napier also agreed that the Cabinet continued to regard the Peninsula as a sideshow in 1809. He believed they would prefer to see Napoleon defeated by a commander more acceptable to the establishment, 'it was more agreeable to the English cabinet to have the French monarch defeated by a monarch in Germany, than by a plebeian insurrection in Spain'. See Napier, *History of the War in the Peninsula*, Vol. 1, p. 360. Since Britain fought in the Revolutionary and Napoleonic Wars with the aim of suppressing revolutionary fervour in France, and discouraging it at home, this theory is well founded.

31. Émile Dard, *Napoleon and Talleyrand*, trans. Christopher R. Turner (London, Philip Allan & Co. Ltd, 1937), p. 199. Talleyrand supposedly showed Metternich correspondence from Fouché and reports from Champagny, detailing their plans to choose a successor who was more favourable to them and Austria if the emperor did not return from Spain. Naturally, the Austrians and Russians were delighted by these intrigues and 'Talleyrand', Metternich wrote, 'agrees that we must not allow Napoleon to be beforehand with us if he decides to declare war upon us', p. 199.

32. R. Ben Jones, *Napoleon Man and Myth* (London, Hodder & Stoughton, 1981), p. 165. This is very revealing as Talleyrand was endorsing what the Allied powers in all seven coalitions raised against France and Napoleon most desired – namely France returning to her pre-1792 borders, thereby restoring the balance of power in Europe. Similar

demands became a constant refrain in peace terms offered to Napoleon from 1813 onwards. Significant evidence exists (including his own memoirs) that Talleyrand intrigued with Britain, Austria, Russia and the Bourbon royal family from 1807 onwards.

33. Louis Cohen, *Napoleonic Anecdotes* (London, Robert Holden & Co. Ltd, 1925), p. 306. After he had dismissed Talleyrand, the emperor scornfully remarked, 'Posterity will grant him no more room than is needed to state that he was a member of every government, that he took twenty oaths of allegiance, and that I was fool enough to be deceived by him', see Frédéric Loliée, *Prince Talleyrand and his Times* (London, John Long Ltd, 1911), p. 370. Nevertheless, considering that the emperor had employed him as foreign minister for seven years, created new offices in order to make him Vice-Grand Elector, Lord High Chamberlain and granted him the principality of Bénévente, this seems unjust to the point of dishonesty on Napoleon's part, see Loliée, *Prince Talleyrand and his Times*, pp. 372–3. In truth, Napoleon relied upon Talleyrand's diplomatic skill, which had contributed to many of his more successful peace treaties. However, the emperor's words were no doubt spoken in anger at this time.

34. Frank McLynn, *Napoleon* (London, Jonathan Cape, 1997), p. 409. Shouting and swearing at Talleyrand like a sergeant major berating a recruit failed to impress those who witnessed the scene, 'onlookers one and all were aghast, and those among them who loved him were profoundly distressed at having to witness a scene which was so derogatory to the dignity of the Crown and of the man of genius who wore it', see Dard, *Napoleon and Talleyrand*, p. 200. It also seemed unfair since he seemed to be the only conspirator who paid the price, when Fouché and others were equally guilty. McLynn believes that, as Fouché knew so many official secrets, Napoleon hesitated to punish him until sure of his ground. Although reproached by the emperor, he retained his position until 1810, McLynn, *Napoleon*, p. 409.

35. Rory Muir, *Britain and the Defeat of Napoleon 1807–1815* (New Haven CT and London, Yale University Press, 1996), p. 86.

36. Jomini, *The Art of War*, p. 20.

Chapter 2

1. Peter Hayman, *Soult – Napoleon's Maligned Marshal* (London, Arms and Armour Press, 1990), p. 17.

2. Ibid., pp. 17–18. 'Roi' is the Portuguese word for king and referred to later allegations that he tried to claim the Portuguese crown. The use of 'Nicolas' as a demeaning nickname was apparently common in rural areas of France at this time. Interestingly, when Napoleon was forced into exile on Elba in 1814, crowds of hostile peasants along the route of his journey shouted 'Nicolas' at him in the Midi area of France.

3. Ibid., pp. 18–19. On occasion, members of the government had difficulty understanding Soult's speech when he spoke in the Chamber as a minister in later life due to his accent.

4. Ibid., p. 19.

5. Ibid., p. 20. During his exile after Napoleon's defeat in 1815, Soult began writing his memoirs but never found the time to cover his complete career during the imperial period. Although he planned to write three volumes, he only completed the first two, which largely dealt with his life during the Revolutionary Wars.

6. David G. Chandler (ed.), *Napoleon's Marshals* (London, Weidenfeld & Nicolson, 1987), p. 459.

7. Ibid., p. 460.
8. Marshal Jean de Dieu Soult, *Memoires du Marechal-General Soult*, 2 vols (publies par son fils, Paris, 1854), Vol. 1, p. 199.
9. Ibid., Vol. 1, p. 208.
10. Hayman, *Soult*, p. 25.
11. Chandler (ed.), *Napoleon's Marshals*, p. 462. Griffith (who wrote the chapter on Soult, 'King Nicolas') believes that Soult was guilty of exaggeration in his memoirs (see *Memoires du Marechal-General Soult*, Vol. 1, pp. 335–59) and mentions mistakes in his text such as the capture of Sir John Moore, who was not taken prisoner at Ostende. Soult's memory of these events while writing his memoirs almost twenty years later may have been at fault here.
12. Chandler (ed.), *Napoleon's Marshals*, pp. 462–3.
13. Soult, *Memoires du Marechal-General Soult*, Vol. 1, p. 69. Swiss soldiers continued to serve in the French army into the imperial period and Soult deserves credit for helping to begin this process.
14. Christopher Duffy, *Eagles Over the Alps – Suvorov in Italy and Switzerland, 1799* (Chicago IL, The Emperor's Press, 1999), pp. 218–19.
15. Soult, *Memoires du Marechal-General Soult*, Vol. 1, p. 538.
16. Hayman, *Soult*, p. 35, here Hayman was using a quotation from Anacharsis Combes, *Histoire anecdotique de Jean-de-Dieu Soult, maréchal-général, duc de Dalmatie, 1769–1851* (Castres, HUC, Léon Bertrand, 1870). It is possible that the wily Massena (notorious for his avarice and looting) may have been complicit in selling or allocating resources elsewhere but Soult clearly believed he had been duped.
17. James Marshall-Cornwall, *Marshal Massena* (London, Oxford University Press, 1965), pp. 66–9. This volume contains numerous references to both alleged and proven financial misappropriation by Massena. Indeed, Napoleon became so incensed by his shameless acts of embezzlement that he simply confiscated the sum of 3 million francs Massena had deposited in a Genoese bank. The Marshal's failure to protest at this implies that he had not acquired the funds legally, pp. 270–1.
18. R.F. Delderfield, *The March of the Twenty-Six* (London, Hodder & Stoughton, 1962), p. 86.
19. Arthur John Butler (ed. and trans.), *The Memoirs of Baron Thiébault*, 2 vols (London, Smith, Elder & Co., 1896), Vol. 2, p. 42.
20. Priscilla Hayter Napier, *The Sword Dance* (London, Joseph, 1971), p. 159. Napier uses a quotation from Soult in French, '*Ah, Monsieur, c'est une autre grande question.*'
21. David G. Chandler, *On the Napoleonic Wars* (London, Greenhill Books, 1999), p. 99. Napoleon knew that he had widespread support in the army and hoped that those he promoted to high rank would bolster his regime.
22. Laurence Currie, *The Bâton in the Knapsack – New Light on Napoleon and his Marshals* (London, John Murray, 1934), p. 11.
23. Delderfield, *The March of the Twenty-Six*, p. 36.
24. Butler (ed. and trans.), *The Memoirs of Baron Thiébault*, Vol. 2, p. 146.
25. Ibid., p. 147. Lannes and Bessières came close to fighting a duel during a lull in the fighting at Aspern-Essling in 1809 and were only prevented by the intervention of Marshal Massena, see Arthur John Butler (ed. and trans.), *The Memoirs of Baron de Marbot* (London, Cassell & Co. Ltd, 1929), p. 215.

26. Butler (ed. and trans.), *The Memoirs of Baron Thiébault*, Vol. 2, p. 178.
27. Ibid., p. 179.
28. Hayman, *Soult*, p. 13.
29. Chandler (ed.), *Napoleon's Marshals*, p. 466. Furthermore, Chandler recorded that while the memory of Austerlitz was commemorated in many forms, Napoleon refused Soult's request to be created 'Duke of Austerlitz' in 1808 as he deemed it his personal triumph, see David G. Chandler, *Austerlitz 1805* (London, Osprey, 1990), pp. 85–6. Hayman concurs with this remarking that 'Austerlitz was reserved for the Emperor himself', see Hayman, *Soult*, p. 81, as does Brigadier Peter Young, *Napoleon's Marshals* (Reading, Osprey Publishing Ltd, 1973), p. 79.
30. Delderfield, *The March of the Twenty-Six*, p. 106. Macdonnell also notes that Soult was extremely keen to be associated with the decisive victory at Austerlitz, see A.G. Macdonell, *Napoleon and his Marshals* (London, Prion, 1996, first edn 1934), p. 99.
31. Chandler (ed.), *Napoleon's Marshals*, pp. 466–7.
32. General Comte de Sainte-Charmans, *Mémoires du Général Comte de Saint-Chamans* (Paris, Librarie Plon, 1896), p. 35.
33. Young, *Napoleon's Marshals*, p. 79.
34. Currie, *The Bâton in the Knapsack*, pp. 77–8.
35. Young, *Napoleon's Marshals*, p. 79.
36. Delderfield, *The March of the Twenty-Six*, p. 126.
37. Chandler (ed.), *Napoleon's Marshals*, p. 467.
38. Christopher Hibbert, *Corunna* (London, B.T. Batsford Ltd, 1961), p. 112. This extract is from a letter Napoleon wrote to King Joseph on 27 December 1808.
39. Major General Sir William Napier, *History of the War in the Peninsula and in the South of France*, 6 vols (London, Frederick Warne and Co., 1851), Vol. 1, p. 340.
40. Hayman, *Soult*, p. 16.
41. Delderfield relays one such gallant incidence during the retreat, 'but even under these appalling conditions the war did not degenerate into the kind of savagery that was now commonplace whenever the French clashed with the Spaniards. At one town the French advance guard heard the cries of women and children coming from a large barn and on opening the doors they found over a thousand half-starved and half-naked camp-followers who had been unable to keep up with the British rate of march. The poor wretches were fed and warmed and a message was sent ahead under a flag of truce to say that they would be returned unharmed the moment the weather mended.', Delderfield, *The March of the Twenty-Six*, p. 143.
42. *Gentleman's Magazine*, Vol. LXXIX (London, John Nichols and Son, 1809), p. 171. This extract, along with those that follow, was taken from the 29th Bulletin of the French Army during this campaign.
43. Ibid.
44. Ibid. Most British accounts agree that the captains of several transports panicked as roundshot fell among them and ran aground to be captured by the French, see Philip Haythornthwaite, *Corunna 1809 – Sir John Moore's Fighting Retreat* (Oxford, Osprey Publishing Limited, 2001), p. 87.
45. Ibid., p. 172.
46. Chandler (ed.), *Napoleon's Marshals*, p. 477, Griffith reinforces his view by referring to the research of Jean Tulard, who stated, 'There has been no serious work on Soult.', Jean

Tulard, *Napoléon – the Myth of the Saviour*, trans. Teresa Waugh (London, Weidenfeld & Nicolson Ltd, 1984, first edn 1977), p. 385.

47. Chandler (ed.), *Napoleon's Marshals*, p. 458.
48. Currie, *The Bâton in the Knapsack*, pp. 77–8.

Chapter 3

1. Arthur John Butler (ed. and trans.), *The Memoirs of Baron Thiébault*, 2 vols (London, Smith, Elder & Co., 1896), Vol. 2, p. 239.
2. Ibid. While the Northern provinces were not plundered as badly as those in central and southern Portugal in 1808, the war drained the resources of the entire nation and the north suffered a severe loss of trade due to the Royal Navy blockade. Even though the Douro Valley was fertile and rich during peacetime, Thiébault's assessment that this was a 'land of plenty' was misleading. In fairness, the region may have been different when he last viewed it but Thiébault must have been aware that it would have suffered since that time. Furthermore, while the coastal roads were well maintained, those further inland were markedly inferior presenting difficulties for a large force equipped with wheeled transport. He must surely have had knowledge of these factors so it seems that his report to the emperor was biased and even dishonest, probably due to Napoleon's stinging criticism of his own actions in Portugal the previous year.
3. Charles Oman, *A History of the Peninsular War, 1807–9*, 7 vols (Oxford, The Clarendon Press, 1902), Vol. 2, p. 19.
4. J.W. Fortescue, *A History of the British Army*, 13 vols (London, Macmillan and Co. Ltd, 1912–20), Vol. 7, p. 113.
5. Ibid. Forjaz argued that the Regency lacked enough muskets to equip 19,000 men, which would have been an adequate force to oppose Soult. However, Fortescue points out that 32,000 muskets were unloaded by the Royal Navy at Lisbon up to September 1808, quoting *Parliamentary Papers*, 1809, p. 898. Admittedly, muskets were in great demand and may have been sent to Almeida, Elvas or elsewhere but the Regency had been supplied with a large amount of arms and munitions and should have been able to equip a sizeable force.
6. Fortescue, *A History of the British Army*, Vol. 7, pp. 114–15.
7. Oman records that in 1809–10 the Lusitanian Legion comprised three infantry battalions, which were each 1,000-men strong and divided into 10 companies. It fielded one small artillery battery and (on paper) possessed a cavalry regiment divided into three squadrons, although the cavalry contingent was probably never up to full strength. At this time, the force totalled around 3,500 men and in 1811 these became part of the Anglo-Portuguese army forming the 7th, 8th and 9th Cazadores. See Oman, *A History of the Peninsular War*, Vol. 2, p. 631.
8. Michael Glover, *A Very Slippery Fellow – The Life of Sir Robert Wilson 1777–1849* (Oxford, Oxford University Press, 1978), p. 48.
9. Ibid., p. 53.
10. Ibid., p. 55, quoting ADMS, ff. 268, 270.
11. Ibid., quoting ADMS, f. 315.
12. Fortescue, *A History of the British Army*, Vol. 7, p. 120.
13. Major General Sir William Napier, *History of the War in the Peninsula and in the South of France*, 6 vols (London, Frederick Warne and Co., 1851), Vol. 2, p. 30.

14. Ibid., p. 21. Fortescue concurred with this view to an extent and he wrote, 'The unfortunate Cradock, who had been told that the main body of the British army was to fight elsewhere, and that only a small force was to be left, not to defend, but to aid in the defence of Portugal, and to embark if the task were found to be impossible, was in a very difficult position, and one which cannot be compared with that of Wellesley a few months later', Fortescue, *A History of the British Army*, Vol. 7, p. 119.

15. Fortescue, *A History of the British Army*, Vol. 7, pp. 119–20.

16. Oman, *A History of the Peninsular War*, Vol. 2, pp. 170–1.

17. Fortescue, *A History of the British Army*, Vol. 7, p. 111. Oman records that 1,500 cannon, 20,000 British muskets and 8 ships-of-the-line were taken by the French along with substantial amounts of ammunition and other supplies – Oman, *A History of the Peninsular War*, Vol. 2, p. 175.

18. Oman, *A History of the Peninsular War*, Vol. 2, p. 176. Oman also elaborated on this stating, 'But Soult, when he had advanced into Portugal, was as much out of touch with the other French corps as if he had been operating in Poland or Naples.', p. 176.

19. Maréchal Jean Baptiste Jourdan, *Mémoires Militaires (Guerre d'Espagne)* (Paris, Ernest Flammarion – Impreimerie de Lagny, 1899), p. 102. Many officers remarked that campaigning in the Peninsula was very different to central Europe where the French army was used to fighting. The countryside was often mountainous, roads were poor and the weather could hamper travel. Even allowing for these conditions, poor maps also held up couriers and, with the French so unpopular, locals were extremely reluctant to provide guides from fear of reprisals.

20. Oman, *A History of the Peninsular War*, Vol. 7, p. 177.

21. Peter Hayman, *Soult – Napoleon's Maligned Marshal* (London, Arms and Armour Press, 1990), p. 101. Oman's figures for II Corps place their number within this broad remit and he estimates the total of II Corps alone at 21,452 on 1 February 1809. With the addition of Lahoussaye's and Lorge's commands, he adds another 2,000 men to this figure, see Oman, *A History of the Peninsular War*, Vol. 7, p. 625.

22. Louis and Antoinette de Sainte-Pierre (eds), *Mémoires du Maréchal Soult: Espagne et Portugal* (Paris, Hachette, 1955), p. 68. Popular feeling against the French ran so high that Spanish and Portuguese commanders were rarely short of volunteers. However, their main problem was that while many of these were enthusiastic, they lacked military training.

23. Pierre le Noble, *Mémoires sur les operations militaries des français en Galice, Portugal et la vallée du Tage en 1809 sous le commandement du Maréchal Soult, duc de Dalmatie, avec un atlas militaire* (Paris, chez Barrois l'aîné, librarie, 1821), pp. 76–9.

24. Joseph de Naylies, *Mémoires sur la guerre d'Espagne pendant les années 1808, 1809, 1810 et 1811* (Paris, Magimel, Anselin et Pochard, 1817), p. 61.

25. Napier, *History of the War in the Peninsula*, Vol. 2, p. 38.

26. Ibid., pp. 63–7. *A chevaux de frise* was a wooden defensive obstruction usually consisting of a long horizontal beam with rows of sharpened stakes protruding at various angles. Often used to block roads, reinforce field fortifications or close up a breach battered in the wall of a fort, it was particularly useful against cavalry as horses usually balked before such a barrier. The literal translation is 'horse of Friesland', the name originating from its initial use by the Frisians.

27. Ibid., pp. 63–7.

28. Ibid., pp. 66–7.
29. Ibid., pp. 41–2.
30. Hayman, *Soult*, p. 103.
31. General Comte de Sainte-Charmans, *Mémoires du Général Comte de Sainte-Charmans* (Paris, Librarie Plon, 1896), pp. 119–21. By 'marauder' Sainte-Charmans did not necessarily mean the word in its harshest sense but was referring to men who left the column (often with permission) in order to forage for supplies. This concurred with the French army policy of 'living off the land', which was viewed as looting by many and was certainly seen as theft by the peasantry, since payment for goods was rarely offered.
32. I.J. Rousseau (ed.), *The Peninsular Journal of Major-General Sir Benjamin D'Urban, 1808–1817* (London, Longmans, Green and Co., 1930), p. 44.
33. Napier, *History of the War in the Peninsula* , Vol. 2, p. 49.
34. Ibid., p. 50.
35. Ibid., p. 51. Eben also recorded that Villaboas, an officer on Freire's staff, was killed on the doorstep of his quarters as he came to appeal to him for protection, pp. 51–2.
36. Hayman, *Soult*, p. 103.
37. Ibid.
38. Jaques Albin Simon Collin de Plancey, *Fastes militaires des Belges, ou Histoire des guerres, sièges, conquêtes, expéditions et faits d'armes, qui ont illustré la Belgique depuis l'invasion de César jusqu'a nos jours*, 4 vols (Bruxelles, au Bureau des fastes militaries, 1835–6), Vol. 4, p. 290. Henri-Antoine Jardon was renowned as the 'Voltigeur General' and Plancey recorded, 'Thus died, at the age of 41 years, one of the bravest of Napoleon's officers, in whom erudition had been replaced by prowess and experience. One could fill a whole book with stories of the feats of Jardon. His soldiers, who loved him as a father, mourned greatly his death. During the Republic, he was the friend of Moreau, of Pichegru, of Souham; under the Empire he had friendly relations with Regnier, Gudin and Soult. He still awaits a monument in his homeland.' Voltigeurs were French light infantrymen who often skirmished with their counterparts to soften up the enemy for a major attack. Oman also wrote of his fall, 'Finding his men checked for a moment, he had seized a musket and charged on foot at the head of his skirmishing line. This was not the place for a brigadier-general, and Jardon died unnecessarily, doing the work of a sub-lieutenant.', see Oman, *A History of the Peninsular War*, Vol. 2, p. 239.

Chapter 4

1. Henry Noel Shore, Baron Teignmouth, *Three Pleasant Springs in Portugal* (London, Sampson Low, Marston & Company, 1899), pp. 198–202. In relation to the city's title, Teignmouth continued, 'It is a pleasant conceit, if not historically true. And the inhabitants lay claim to the distinction on the strength of the brave defence their city made when besieged by the troops of Dom Miguel, the usurper, in 1833.' He also admitted that Porto changed hands twice during 1809, claiming, 'Few towns in Europe have been the scene of more stirring events, or of more fighting and bloodshed, than Oporto.'
2. *The Times*, 17 April 1809, p. 3. For further comment on these murders see Luís António de Oliveira Ramos, 'Os afrancesados do Porto', *Revista de história*, Vol. 3 (1980), pp. 115–26. According to Oman, the bishop said words to the effect that, 'he could not stand in the way of the righteous vengeance of the people upon traitors', see Charles Oman, *A History*

of the Peninsular War, 1807–9, 7 vols (Oxford, The Clarendon Press, 1902),Vol. 2, p. 242. Napier also records that passions in the city had reached a fever pitch with the approach of Soult's army, with priests, monks and reactionaries inciting hatred against the French, see Major General Sir William Napier, *History of the War in the Peninsula and in the South of France*, 6 vols (London, Frederick Warne and Co., 1851), Vol. 2, p. 56.

3. 'It is supposed that about 15 ships, having on board 3000 pipes of wine, were in the harbour when the French took possession of the place. On the 27th, when the British left Oporto, the state of the weather was such, that no vessel could possibly cross the bar.', *The Times*, 15 April 1809, p. 3. However, Oman believed that at least thirty merchant ships lay stranded in Porto, see Oman, *A History of the Peninsular War*, Vol. 2, p. 242. Napier also claims the batteries on the Serra do Pilar contained as many as fifty guns, p. 56.

4. Oman, *A History of the Peninsular War*, Vol. 2, pp. 240–1. Napier puts the figure at 50,000, *History of the War in the Peninsula*, Vol. 2, p. 56.

5. Pierre le Noble, *Mémoires sur les operations militaries des français en Galice, Portugal et la vallée du Tage en 1809 sous le commandement du Maréchal Soult, duc de Dalmatie, avec un atlas militaire* (Paris, chez Barrois l'aîné, librarie, 1821), p. 161.

6. Accounts of this incident differ with some French sources claiming that the Portuguese lured Foy into a trap while he was openly carrying a white flag. Others insist that he carried a second message for the Bishop, though this seems unlikely if Soult deemed it so unsafe to send a Frenchman that he chose a prisoner as his initial emissary. Oman believed that the Portuguese acted correctly in any case, since these officers had no right to ride into enemy lines even during a truce. See Oman, *A History of the Peninsular War*, Vol. 2, p. 243 and Napier, *History of the War in the Peninsula*, Vol. 2, p. 57.

7. David Gates, *The Spanish Ulcer* (London, George Allen & Unwin, 1986), p. 141. Chalot's garrison included several hundred sick and wounded from Soult's army and he surrendered 23 officers and 800 men along with 60 wagons, 339 horses and part of Soult's military treasury valued at £6,000. See Digby Smith, *The Greenhill Napoleonic Wards Data Book – Actions and Losses in Personnel, Colours, Standards and Artillery, 1792–1815* (London, Greenhill Books, 1998), p. 283.

8. Napier, *History of the War in the Peninsula*, Vol. 2, p. 58 and Oman, *A History of the Peninsular War*, Vol. 2, p. 243.

9. Napier, *History of the War in the Peninsula*, Vol. 2, p. 59, Oman, *A History of the Peninsular War*, Vol. 2, p. 246 and Gates, *The Spanish Ulcer*, p. 141.

10. Auguste Bigarré, *Mémoires du Général Bigarré, aide-de-camp due Roi Joseph, 1775–1813* (Paris, Ernest Kolb, Chailley, 1903), pp. 241–2.

11. Both Napier and Gates claim 4,000 were lost in this incident, see Napier, *History of the War in the Peninsula*, Vol. 2, p. 59 and Gates, *The Spanish Ulcer*, p. 141.

12. Napier recorded that the French had their own grievances to avenge, 'exasperated by long hardships, and prone like all soldiers to ferocity and violence during an assault, became frantic with fury when in one of the principal squares they found several of their comrades, who had been made prisoners, fastened upright and living, but with their eyes burst, their tongues torn out, and their other members mutilated and gashed: those that beheld them spared none.', Napier, *History of the War in the Peninsula*, Vol. 2, p. 60.

13. Joseph de Naylies, *Mémoires sur la guerre d'Espagne pendant les années 1808, 1809, 1810 et 1811* (Paris, Magimel, Anselin et Pochard, 1817), pp. 99–100. Fortescue summed up the aftermath of the First Battle of Porto effectively, 'The French soldiers … passed for a time completely out of control, and indemnified themselves for past hardships, sufferings and humiliations by sacking the city from cellar to garret, with the usual accompaniments of rape, drunkenness, and wanton destruction', see J.W. Fortescue, *A History of the British Army*, 13 vols (London, Macmillan and Co. Ltd, 1912–20), Vol. 7, p. 134.

14. Oman, *A History of the Peninsular War*, Vol. 2, p. 248. Here Oman refers to two sieges undertaken by Wellington in Spain during 1812 and 1813. The storming of Badajoz by the British army is particularly notorious as soldiers, maddened by their appalling losses, sacked the town for two to three days committing many depredations. The fact that those who suffered the most were Spanish (British allies) made the incident even worse. Wellington had to erect gallows to restore discipline and talk about the siege arouses strong emotions in Badajoz even today.

15. *Literary Panorama and National Register 1809*, Vol. 6, April–August (London, printed by Cox, Son, and Baylis for C. Taylor, 1809), pp. 581–2.

16. Ibid. The article ended with the following statement, 'There is too much reason to believe that this information is true: as it is corroborated by the following article which has appeared in the French gazettes, dated *Bayonne, April 30*. – According to a letter from Madrid, arrived this morning, the Duke of Dalmatia took Oporto by storm, and put the whole garrison to the sword, for having put to death *two* French *parlementaires*.'

17. Fortescue, *A History of the British Army*, Vol. 7, pp. 136–7.

18. René Chartrand, *Oldest Allies – Alcantara 1809* (Oxford, Osprey Publishing Ltd, 2012), pp. 31–2.

19. Smith, *The Greenhill Napoleonic Wards Data Book* , pp. 283–4. Smith records that Victor reported 300 killed or wounded but I Corps probably suffered in the region of 700 casualties according to other sources. Estimates of Spanish losses vary but most are in the region of 8,000 killed or wounded with 2,000 taken prisoner. The number of cannon captured by the French was between 16 and 20 and at least 9–12 colours were taken. This battle saw Cuesta's army completely dispersed and it was days before the Spanish could assemble as much as a battalion to form the basis of a new army. Nevertheless, by April Cuesta had amassed a force of 20,000 infantry and 3,000 cavalry.

20. See Michael Glover, *A Very Slippery Fellow – The Life of Sir Robert Wilson 1777–1849* (Oxford, Oxford University Press, 1978), p. 58, Fortescue, *A History of the British Army*, Vol. 7, pp. 135–6 and Chartrand, *Oldest Allies*, p. 60. Chartrand emphasises that, while events between January and March were influential, it was the capture of Alacantara on 12 April that really worried the marshal, which led to a serious action to dislodge them on 14 May.

21. Fortescue, *A History of the British Army*, Vol. 7, p. 140. This extract is from Cradock's last letter to Castlereagh while he retained command in Portugal.

22. See Smith, *The Greenhill Napoleonic Wards Data Book*, p. 284, Napier, *History of the War in the Peninsula*, Vol. 2, p. 60, Fortescue, *A History of the British Army*, Vol. 7, p. 134 and Oman, *A History of the Peninsular War*, Vol. 2, p. 249.

23. Oman, *A History of the Peninsular War*, Vol. 2, p. 249. Oman actually went further in his summary of Soult's predicament, writing, 'The main task which his master had set

192 Wellington Against Soult

before him, the capture of Lisbon, he was never able to contemplate, much less take in hand.'

24. Lloyd's List printed that the following vessels (along with the names of their captains/masters) had been captured by the French at Porto, 'The Little Mary, Brooks; Atalanta Batterbye; Mary, Beck; Favorite, Liddell; Phœnix, Tomlinson; Anna, Palmer; Lord Howick, Anderson; Noah, Bowman; Progress, Barker; Charlotte, Watson; Aquilon, Thomas; John, Haywood; Unity, Gardner; Elizabeth, Henderson; Queen, Marshall; Harmony, Penson (all fully laden, except the Charlotte, which had only about 50 Pipes of Wine on board) were taken in Oporto by the French on the 29th of March – the two latter are since lost. – Some Portugueze and Neutral Vessels, bound to England, were also taken.' See Lloyd's List, 1809, No. 4353 (London, printed by W. Phillips), Friday, 19 May 1809 (no page numbers).

Chapter 5

1. Elizabeth Longford, *Wellington – The Years of the Sword* (London, World Books, 1971), p. 21. The British army had a poor reputation in Great Britain at the end of the eighteenth century. While officers had high status in society, the army was regarded as a poor career for talented gentlemen and the rank and file were looked down upon as many enlisted because of unemployment, a wish to avoid gaol or for the alcohol ration. Private soldiers received lower wages than labourers at this time and the public failed to appreciate the army's services until the end of the Napoleonic Wars, the great victory at Waterloo 1815 doing much to change attitudes.

2. Philip Guedalla, *The Duke* (London, Hodder & Stoughton, 1933), p. 27.

3. J.W. Fortescue, *A History of the British Army*, 13 vols (London, Macmillan and Co. Ltd, 1912–20), Vol. 5, p. 25. Fortescue comments on Wellesley's usual reluctance to attack the Mahrattas when they had mounted a prepared defence as he recognised their skill in choosing positions that were 'confoundedly strong and difficult of access'. Yet, at Assaye he felt he had no choice. See p. 24.

4. John Wilson Croker, *The Croker Papers: The Correspondence and Diaries of John Wilson Croker, Secretary to the Admiralty from 1809 to 1830*, 3 vols (London, John Murray, 1885), Vol. 1, p. 354.

5. Writing to Major Malcolm from camp on 26 September 1803, a triumphant Wellesley stated, 'Our loss has been very severe; but we have got more than 90 guns, 70 of which are the finest brass ordnance I have ever seen. The enemy, in great consternation, are gone down the Ghauts, Stephenson follows them tomorrow ... It is reported that Jardoon Rao is missing. They say that Scindiah and Ragojee are stupefied by their defeat ... their baggage was plundered by their own people, and many of their troops are gone off', see Second Duke of Wellington (ed.), *Supplementary Despatches, Correspondence, and Memoranda of Field Marshal the Duke of Wellington*, 15 vols (London, John Murray, 1858–72), Vol. 4, pp. 180–1.

6. G.R. Gleig, *Life of Wellington* (London, Longman, Green, Longman and Roberts, 1862), pp. 430–1.

7. David Buttery, *Wellington Against Junot – The First Invasion of Portugal 1807–1808* (Barnsley, Pen & Sword Books Ltd, 2011) , pp. 144–7; see also Chapter 9 for details and comment on the Convention of Sintra and the resulting Inquiry, pp.134–48.

8. *Cobbett's Parliamentary Debates*, Vol. 12, 19 Jan–7 March 1809 (London, T.C. Hansard, 1809), p. 312.

9. Second Duke of Wellington (ed.), *Supplementary Despatches*, Vol. 6, p. 225 – Viscount Castlereagh to Sir Arthur Wellesley from Downing Street, London, 11 April 1809.

10. Opinion is divided over Cradock's abilities and historian Jac Weller was surprised that Sir Arthur was one of his few supporters 'treating him with both respect and consideration' as most contemporaries and historians considered him timorous and ineffectual due to his lack of offensive action in 1809, Jac Weller, *Wellington in the Peninsula 1808–1814* (London, Purnell Book Services Ltd, 1973, first edn 1962), p. 70. Yet, some historians take a more generous view, acknowledging that 'Cradock had some reason to complain. He had done excellent work with inadequate means in the face of no ordinary difficulties, and he was summarily and unceremoniously superseded.', Alexander Innes Shand, *The War in the Peninsula 1808–1814* (London, Seeley and Co. Ltd, 1898), p. 68. Although undoubtedly biased, General Lord Howden (Cradock's only son) later wrote about his father's replacement, commenting 'Of Sir John Cradock's feelings at such a moment, just as he was about to reap the reward of several months labour and anxiety, it is unnecessary to make any remark – they can be imagined without much difficulty …', *United Service Magazine*, 1839, Part III, p. 97.

11. I.J. Rousseau (ed.), *The Peninsular Journal of Major-General Sir Benjamin D'Urban, 1808–1817* (London, Longmans, Green and Co., 1930), p. 50. D'Urban wrote this entry on 10 April 1809.

12. Second Duke of Wellington (ed.), *Supplementary Despatches*, Vol. 6, p. 774.

13. Sir Charles Oman, *Wellington's Army 1809–1814* (London, Greenhill Books, 2006, first edn 1913), p. 231.

14. Oman, *Wellington's Army*, pp. 229–31. Also, Colonel H.C.B. Rogers, *Wellington's Army* (Shepperton, Ian Allen Printing Ltd, 1979), p. 74. Rogers believed the Portuguese cavalry were inferior to the infantry and that three regiments were obliged to fight on foot due to lack of horses.

15. Rogers, *Wellington's Army*, p. 74. Line regiments were given blue and white uniforms but Caçadores had brown uniforms signifying their elite status. While their accoutrements emulated the British rifle regiments, only a portion of these units had been issued the Baker rifle at this time and most still carried muskets in 1809.

16. Sir Charles Oman, *Wellington's Army 1809–1814* (London, Greenhill Books Ltd, 2006), p. 235.

17. *Scots Magazine and Edinburgh Literary Miscellany*, May 1809, Vol. 71, p. 382. The *London Chronicle* also quoted extracts, commenting sarcastically, 'This is certainly a very petty sample of Portuguese valour and enthusiasm', Vol. 105, 24 April 1809, p. 292. Both of these British sources drew upon the original article printed in the *Lisbon Gazette* for this information. The proclamation was issued from Beresford's headquarters, then at Calhariz on 2 April. Ensign John Aitchison also commented, 'All accounts agree that it was want of proper example that caused the fall of Oporto, and there is very little doubt that had 1,000 British soldiers been in that own it would *yet* have been possessed by the Portuguese.', W.F.K. Thompson (ed.), *An Ensign in the Peninsular War – The Letters of John Aitchison* (London, Michael Joseph Ltd, 1994, first edn 1981), p. 36.

18. *The London Chronicle*, Vol. 105, Tuesday, 16 May–Wednesday, 17 May 1809, p. 467. The *Chronicle* recorded that 'The following persons had been arrested at Lisbon, suspected

of treasonable communication: BIAZ FRANCISCO LIMA; MOUN, a Captain in the Portuguese navy; **SALES, an eminent merchant, at whose palace General BERESFORD** lodged; Mr. PAYRA, his wife, and her father, Monsieur Rollin, formerly a French Consul in the reign of Louis XVI; the Chief Magistrate of Abrantes, and many others. Doctor Payra, one of the Physicians of the Prince Regent, underwent the first part of his sentence, to be whipped, and afterwards transported to Angola …'.

19. Wordsworth used less guarded language in a private letter, commenting, 'We see, from the events which have taken place at Oporto and at Lisbon, that victory after victory in the field turns to no account, if the affections of the people are alienated by tyranny. There would have been little occasion for General Beresford's proclamations, and those of the Portuguese government complaining of reports to the prejudice of the English, if it had not been for D. and W's cursed Conventions …', see Daniel Stuart, *Letters from the Lake Poets, Samuel Taylor Coleridge, William Wordsworth, Robert Southey, to Daniel Stuart, Editor of The Morning Post and The Courier, 1800–1838* (London, West, Newman and Co. (printed for private circulation), 1889), pp. 341–4 (fifth letter posted on 6 May 1809). D and W are generals Dalrymple and Wellesley. For Wordsworth's tract on Sintra see William Wordsworth, *Wordsworth's Tract on the Convention of Cintra* (London, Humphrey Milford, 1915, first edn 1809).

20. Oman, *A History of the Peninsular War*, Vol. 2, p. 292. Wellesley wrote similar statements to Castlereagh and Oman divined that, 'In short, he had fathomed the great secret, that Napoleon's military power – vast as it was – had its limits: that the Emperor could not send to Spain a force sufficient to hold down every province of a thoroughly disaffected country and also provide (over and above the garrisons) a field army large enough to beat the Anglo-Portuguese and capture Lisbon.', pp. 293–4.

Chapter 6

1. Louis and Antoinette de Sainte-Pierre (eds), *Mémoires du Maréchal Soult: Espagne et Portugal* (Paris, Hachette, 1955), p. 78.
2. Manuel Pinheiro Chagas, *Historia de Portugal*, 8 vols (Empreza da Historia de Portugal, Livraria Moderna, 1903), Vol. 8, p. 8. Some of Soult's contemporaries expressed similar views arguing that he should not have paused on the Douro and that an immediate march on Lisbon would been wiser, see Arthur John Butler (ed. and trans.), *The Memoirs of Baron Thiébault*, 2 vols (London, Smith, Elder & Co., 1896), Vol. 2, p. 256.
3. Charles Oman, *A History of the Peninsular War, 1807–9*, 7 vols (Oxford, The Clarendon Press, 1902), Vol. 2, p. 273.
4. Peter Hayman, *Soult – Napoleon's Maligned Marshal* (London, Arms and Armour Press, 1990), p. 111.
5. Major General Sir William Napier, *History of the War in the Peninsula and in the South of France*, 6 vols (London, Frederick Warne and Co., 1851), Vol. 2, p. 454, from Captain Brotherton's letter to Colonel Donkin (Quarter Master General), 17 March 1809. Cradock also wrote to Lord Castlereagh in a similar vein, stating, 'It also appears to be the object of the enemy to ingratiate himself with the populace of Oporto, *by even feeding them*, and granting further indulgences.' From a letter dated 20 April 1809, 'It is also said that a Portuguese legion, to consist of *six thousand men*, has been instituted.', pp. 454–5.

6. Oman, *A History of the Peninsular War*, Vol. 2, pp. 275–6. Considering that Soult despised his nickname (see Chapter 2), shouts of '*Viva o Roi Jean*' ('Long live King John') would be more likely had he endorsed these events. Oman cites Pierre le Noble, *Mémoires sur les operations militaries des français en Galice, Portugal et la vallée du Tage en 1809 sous le commandement du Maréchal Soult, duc de Dalmatie, avec un atlas militaire* (Paris, chez Barrois l'ainé, librarie, 1821), p. 120 and Fantin des Odoards, *Journal du Général Fantin des Odoards – Etapes d'un Officer de la Grande Armee 1800–1830* (Paris, Libraire Plon, E. Plon, Nourrit et Cie Imprimeurs-Éditeurs, 1895), p. 213, Oman, *A History of the Peninsular War*, Vol. 2, p. 227, as sources for the replacement of church silver and Soult's proclamations. Fantin des Odoards expressed his shock at seeing these posters, thinking such a scheme was madness because of widespread Portuguese opposition to the French.

7. Alexander Innes Shand, *The War in the Peninsula 1808–1814* (London, Seeley and Co. Ltd, 1898), p. 66. Some Portuguese sources are voluble in their condemnation of both Britain and France with statements like, 'It is not surprising that, according to popular tradition, the arrival of the French and the English were seen at the time as two different invasions and were both equally detested. More than once in village wells, where the haphazard revenge of the countryfolk buried bodies of the invading foreigners, the red uniforms of the English intermingled with the hated uniforms of Napoleon's soldiers.', Pinheiro Chagas, *Historia de Portugal*, Vol. 8, p. 27.

8. Pinheiro Chagas, *Historia de Portugal*, Vol. 8, pp. 13 and 26. Many among the nobility and gentry favoured France due to her more enlightened system before the First Invasion of Portugal. Furthermore, many of those who stayed after the flight of the Regent did not lament the Braganza's departure but fighting during 1808 virtually united the common people against the French. Feeling ran so high that those who did possess pro-French sentiments were unlikely to admit it for fear of reprisals.

9. Delderfield placed Soult's ambitions in context, declaring, 'It was, of course, Napoleon's fault that he was a victim of this obsession. Napoleon had made his brother-in-law Murat a king and at the same time had refused to make him, Soult, His Grace the Duke of Austerlitz. If Murat could rule Naples then Nicholas Soult was sure he could rule Portugal …', R.F. Delderfield, *The March of the Twenty-Six* (London, Hodder & Stoughton, 1962), p. 146.

10. Napier, *History of the War in the* Peninsula, Vol. 2, p. 97.

11. *The Despatches of Field Marshal the Duke of Wellington During his Various Campaigns*, compiled by Lieutenant Colonel Gurwood, 13 vols (London, John Murray, 1834–8), Vol. 4, p. 276. Extract from a letter to Castlereagh dated 27 April 1809 (his first meeting with Argenton was 25 April).

12. Ibid.

13. Oman, *A History of the Peninsular War*, Vol. 2, p. 634, extract from a letter from Wellesley to Castlereagh, written from Villa Nova, 15 May 1809.

14. Ibid., p. 284. There were groups and societies in France dedicated to the overthrow of Napoleon, although few had much support at this time. According to Napier, if the conspirators failed to get the concessions they wanted from the emperor they would replace him with Marshal St Cyr, see Napier, *History of the War in the Peninsula*, Vol. 2, p. 96.

15. Oman, *A History of the Peninsular War*, Vol. 2, p. 634, extract from a letter from Wellesley to Castlereagh, written from Villa Nova, 15 May 1809.

16. Colonel James J. Graham, *Military ends and moral means: exemplifying the higher influences affecting military life and character; the motives to enlistment; the use of stratagems in war; the necessity of standing armies; and the duties of a military force aiding the civil power* (London, Smith, Elder and Co., 1864), p. 444.

17. Hayman, *Soult*, p. 116.

18. Arthur John Butler (ed. and trans.), *The Memoirs of Baron Thiébault*, 2 vols (London, Smith, Elder & Co., 1896), Vol. 2, p. 259.

19. Delderfield, *The March of the Twenty-Six*, pp. 146–7.

20. Henry Colburn and Richard Bentley, *Memoirs of the Duchess d'Abrantès* (Madame Junot), 8 vols (London, Henry Colburn and Richard Bentley, 1831–5), Vol. 6, pp. 324–7.

21. J.M. Thompson (ed.), *Letters of Napoleon* (Oxford, Basil Blackwell, 1934), p. 249, taken from a letter written at Schönbrunn and dated 26 September 1809.

22. Ibid. From Latin, the words *proprio motu* translate as 'own motion' and *lèse-majesté* translates from French as 'aggrieved majesty' (or to give offence to the sovereign).

23. Ibid., p. 250. Napoleon was outraged by the conspiracy and ordered his Minister of Police to carry out a full investigation, writing, 'I send you a letter from the Duke of Dalmatia, and the inquiry of a Lieutenant of Gendarmerie into a strange and altogether extraordinary event. A certain Argenton, an adjutant-major in the 18th Dragoon regiment in Spain, who has served with us, who fought through the Egyptian campaign, whom I do not know personally, but who had the reputation of being a faithful and reliable man, has, how I know not, been led away by the English. You will see, by several letters taken from him, and which I send you, that his wife's relations live at Tours. You will collect information as to his family. Colonel Lafitte, who is mixed up in this business, is one of the most faithful of soldiers, a man whom everyone is ready to answer for. The whole business is a very strange one.', Lady Mary Lloyd (ed. and trans.), *New Letters of Napoleon I, Omitted from the Edition Published Under the Auspices of Napoleon III [by Napoleon I, Emperor of the French]* (New York, D. Appleton, 1897), p. 131, taken from a letter to Comte Fouché, Minister of Police and dated Schönbrunn, 30 June 1809.

24. Sainte-Pierre (eds), *Mémoires du Maréchal Soult*, pp. 111–12.

25. Ibid., p. 114.

26. See Arthur John Butler (ed. and trans.), *The Memoirs of Baron de Marbot Late Lieutenant-General in the French Army*, 2 vols (London, Longmans, Green and Co., 1892), Vol. 2, p. 365 and Maréchal Jean Baptiste Jourdan, *Mémoires Militaires (Guerre d'Espagne)* (Paris, Ernest Flammarion – Impreimerie de Lagny, 1899), p. 191.

27. Colburn and Bentley, *Memoirs of the Duchess d'Abrantès*, Vol. 6, pp. 324–7. Madam d'Abrantes' acknowledged that one of Soult's supporters wrote the biography she found. Her own account is very entertaining and she introduced the subject of the Second Invasion of Portugal in the following manner, 'The adventure of the second expedition to Portugal happened about the same time; I call it an adventure, because the facts were perfectly romantic. That gleam of ambition, the undefined shadow of which was thrown across his path by one of his captains, was one of the most extraordinary incidents of Napoleon's reign.'

28. Ibid.

29. Butler (ed. and trans.), *The Memoirs of Baron Thiébault*, Vol. 2, pp. 257 and 259. Also Hayman, *Soult*, pp. 114 and 123 for comment on Thiébault's bias.
30. *United Service Magazine*, 1858, Part I, p. 209. The line *doué de tres peu d'esprit, fort passionné, à une ambition sans bornes* translates as 'endowed with very little wit, very passionate and a boundless ambition'.
31. Napier, *History of the War in the Peninsula*, Vol. 2, p. 98.
32. Oman, *A History of the Peninsular War*, Vol. 2, p. 278. Strictly speaking, the spelling 'hare-brained' is more correct for a wild and foolish action.
33. Hayman, *Soult*, p. 112. Oman also agrees that many rumours about Soult's intentions were put about by his detractors but does believe that he had serious aspirations to be king, Oman, *History of the War in the Peninsula*, Vol. 2, p. 273.
34. Sainte-Pierre (eds), *Mémoires du Maréchal Soult*, p. 90.

Chapter 7

1. J.W. Fortescue, *A History of the British Army*, 13 vols (London, Macmillan and Co. Ltd, 1912–20), Vol. 7, pp. 148–9 and 154.
2. W.F.K. Thompson (ed.), *An Ensign in the Peninsular War – The Letters of John Aitchison* (London, Michael Joseph Ltd, 1994, first edn 1981), p. 35. This letter was dated 12 April 1809 and written from Carregado. There were widespread rumours that General Sebastiani was in the region but Aitchison later corrected himself in a letter on 24 April, stating that the general in question was actually Lapisse. He also commented, 'notwithstanding Lisbon is almost to a certainty lost by our advance.', p. 36.
3. Major General Sir William Napier, *History of the War in the Peninsula and in the South of France*, 6 vols (London, Frederick Warne and Co., 1851), Vol. 2, p. 100.
4. Fantin des Odoards, *Journal du Général Fantin des Odoards – Etapes d'un Officer de la Grande Armee 1800–1830* (Paris, Libraire Plon, E. Plon, Nourrit et Cie Imprimeurs-Éditeurs, 1895), p. 226.
5. Charles Oman, *A History of the Peninsular War, 1807–9*, 7 vols (Oxford, The Clarendon Press, 1902), Vol. 2, p. 265.
6. Maréchal Jean Baptiste Jourdan, *Mémoires Militaires (Guerre d'Espagne)* (Paris, Ernest Flammarion – Impreimerie de Lagny, 1899), p. 259.
7. René Chartrand, *Oldest Allies – Alcantara 1809* (Oxford, Osprey Publishing Ltd, 2012), pp. 50–1.
8. Fortescue, *A History of the British Army*, Vol. 7, p. 143. Oman believed that Lapisse's decision to deviate from Napoleon's plan and unite with I Corp was almost entirely due to Wilson's daring and aggressive actions along the frontier, Oman, *A History of the Peninsular War*, Vol. 2, pp. 261–2.
9. Napier, *History of the War in the Peninsula*, Vol. 2, pp. 80–1.
10. *United Service Magazine*, 1831, Part I, pp. 226–7.
11. Napier, *History of the War in the Peninsula*, Vol. 2, p. 81.
12. Oman, *A History of the Peninsular War*, Vol. 2, p. 271.
13. Napier, *History of the War in the Peninsula*, Vol. 2, pp. 100–1.
14. I.J. Rousseau (ed.), *The Peninsular Journal of Major-General Sir Benjamin D'Urban, 1808–1817* (London, Longmans, Green and Co., 1930), p. 51.
15. Lieutenant General Sir William Warre, *Letters from the Peninsula 1808–1812* (London, John Murray, 1909), in a letter to his father from Thomar, 27 April 1809. For an

alternative view, Ensign Aitchison was less sure of his Allies' soldiers, commenting, 'It will not perhaps be quite fair to judge the merits of the Portuguese troops by their appearance, but compared with the men of our army the contrast is certainly very striking. There are a great proportion of boys amongst them and they are all I believe newly raised. On this account the propriety of incorporating them with our troops appears to be very questionable, for but a few young soldiers of any nation will stand fire well and if they are at once thrown into confusion and retire this confusion will soon spread amongst the veterans and the bad effects are incalculable.', Thompson (ed.), *An Ensign in the Peninsular War*, pp. 39–40.

16. *The Despatches of Field Marshal the Duke of Wellington During his Various Campaigns*, compiled by Lieutenant Colonel Gurwood, 13 vols (London, John Murray, 1834–8), Vol. 3, pp. 216–18. Fortescue believed that Wellesley was confident that Beresford and Silveira would have the capability of acting offensively but also recorded Sir Arthur's words of caution, 'Remember,' he wrote to Beresford, '... that you are the commander-in-chief, and must not be beaten; therefore do not undertake anything with your troops unless you have some strong hope of success.', Fortescue, *A History of the British Army*, Vol. 7, p. 153.

17. Napier, *History of the War in the Peninsula*, Vol. 2, p. 102.

18. Fortescue, *A History of the British Army*, Vol. 7, p. 156.

19. *United Service Magazine*, 1829, p. 660. This extract was taken from a series of letters printed by the journal relating to 'A Hussar's Life on Service' and under the title 'An Account of the British Campaign 1809, Under Sir A. Wellesley, in Portugal and Spain', from the revised journal of an officer of the staff of the army. The anonymous officer went on to acknowledge that, 'The exasperation of the French was not wholly uncalled-for, as the atrocities committed on the stragglers and sick were horrible, amounting often, besides shocking lingering deaths, to frightful mutilations.' The phrase *hors de la loi* translates into English as 'outside the law'.

Chapter 8

1. J.W. Fortescue, *A History of the British Army 1807–9*, 13 vols (London, Macmillan and Co. Ltd, 1912–20), Vol. 7, p. 160 and Charles Oman, *A History of the Peninsular War, 1807–9*, 7 vols (Oxford, The Clarendon Press, 1902), Vol. 2, p. 337. Napier believed that Soult moved his headquarters and commented that the 'Serra rock' (the hill that the convent was built upon) obscured his view of the upper river but provided an excellent viewpoint of the estuary, Major General Sir William Napier, *History of the War in the Peninsula and in the South of France*, 6 vols (London, Frederick Warne and Co., 1851), Vol. 2, p. 105.

2. W.F.K. Thompson (ed.), *An Ensign in the Peninsular War – The Letters of John Aitchison* (London, Michael Joseph Ltd, 1994, first edn 1981), p. 39. Aitchison also feared the army would suffer significant losses if they tried to attack here, as Wellesley would hesitate to bombard Porto because of inevitable civilian casualties and widespread destruction of property. He believed Sir Arthur would march upriver and attempt to cross at Lamego. A cavalry officer who rode in Wellesley's vanguard expressed similar doubts, writing, 'As we advanced on the high road to Oporto, this report of the destruction of the bridge was confirmed, and doubts came fast and thick upon us, respecting the passage of the Douro ...' and he also voiced his opinion that, 'The passage of a river in the front of an

enemy is allowed to be the most difficult of military operations ...', see *United Service Magazine*, (1829), Part II, p. 660.

3. Fortescue, *A History of the British Army*, Vol. 7, p. 158. Fortescue visited Porto during the early twentieth century and commented that the remains of the wall were still there but the main building was being extended with another storey (possibly two) about to be added.

4. Alexander Innes Shand, *The War in the Peninsula 1808–1814* (London, Seeley and Co. Ltd, 1898), p. 72. Colonel Waters was renowned as a capable and resourceful man. Exploring officers were solitary scouts who explored terrain and sought intelligence in full uniform in order to avoid accusations of spying, since spies were routinely executed. Captured on one occasion, he refused to give the French his parole and was tied to a gun carriage and placed under guard but managed to escape. When informed that Waters was setting out on a risky venture to secure these wine barges under the enemy's watch, Wellesley confidently remarked that the Colonel would soon rejoin them.

5. Fortescue, *A History of the British Army*, Vol. 7, p. 159. There are other versions of this statement such as, '"Let the men embark," said the general brusquely, when someone suggested difficulties', Innes Shand, *The War in the Peninsula 1808–1814*, p. 72.

6. Oman, *A History of the Peninsular War*, Vol. 2, p. 336.

7. Fortescue, *A History of the British Army*, Vol. 7, pp. 159–60.

8. Oman, *A History of the Peninsular War*, Vol. 2, p. 338. Oman took this quotation from the diary of Captain Lane that had been sent to him by Colonel Whinyates of the Royal Artillery.

9. Thomas Bunbury, *Reminiscences of a Veteran, being Personal and Military Adventures in Portugal, Spain, France, Malta, New South Wales, Norfolk Island, New Zealand, the Andaman Islands and India* (London, Charles J. Skeet, 1861), pp. 31–4. Bunbury also recalled how the enemy lost heart when a German rifleman shot a French officer as he climbed up onto the wall, who then abruptly tumbled backward into their ranks.

10. Ibid. During this period, bandsman were used to spur the men on with the beating of drums (sometimes a martial tune was played by an entire band) and the French were renowned for using drummers to play the *pas des charge* for this purpose. As a young officer, Bunbury was excited rather than repulsed by the fighting, recalling, 'This being the first time I was under fire, I may be asked what were my feelings on the occasion. Being a giddy, hare-brained fellow, I do not suppose that I reflected at all upon the matter. It seemed to me capital fun.'

11. Oman, *A History of the Peninsular War*, Vol. 2, p. 339.

12. Napier, *History of the War in the Peninsula*, Vol. 2, p. 106.

13. Surgeon Thomas Wakley (ed.), 'Biographical Sketch of G. J. Guthrie, Esq., F.R.S, Late President of the College of Surgeons' (1850), *Lancet*, No. 1398, Vol. 1, pp. 726–36. The Portuguese 16th Regiment commanded by Colonel Machado also took part in this action, and was praised by Wellesley for the part they played, see *Gazeta del Gobierno*, Núm. 32, Del Lúnes, 29 de Mayo de 1809, pp. 540–1, which printed a letter from Don Miguel Persira Forjaz to Sir Arthur Wellesley.

14. Wakley (ed.), 'Biographical Sketch of G. J. Guthrie, Esq.', pp. 726–36.

15. Ibid. For a more modern account see Raymond Hurt, 'George Guthrie (1785–1856): surgeon to the Duke of Wellington, and a pioneer thoracic surgeon' (February 2007), *Journal of Medical Biography*, Vol. 15, No. 1, pp. 38–44.

16. *Gazeta del Gobierno*, Núm. 32, Del Lúnes, 29 de Mayo de 1809, pp. 540–1, letter between Don Miguel Persira Forjaz and Sir Arthur Wellesley with a slightly different version printed in the *Gazeta Extraordinaria del Gobierno*. Forjaz mistakenly believed that Loison was present in Porto during the battle when he was actually retreating from Amarante at the time.

17. Oman, *A History of the Peninsular War*, Vol. 2, p. 339. Oman wrote that the British suffered accordingly - 1/3rd – 50 casualties, 2/48th – 17 casualties and 2/66th – 10 casualties.

18. Colonel K.H. Leslie, *Military Journal of Colonel K.H. Leslie whilst serving with the 29th Regt in the Peninsula, and the 60th Rifles in Canada, etc, 1807–1832* (Aberdeen, Aberdeen University Press, 1887), p. 113.

19. Fortescue, *A History of the British Army*, Vol. 7, pp. 161–2. In Fortescue's opinion, 'but the unhappy man, as useless and inefficient in Portugal as in India, simply stood and looked at them'.

20. Captain Peter Hawker, *Journal of a Regimental Officer during the Recent Campaigns in Portugal and Spain under Viscount Wellesley* (London, Johnson, 1810), pp. 53–6. By the word 'pieces' Hawker was of course referring to muskets.

21. Pierre le Noble, *Mémoires sur les operations militaries des français en Galice, Portugal et la vallée du Tage en 1809 sous le commandement du Maréchal Soult, duc de Dalmatie, avec un atlas militaire* (Paris, chez Barrois l'aîné, librarie, 1821), p. 249.

22. Oman, *A History of the Peninsular War*, Vol. 2, p. 341.

23. Fortescue, *A History of the British Army*, Vol. 7, pp. 162–3. According to Napier, 'If Murray had fallen upon the disordered crowds their discomfiture would have been complete; but he suffered column after column to pass without even a cannon-shot, and seemed fearful lest they should turn and push him into the river.', *History of the War in the Peninsula*, Vol. 2, p. 107. Oman was also critical of Murray and believed that an advance by infantry in support of Stewart might have totally overwhelmed the French rearguard, *A History of the Peninsular War*, Vol. 2, p. 341.

24. Lieutenant George Wood, *The Subaltern Officer: a Narrative* (London, S. and B. Bentley, 1826), p. 78.

25. *United Service Magazine*, 1870, Part II, p. 569, this is a quotation from the Malmesbury Letters written by Captain George Bowles of the Coldstream Guards (later General Sir G. Bowles, KCB).

26. Fortescue, *A History of the British Army*, Vol. 7, p. 163 and Oman, *A History of the Peninsular War*, Vol. 2, pp. 341–2. Digby Smith records slightly different figures with Bodart claiming French losses as 3 generals, 36 officers and 600 men killed, wounded or captured. Citing Oman, Napier, Robinson and Martinien, he estimates Allied losses at 23 killed, 18 wounded and 6 missing, Digby Smith, *The Greenhill Napoleonic Wards Data Book – Actions and Losses in Personnel, Colours, Standards and Artillery, 1792–1815* (London, Greenhill Books, 1998), p. 302.

27. Second Duke of Wellington (ed.), *Supplementary Despatches, Correspondence, and Memoranda of Field Marshal the Duke of Wellington*, 15 vols (London, John Murray, 1858–72), Vol. 6, pp. 260–1.

28. *Gazeta Extraordinaria del Gobierno*, Del Mártes, 30 de Mayo de 1809, pp. 545–8. Forjaz appears to have written this letter outside the city in a field surrounded by the bodies of French soldiers killed in the pursuit. He recorded that his battalion (Portuguese

16th Regiment) was praised for their valour during the action. Casualties included Ensign Vasconcelos, who was killed along with a number of private soldiers, and Lieutenant Verissimo, who was gravely wounded.

29. Don Miguel Persira Forjaz wrote that British and Portuguese troops under Wellesley had marched swiftly from Coimbra, 'without stopping even to eat. The baggage remained in Aveiro.', *Gazeta Extraordinaria del Gobierno*, pp. 545–8.

Chapter 9

1. Charles Oman, *A History of the Peninsular War, 1807–9 ,* 7 vols (Oxford, The Clarendon Press, 1902), Vol. 2, p. 273.
2. Ibid., p. 345.
3. Major General Sir William Napier, *History of the War in the Peninsula and in the South of France*, 6 vols (London, Frederick Warne and Co., 1851), Vol. 2, p. 108 and Oman, *A History of the Peninsular War,* Vol. 2, p. 346.
4. Ibid., p. 109 and Alexander Innes Shand, *The War in the Peninsula 1808–1814* (London, Seeley and Co. Ltd, 1898), p. 74.
5. Oman, *A History of the Peninsular War*, Vol. 2, p. 634 –Wellesley to Castlereagh, 15 May 1809. Hayman records that Soult's detractors found Argenton's escape difficult to credit, many believing that the marshal simply ordered him released to avoid the embarrassment of a court martial. Considering that vengeful peasants and guerrillas prowled in the wake of the retreat, leaving a French officer to his own devices in this wild region was tantamount to a death sentence anyway. It is remarkable that Argenton managed to evade capture and seek the protection of the British army.
6. Lady Mary Lloyd (ed. and trans.), *New Letters of Napoleon I, Omitted from the Edition Published Under the Auspices of Napoleon III [by Napoleon I, Emperor of the French]* (New York, D. Appleton, 1897), p. 132. This extract is taken from a letter to Comte Fouché, Minister of Police and dated Schönbrunn, 14th July 1809.
7. Second Duke of Wellington (ed.), *Supplementary Despatches, Correspondence, and Memoranda of Field Marshal the Duke of Wellington*, 15 vols (London, John Murray, 1858–72), Vol. 6, July 1807–December 1810, p. 230. This is taken from the Deposition of the Secretary of the late Governor of Oporto and dated 13 May 1809. The informant believed that Soult would retire towards Braganza and that he personally witnessed some powder and tumbrils being destroyed. This he did, 'under the assurance of being hanged if not true …', as this letter's writer laconically admitted.
8. *London Chronicle*, Saturday, 20 May–Monday, 22 May 1809, Vol. 105, No. 7867, p. 483.
9. I.J. Rousseau (ed.), *The Peninsular Journal of Major-General Sir Benjamin D'Urban, 1808–1817* (London, Longmans, Green and Co., 1930), p. 53.
10. Napier, *History of the War in the Peninsula*, Vol. 2, p. 110.
11. Alexander Innes Shand, *The War in the Peninsula 1808–1814* (London, Seeley and Co. Ltd, 1898), p. 74.
12. A.V. Arnault, A. Jay, E. Jouy and J. Novrins, *Biographie nouvelle des contemporains, ou Dictionnaire historique et raisonné de tous les hommes qui, depuis la Révolution Française, ont acquis de la célébrité par leurs actions, leurs écrits, leurs erreurs ou leurs crimes, soit en France, soit dans les pays étrangers; précédée d'un tableau par ordre chronologique des époques célèbres et des événemens remarquables, tant en France qu'à l'étranger, depuis 1787 jusqu'à ce jour, et d'une table alphabétique des assemblées législatives, à partir de l'assemblée*

constituante jusqu'aux dernières chambres des pairs et des députés et autres hommes de lettres, magistrats et militaires (Paris, à La Librairie Historique, 1820–5), pp. 463–5. Napier translated the same passage thus, 'I have chosen you from the whole army to seize the Ponte Nova, which has been cut by the enemy; select a hundred grenadiers and twenty-five horsemen, endeavour to surprise the guards and secure the passage of the bridge. If you succeed, say so, but send no other report, your silence will suffice.', Napier, *History of the War in the Peninsula*, Vol. 2, p. 111.

13. Anonymous (ed.), *Strictures on certain passages of Lieut.-Col. Napier's History of the Peninsular War, which relate to the military opinions and conduct of General Lord Viscount Beresford* (London, Longman, Rees, Orme, Brown and Green, 1831), p. 95. For Napier's account see *History of the War in the Peninsula*, Vol. 2, p. 111. Some French sources assert that there was a sharp exchange of fire and a serious hand-to-hand struggle before the Portuguese conceded the bridge to the enemy, see Arnault et al., *Biographie nouvelle des contemporains*, pp. 463–5.

14. Arnault et al., *Biographie nouvelle des contemporains*, pp. 463–5.

15. Ibid. Nevertheless, some dispute such accounts claiming that Portuguese defence was almost as poor as it had been at the Ponte Nova, 'as stated in a Memoire written and published by an officer of Soult's army, that the gallant Major Dulong and seventeen others, were wounded at this spot. As the post is a strong one, it is clear that the defenders could have done little more than have discharged their arms and fled.', Anonymous (ed.), *Strictures on certain passages of Lieut.-Col. Napier's History of the Peninsular War*, p. 96.

16. Arnault et al., *Biographie nouvelle des contemporains*, pp. 463–5. Miraculously, Dulong survived and was eventually promoted Colonel of the 12th Light Infantry Regiment. He went on to serve with distinction in Spain, notably at Rio Barbata, and Soult praised him in dispatches to the Minister for War. After the Peninsular War, he was accepted into the Imperial Guard.

17. W.F.K. Thompson (ed.), *An Ensign in the Peninsular War – The Letters of John Aitchison* (London, Michael Joseph Ltd, 1994, first edn 1981), p. 43.

18. Julian Rathbone, *Wellington's War – His Peninsular Dispatches* (Bury St Edmunds, Book Club Associates, 1984), p. 48.

19. Joseph de Naylies, *Mémoires sur la guerre d'Espagne pendant les années 1808, 1809, 1810 et 1811* (Paris, Magimel, Anselin et Pochard, 1817), pp. 130–3.

20. Oman, *A History of the Peninsular War*, Vol. 2, p. 353.

21. J.S. Cooper, *Rough Notes of Seven Campaigns in Portugal, Spain, France and America during the Years 1809–1815* (London, Staplehurst, 1996, first edn 1869), pp. 12–13. He went on to relate an incident when a wine store was looted and, 'The owner, finding this out, ran and brought an officer of the Fifty-Third, who caught one of our company named Brown in the act of handing out the wine in camp kettles. Seizing Brown by the collar, the officer shouted, "Come out you rascal and give me your name!" Brown … gave his name as Brennan; then, knocking the officer down, he made his escape and was not found out.'

22. Thompson (ed.), *An Ensign in the Peninsular War*, p. 43. Aitchison claimed that at least 300 prisoners were taken during this engagement.

23. I.J. Rousseau (ed.), *The Peninsular Journal of Major-General Sir Benjamin D'Urban, 1808–1817* (London, Longmans, Green and Co., 1930), p. 54.

24. Anonymous, *Camden Miscellany*, Vol. 18 (London, Offices of the Royal Historical Society, 1948), p. 12. This quotation is drawn from the chapter 'Some Letters of the Duke of Wellington to his Brother William Wellesley-Pole', edited by Professor Sir Charles Webster. Wellesley wrote this letter at Porto and dated it 22 May 1809. Webster judged that the village of Milgapey was the small hamlet near the Saltador bridge. Many of Wellesley's contemporaries agreed that Soult's forced withdrawal went some way to avenging Corunna.

25. Oman, *A History of the Peninsular War*, Vol. 2, pp. 361 (losses) and 364 (quotation). Other historians place French total losses between 4,000 and 6,000 men. For example, Michael Glover estimates total French losses at 4,000 with Allied losses about a tenth of that figure, *Wellington as Military Commander* (London, Penguin Books, 2001), p. 123, while Peter Hayman places total French losses at 6,000 men, *Soult – Napoleon's Maligned Marshal* (London, Arms and Armour Press, 1990), pp. 119–20. Regarding the number of guns lost, Soult began the invasion with fifty-four guns but sent many back to Tuy after his repulse on the Minho. Having entered Portugal with twenty-two cannon it is likely that he added some Portuguese guns to his artillery captured at Porto so it is difficult to be precise.

26. Naylies, *Mémoires*, p. 130.

27. Raymond Horricks, *Marshal Ney – The Romance and the Real* (London, Archway Publishing Company, 1982), p. 95. Horricks related that there 'was a violent altercation during which Ney half-drew his sword and threatened Soult with a duel; whereupon their staff-officers hastily intervened'.

28. Arthur John Butler (ed. and trans.), *The Memoirs of Baron Thiébault*, 2 vols (London, Smith, Elder & Co., 1896), Vol. 2, p. 259. Thiébault wrote that Delaborde was disillusioned because of the way in which the Second Invasion of Portugal had been conducted and returned to France due to ill-health. When Thiébault asked whether he would speak out about what he had witnessed, Delaborde responded, 'My mind is irrevocably made up on that head. If I am questioned, I shall tell everything; if not, I shall say nothing.' In the event, Napoleon failed to question him and this honest old soldier was true to his word.

29. Hayman, *Soult*, pp. 124–5.

30. Horricks, *Marshal Ney*, p. 95.

31. Hayman, *Soult*, p. 23, Napoleon made this remark to Baron de Jomini (the famed military analyst) in direct reference to this notorious disagreement in Galicia.

32. Ibid., p. 115.

Chapter 10

1. Anonymous (ed.), *De Quincey to Wordsworth: a biography of a relationship/John E. Jordan; with the letters of Thomas De Quincey to the Wordsworth family* (Los Angeles CA, University of California Press and London, Cambridge University Press, 1962), pp. 176–7.

2. W.F.K. Thompson (ed.), *An Ensign in the Peninsular War – The Letters of John Aitchison* (London, Michael Joseph Ltd, 1994, first edn 1981), p. 43.

3. *Monthly Magazine; or, British Register*, 1809, Part II, No. 188 (1 of Vol. 28), p. 101.

4. Ibid.

5. Andrew Roberts, *Napoleon & Wellington* (London, Weidenfield & Nicolson, 2001), p. 262, here Roberts is using a quotation from Philip Henry Stanhope, *Notes of Conversations with the Duke of Wellington, 1831–1851* (London, John Murray, 1889).

6. Roberts, *Napoleon & Wellington*, p. 174. For example, Wellesley saw a brief opportunity to assail Marmont's army at Salamanca in 1812 as the opposing armies marched parallel with one another and seized the opportunity, winning a remarkable victory.

7. Godfrey Davies, 'The Whigs and the Peninsular War' (1919), *Transactions of the Royal Historical Society*, Vol. 2, 4th Series, pp. 121–2. Earl Grey was a leading Whig politician at this time.

8. Anonymous, *Camden Miscellany*, Vol. 18 (London, Offices of the Royal Historical Society, 1948), p. 13. This was a letter to his brother William from Castelo Branco and dated 1 July 1809.

9. *Cobbett's Parliamentary Debates*, Vol. 15, 23 January–1 March 1810 (London, T.C. Hansard, 1810), p. 444. The Battle of Talavera, 27–8 July 1809, was Wellesley's first major success in Spain against a much larger force under Marshals Victor and Jourdan with King Joseph in attendance. He withstood repeated attacks despite receiving poor support from General Cuesta's Spanish forces but the French ultimately withdrew after suffering heavy losses. Wellesley had hoped to march on Madrid but the advance of armies under Soult and Ney, along with Spanish failures to re-supply his army, persuaded him to withdraw towards the Portuguese frontier.

10. Ibid., p. 448.

11. Ibid., p. 449.

12. Ibid., p. 450.

13. Ibid., p. 451.

14. J.W. Fortescue, *A History of the British Army*, 13 vols (London, Macmillan and Co. Ltd, 1912–20), Vol. 7, p. 163. Fortescue also accuses Soult of carelessness but allows him the partial excuse of having been sick the night before the passage of the Douro.

15. Ibid.

16. Charles Oman, *A History of the Peninsular War, 1807–9* , 7 vols (Oxford, The Clarendon Press, 1902), Vol. 2, p. 333.

17. Antoine-Henri, Baron de Jomini, *The Art of War* (New York, Dover Publications Inc., 2007, first edn 1862), p. 229.

18. Fortescue, *A History of the British Army*, Vol. 7, p. 163.

19. Michael Glover, *Wellington as Military Commander* (London, Penguin Books, 2001), p. 123.

20. Oman, *A History of the Peninsular War*, Vol. 2, pp. 301–2. Oman elaborates on this theory by suggesting that Wellesley would have destroyed Marmont's army at Salamanca in 1812 if he had used his cavalry more wisely and believed Napoleon would have done so in his place. Likewise, he thought Wellesley could never have inflicted a defeat like that of Jena in 1806 on the Prussians where huge losses were inflicted upon them by Murat's cavalry pursuit (to whom Napoleon permitted a virtual free hand). For a detailed analysis of Wellesley's use of cavalry, see Ian Fletcher, *Galloping at Everything – The British Cavalry in the Peninsular War and at Waterloo 1808–1815 – a Reappraisal* (Staplehurst, Spellmount Publishers Ltd, 1999).

21. Oman, *A History of the Peninsular War*, Vol. 2, p. 363. This was praise indeed from the foremost historian of the Peninsular War as it invites comparisons with Wellesley's

victories at Talavera in 1809, Salamanca in 1812 and Vittoria in 1813, among others. The fact that Wellesley inflicted significant damage on an entire French corps and ejected the French from Portugal in return for relatively small losses makes this achievement stand out when compared with battles where enormous casualties were inflicted with less strategic gain.

22. Christopher Hibbert, *Wellington – a Personal History* (London, Harper Collins Publishers, 1997), p. 91, this quotation is taken from Wellington Papers, Stratfield Saye: Joan Wilson, *A Soldier's Wife: Wellington's Marriage* (Worthing, Littlehampton Book Services Ltd, 1987), p. 124. For information about the Wellesley family retaining the title and using the name of Douro up to the current day (written by a relative of the Great Duke) see Jane Wellesley, *Wellington – A Journey Through My Family* (London, Weidenfeld & Nicolson, 2008).

23. Elizabeth Longford, *Wellington – The Years of the Sword* (London, World Books, 1971), pp. 315–16.

24. *Brooklyn Daily Eagle*, Saturday, 3 April 1937, p. 1. For a detailed view of the itinerary of this event see – Anonymous, *Official Programme of the Coronation Tattoo Aldershot: Held at Rushmoor, Aldershot June 10th, 11th, 12th, 15th, 16th, 17th, 18th, 19th, 1937* (Aldershot, Gale and Polden, 1937). This publication is now rare but can be found at the British Library: Humanities and Social Sciences, St Pancras Reading Rooms: Shelfmark: YD.2010.b.3247.

25. *Illustrated London News*, Saturday, 12 June 1937, Issue 5121, pp. 1082–3.

26. Howard N. Cole, *The Story of Aldershot: A History of the Civil and Military Towns* (Aldershot, Southern Books, 1980), p. 223.

27. *Parliamentary Debates – House of Commons Official Report, Ninth Volume of Session 1936–37, Fifth Series – Vol. 325* (London, His Majesty's Stationery Office, 1937), pp. 180–1. The Secretary of State for the War Office was the Right Honourable Leslie Hore-Belisha MP.

28. General Comte de Sainte-Chamans, *Mémoires du Général Comte de Saint-Chamans* (Paris, Librarie Plon, 1896), pp. 149–50.

29. Alexander Innes Shand, *The War in the Peninsula 1808–1814* (London, Seeley and Co. Ltd, 1898), p. 75. Dupont surrendered his entire army at Bailén 21 July 1808, which amounted to 18,000 men with the addition of Vedel's troops who also capitulated. General Junot suffered a serious defeat when he mounted a poorly conducted assault on Wellesley's position on 21 August 1808. He lost 2,500 men in return for around 700 Allied casualties and the extent of the defeat led to him seeking an armistice and evacuating Portugal.

30. Fortescue, *A History of the British Army*, Vol. 7, p. 170.

31. Oman, *A History of the Peninsular War*, Vol. 2, pp. 361–2.

32. For an excellent account of the Battle of Aspern-Essling see F. Loraine Petre, *Napoleon and the Archduke Charles* (London, Greenhill Books, 1991, first edn 1909).

33. Peter Hayman, *Soult – Napoleon's Maligned Marshal* (London, Arms and Armour Press, 1990), p. 165. Another version of what Soult said is as follows, 'Those infantry were beaten but they just didn't know it.' While the French left the British in possession of the battlefield, the near parity of the casualty figures meant their claim of victory was not entirely unjustified and who won is still open to debate. Revealingly, Wellington proved reluctant to allow Beresford an independent command on this scale again.

34. Stanhope, *Notes of Conversations with the Duke of Wellington*, p. 90.
35. Laurence Currie, *The Bâton in the Knapsack – New Light on Napoleon and his Marshals* (London, John Murray, 1934), pp. 77–8.
36. Colonel James J. Graham, *Military ends and moral means: exemplifying the higher influences affecting military life and character; the motives to enlistment; the use of stratagems in war; the necessity of standing armies; and the duties of a military force aiding the civil power* (London, Smith, Elder and Co., Cornhill, 1864), p. 209.
37. For opposing views on Soult's performance during the Hundred Days Campaign see Stephen Coote, *Napoleon and the Hundred Days* (London, Simon & Schuster UK Ltd, 2004), p. 215, where Coote accuses Soult of incompetent staff work which made a significant contribution to the French defeat. In contrast, Hayman, *Soult*, p. 232 (and Chapter 18 in general) acknowledges that Soult made errors but that the ultimate responsibility for the defeat lay with Napoleon himself. Hayman illustrates this by Napoleon's refusal to blame Soult for the outcome and summary of him as 'an excellent major general' during the campaign while in exile on St Helena.
38. Coote, *Napoleon and the Hundred Days*, p. 247. For Gourgaud's account of the incident see Dr Barry E. O'Meara, *Napoleon in Exile; or, A Voice from St. Helena. The Opinions and Reflections of Napoleon on the most important events of his life and government in his own words*, 2 vols (Philadelphia PA, 1822), Vol. 2, pp. 161–2.
39. The Battle of Toulouse took place on 10 April 1814 with Soult attempting to prevent the British (under Wellington) from taking the city. He retreated the following day and it was only shortly afterwards that both sides were informed that Napoleon had abdicated some days earlier on 6 April.
40. Currie, *The Bâton in the Knapsack*, p. 78.
41. Marshal Jean de Dieu Soult, *Memoires du Marechal-General Soult*, 2 vols (publies par son fils, Paris, 1854), Vol. 1, p. 298.
42. Hayman, *Soult*, p. 255.
43. Ibid., p. 256.
44. Ibid., p. 255.

Bibliography

CONTEMPORARY/PRIMARY SOURCES

Archives and Libraries
The British Library
The National Army Museum
The University of Leicester (David Wilson Library)

Newspapers and Periodicals
Annual Register
Brooklyn Daily Eagle
Cobbett's Parliamentary Debates
Gazeta del Gobierno
Gazeta Extraordinaria del Gobierno
Gentleman's Magazine
Lisbon Gazette
Literary Panorama and National Register
Lloyd's List
London Chronicle
Monthly Magazine or British Register
Parliamentary Debates – House of Commons Official Report
Scots Magazine and Edinburgh Literary Miscellany
The Times
United Service Magazine

Books
Abrantes, Duchess d', Laure Junot, *Mémoires de Madame la duchesse d'Abrantes: ou Souvenirs sur Napoléon le Directoire, le Consulat, l'Empire et la Restoration*, 18 vols, Paris, La Haye Vervloet, 18315
Anonymous, *Camden Miscellany*, Vol. 18, London, Offices of the Royal Historical Society, 1948
Anonymous (ed.), *De Quincey to Wordsworth: a biography of a relationship/John E. Jordan; with the letters of Thomas De Quincey to the Wordsworth family*, Los Angeles CA, University of California Press and London, Cambridge University Press, 1962
Anonymous (ed.), *Strictures on certain passages of Lieut.-Col. Napier's History of the Peninsular War, which relate to the military opinions and conduct of General Lord Viscount Beresford*, London, Longman, Rees, Orme, Brown and Green, 1831

Arnault, A.V., Jay, A., Jouy, E. and Novrins, J., *Biographie nouvelle des contemporains, ou Dictionnaire historique et raisonné de tous les hommes qui, depuis la Révolution Française, ont acquis de la célébrité par leurs actions, leurs écrits, leurs erreurs ou leurs crimes, soit en France, soit dans les pays étrangers; précédée d'un tableau par ordre chronologique des époques célèbres et des événemens remarquables, tant en France qu'à l'étranger, depuis 1787 jusqu'à ce jour, et d'une table alphabétique des assemblées législatives, à partir de l'assemblée constituante jusqu'aux dernières chambres des pairs et des députés et autres hommes de lettres, magistrats et militaires*, Paris, à La Librairie Historique, 1820–5

Bigarré, Auguste, *Mémoires du Général Bigarré, aide-de-camp due Roi Joseph, 1775–1813*, Paris, Ernest Kolb, Chailley, 1903

Bunbury, Thomas, *Reminiscences of a Veteran, being Personal and Military Adventures in Portugal, Spain, France, Malta, New South Wales, Norfolk Island, New Zealand, the Andaman Islands and India*, London, Charles J. Skeet, 1861

Butler, Arthur John (ed. and trans.), *The Memoirs of Baron de Marbot Late Lieutenant-General in the French Army*, 2 vols, London, Longmans, Green and Co., 1892

Butler, Arthur John (ed. and trans.), *The Memoirs of Baron de Marbot*, London, Cassell & Co. Ltd, 1929

Butler, Arthur John (ed. and trans.), *The Memoirs of Baron Thiébault*, 2 vols, London, Smith, Elder & Co., 1896

Byron, George, *The Complete Poetical Works of Lord Byron*, 3 vols, London, George Routledge and Sons, 1886

Colburn, Henry and Bentley, Richard, *Memoirs of the Duchess d'Abrantès* (Madame Junot), 8 vols, London, Henry Colburn and Richard Bentley, 1831–5

Cooper, J.S., *Rough Notes of Seven Campaigns in Portugal, Spain, France and America during the Years 1809–1815*, London, Staplehurst, 1996 (first edn 1869)

Croker, John Wilson, *The Croker Papers: The Correspondence and Diaries of John Wilson Croker, Secretary to the Admiralty from 1809 to 1830*, 3 vols, London, John Murray, 1885

Gleig, G.R., *Life of Wellington*, London, Longman, Green, Longman and Roberts, 1862

Hawker, Captain Peter, *Journal of a Regimental Officer During the Recent Campaigns in Portugal and Spain under Viscount Wellesley*, London, Johnson, 1810

Jomini, Baron de Antoine-Henri, *The Art of War*, New York, Dover Publication Inc., 2007 (first edn 1862)

Jourdan, Maréchal Jean Baptiste, *Mémoires Militaires (Guerre d'Espagne)*, Paris, Ernest Flammarion – Impreimerie de Lagny, 1899

Leslie, Colonel K.H., *Military Journal of Colonel K.H. Leslie whilst serving with the 29th Regt in the Peninsula, and the 60th Rifles in Canada, etc, 1807–1832*, Aberdeen, Aberdeen University Press, 1887

Napier, Major General Sir William, *History of the War in the Peninsula and in the South of France*, 6 vols, London, Frederick Warne and Co., 1851 de Naylies, Joseph, *Mémoires sur la guerre d'Espagne pendant les années 1808, 1809, 1810 et 1811*, Paris, Magimel, Anselin et Pochard, 1817

Noble, Pierre, le, *Mémoires sur les operations militaires des français en Galice, Portugal et la vallée du Tage en 1809 sous le commandement du Maréchal Soult, duc de Dalmatie, avec un atlas militaire*, Paris, chez Barrois l'ainé, librarie, 1821

des Odoards, Fantin, *Journal du Général Fantin des Odoards – Etapes d'un Officier de la Grande Armee 1800–1830*, Paris, Libraire Plon, E. Plon, Nourrit et Cie Imprimeurs-Éditeurs, 1895

O'Meara, Dr Barry E., *Napoleon in Exile; or, A Voice from St. Helena. The Opinions and Reflections of Napoleon on the most important events of his life and government in his own words*, 2 vols, Philadelphia PA, 1822

de Plancey, Jaques Albin Simon Collin, *Fastes militaires des Belges, ou Histoire des guerres, sièges, conquêtes, expéditions et faits d'armes, qui ont illustré la Belgique depuis l'invasion de César jusqu'a nos jours*, 4 vols, Bruxelles, au Bureau des fastes militaries, 1835–6

Rousseau, I.J. (ed.), *The Peninsular Journal of Major-General Sir Benjamin D'Urban, 1808–1817*, London, Longmans, Green and Co., 1930

de Sainte-Chamans, General Comte, *Mémoires du Général Comte de Saint-Chamans*, Paris, Librarie Plon, 1896

de Sainte-Pierre, Louis and Antoinette (eds), *Mémoires du Maréchal Soult: Espagne et Portugal*, Paris, Hachette, 1955

Soult, Marshal Jean de Dieu, *Memoires du Marechal-General Soult*, 2 vols, publies par son fils, Paris, 1854

Stanhope, Philip Henry, *Notes of Conversations with the Duke of Wellington, 1831–1851*, London, John Murray, 1889

Stuart, Daniel, *Letters from the Lake poets, Samuel Taylor Coleridge, William Wordsworth, Robert Southey, to Daniel Stuart, editor of The Morning Post and The Courier, 1800–1838*, London, West, Newman and Co. (printed for private circulation), 1889

Thompson, J.M. (ed.), *Letters of Napoleon*, Oxford, Basil Blackwell, 1934

Thompson, W.F.K. (ed.), *An Ensign in the Peninsular War – The Letters of John Aitchison*, London, Michael Joseph Ltd, 1994 (first edn 1981)

Warre, Lieutenant General Sir William, *Letters from the Peninsula 1808–1812*, London, John Murray, 1909

Wellington, Field Marshal Arthur, Duke of, *The Despatches of Field Marshal the Duke of Wellington During his Various Campaigns*, compiled by Lieutenant Colonel Gurwood, 13 vols, London, John Murray, 1834–8

Wellington, Second Duke of (ed.), *Supplementary Despatches, Correspondence, and Memoranda of Field Marshal the Duke of Wellington*, 15 vols, London, John Murray, 1858–72

Wood, Lieutenant George, *The Subaltern Officer: A Narrative*, London, S. and B. Bentley, 1826

Wordsworth, William, *Wordsworth's Tract on the Convention of Cintra*, London, Humphrey Milford, 1915 (previously published 1809)

SECONDARY SOURCES

Books

Anonymous, *Napoleon and the Marshals of the Empire*, 2 vols, Philadelphia PA, J.B. Lippincott, 1858

Anonymous, *Official Programme of the Coronation Tattoo Aldershot: Held at Rushmoor, Aldershot June 10th, 11th, 12th, 15th, 16th, 17th, 18th, 19th, 1937*, Aldershot, Gale and Polden, 1937

Buttery, David, *Wellington Against Junot – The First Invasion of Portugal 1807–1808*, Barnsley, Pen & Sword Books Ltd, 2011

Chandler, David G., *Austerlitz 1805*, London, Osprey, 1990

Chandler, David G., *The Campaigns of Napoleon*, London, Weidenfeld & Nicolson, 1967

Chandler, David G. (ed.), *Napoleon's Marshals*, London, Weidenfeld & Nicolson, 1987

Chandler, David G., *On the Napoleonic Wars*, London, Greenhill Books, 1999

Chartrand, René, *Oldest Allies – Alcantara 1809*, Oxford, Osprey Publishing Ltd, 2012

Cohen, Louis, *Napoleonic Anecdotes*, London, Robert Holden & Co. Ltd, 1925

Cole, Howard N., *The story of Aldershot: a History of the Civil and Military Towns*, Aldershot, Southern Books, 1980

Combes, Anacharsis, *Histoire anecdotique de Jean-de-Dieu Soult, maréchal-général, duc de Dalmatie, 1769–1851*, Castres, HUC, Léon Bertrand, 1870

Coote, Stephen, *Napoleon and the Hundred Days*, London, Simon & Schuster UK Ltd, 2004

Currie, Laurence, *The Bâton in the Knapsack – New Light on Napoleon and his Marshals*, London, John Murray, 1934

Dard, Émile and Turner, Christopher R. (trans.), *Napoleon and Talleyrand*, London, Philip Allan & Co. Ltd, 1937

Delderfield, R.F., *Imperial Sunset – The Fall of Napoleon, 1813–14*, London, Hodder & Stoughton, 1968

Delderfield, R.F., *The March of the Twenty-Six*, London, Hodder & Stoughton, 1962

Duffy, Christopher, *Eagles Over the Alps – Suvorov in Italy and Switzerland, 1799*, Chicago IL, The Emperor's Press, 1999

Esdaile, Charles, *Peninsular Eyewitness – the Experience of War in Spain and Portugal 1808–1813*, Barnsley, Pen & Sword Books Ltd, 2008

Fletcher, Ian, *Galloping at Everything – The British Cavalry in the Peninsular War and at Waterloo 1808–1815 – a Reappraisal*, Staplehurst, Spellmount Publishers Ltd, 1999

Fortescue, Sir John W., *A History of the British Army*, 13 vols, London, Macmillan and Co. Ltd, 1912–20

Gates, David, *The Spanish Ulcer*, London, George Allen & Unwin, 1986

Girod de l'Ain, Maurice, *Vie militaire du général Foy. Ouvrage accompagné de deux portraits en héliogravure, six cartes et trois fac-simile d'autographes*, Paris, E. Plon, Nourrit et Cie, 1900

Glover, Michael, *Britannia Sickens – The Convention of Cintra*, London, Leo Cooper, 1970

Glover, Michael, *Legacy of Glory – The Bonaparte Kingdom of Spain 1808–1813*, London, Leo Cooper, 1972

Glover, Michael, *The Peninsular War 1807–1814*, London, Penguin Group, 2001 (first edn 1974)

Glover, Michael, *A Very Slippery Fellow – The Life of Sir Robert Wilson 1777–1849*, Oxford, Oxford University Press, 1978

Glover, Michael, *Wellington as Military Commander*, London, Penguin Books, 2001 (first edn 1968)

Graham, Colonel James J., *Military ends and moral means: exemplifying the higher influences affecting military life and character; the motives to enlistment; the use of stratagems in war; the necessity of standing armies; and the duties of a military force aiding the civil power*, London, Smith, Elder and Co., Cornhill, 1864

Guedalla, Philip, *The Duke*, London, Hodder & Stoughton, 1933

Esdaile, Charles, *The Peninsular War*, London, Penguin Books, 2003

Hargreaves-Mawdsley, William Norman (ed.), *Spain under the Bourbons 1700–1833*, London, Macmillan, 1973

Hayman, Peter, *Soult – Napoleon's Maligned Marshal*, London, Arms and Armour Press, 1990

Haythornthwaite, Philip, *Corunna 1809 – Sir John Moore's Fighting Retreat*, Oxford, Osprey Publishing Ltd, 2001

Haythornthwaite, Philip J., *The Napoleonic Source Book*, London, Guild Publishing, 1990

Hibbert, Christopher, *Corunna*, London, B.T. Batsford Ltd, 1961

Hibbert, Christopher, *Wellington – a Personal History*, London, Harper Collins Publishers, 1997

Horricks, Raymond, *Marshal Ney – The Romance and the Real*, London, Archway Publishing Co., 1982

Humble, Richard, *Napoleon's Peninsular Marshals*, London, Purcell Book Services Ltd, 1973

Innes Shand, Alexander, *The War in the Peninsula 1808–1814*, London, Seeley and Co. Ltd, 1898

Jones, R. Ben, *Napoleon Man and Myth*, London, Hodder & Stoughton, 1981 (first edn 1977)

Lloyd, Lady Mary (ed. and trans.), *New Letters of Napoleon I, Omitted from the Edition Published Under the Auspices of Napoleon III [by Napoleon I, Emperor of the French]*, New York, D. Appleton, 1897

Loliée, Frédéric, *Prince Talleyrand and his Times*, London, John Long Ltd, 1911

Longford, Elizabeth, *Wellington – The Years of the Sword*, London, World Books, 1971

Macdonell, A.G., *Napoleon and his Marshals*, London, Prion, 1996 (first edn 1934)

McLynn, Frank, Napoleon, London, Jonathan Cape, 1997

Marshall-Cornwall, James, *Marshal Massena*, London, Oxford University Press, 1965

Muir, Rory, *Britain and the Defeat of Napoleon 1807–1815*, New Haven CT and London, Yale University Press, 1996

Muir, Rory, *Wellington: the Path to Victory, 1769–1814*, New Haven CT, Yale University Press, 2013

Napier, Priscilla Hayter, *The Sword Dance*, London, Joseph, 1971

Oman, Charles, *A History of the Peninsular War*, 1807–9, 7 vols, Oxford, The Clarendon Press, 1902

Oman, Sir Charles, *Wellington's Army 1809–1814*, London, Greenhill Books, 2006 (first edn 1913)

Petre, F. Loraine, *Napoleon and the Archduke Charles*, London, Greenhill Books, 1991 (first edn 1909)

Pinheiro Chagas, Manuel, *Historia de Portugal*, 8 vols, Lisboa, Empreza da Historia de Portugal, Livraria Moderna, 1903

Rathbone, Julian, *Wellington's War – His Peninsular Dispatches*, Bury St Edmunds, Book Club Associates, 1984

Roberts, Andrew, *Napoleon & Wellington*, London, Weidenfield & Nicolson, 2001

Rogers, Colonel H.C.B., *Wellington's Army*, Shepperton, Ian Allen Printing Ltd, 1979

Rudorff, Raymond, *War to the Death – the Sieges of Saragossa 1808–1809*, London, W. & J. Mackay Limited, 1974

Sitwell, Sacheverell, *Portugal and Madeira*, B.T. Batsford Ltd, 1954

Smith, Digby, *The Greenhill Napoleonic Wars Data Book – Actions and Losses in Personnel, Colours, Standards and Artillery, 1792–1815*, London, Greenhill Books, 1998

Teignmouth, Henry Noel Shore, Baron, *Three Pleasant Springs in Portugal*, London, Sampson Low, Marston & Co., 1899

Tulard, Jean, *Napoléon – the Myth of the Saviour*, trans. Teresa Waugh, London, Weidenfeld & Nicolson Ltd, 1984 (first edn 1977)

Weller, Jac, *Wellington in the Peninsula 1808–1814*, London, Purnell Book Services Ltd, 1973 (first edn 1962)

Wellesley, Jane, *Wellington – A Journey Through My Family*, London, Weidenfeld & Nicolson, 2008

Wilson, Joan, *A Soldier's Wife: Wellington's Marriage*, Worthing, Littlehampton Book Services Ltd, 1987

Young, Brigadier Peter, *Napoleon's Marshals*, Reading, Osprey Publishing Ltd, 1973

Magazines and Journals

Davies, Godfrey, 'The Whigs and the Peninsular War' (1919), *Transactions of the Royal Historical Society*, Vol. 2, 4th Series, pp. 121–2

Hurt, Raymond, 'George Guthrie (1785–1856): surgeon to the Duke of Wellington, and a pioneer thoracic surgeon' (Feburary 2007), *Journal of Medical Biography*, Vol. 15, No. 1, pp. 38–44

Ramos, Luís António de Oliveira, 'Os afrancesados do Porto' (1980), *Revista de história*, Universidade do Porto – Faculdade de Letras, Vol. 3, pp. 115–25

Wakley, Surgeon Thomas (ed.), 'Biographical Sketch of G. J. Guthrie, Esq., F.R.S, Late President of the College of Surgeons' (1850), *Lancet*, No. 1398, Vol. 1, pp. 726–36

Index